INDELIBLE
CITY

INDELIBLE CITY

DISPOSSESSION

and

DEFIANCE

IN HONG KONG

LOUISA LIM

RIVERHEAD BOOKS · NEW YORK · 2022

RIVERHEAD BOOKS
An imprint of Penguin Random House LLC
penguinrandomhouse.com

Copyright © 2022 by Louisa Lim
Penguin supports copyright. Copyright fuels creativity, encourages diverse voices,
promotes free speech, and creates a vibrant culture. Thank you for buying an authorized
edition of this book and for complying with copyright laws by not reproducing, scanning,
or distributing any part of it in any form without permission. You are supporting writers
and allowing Penguin to continue to publish books for every reader.

Grateful acknowledgment is made for permission from MC Yan to reprint the lyrics from "2019."

Photo on page 267 reprinted by permission of Patrick Cummins.

Riverhead and the R colophon are registered trademarks of Penguin Random House LLC.

Library of Congress Cataloging-in-Publication Data
Names: Lim, Louisa, author.
Title: Indelible city : dispossession and defiance in Hong Kong / Louisa Lim.
Other titles: Dispossession and defiance in Hong Kong
Description: New York : Riverhead, 2022. |
Includes bibliographical references.
Identifiers: LCCN 2021039690 (print) | LCCN 2021039691 (ebook) |
ISBN 9780593191811 (hardcover) | ISBN 9780593191835 (ebook)
Subjects: LCSH: Protest movements—China—Hong Kong—History. |
Hong Kong (China)—Social conditions. | Dissenters—China—Hong Kong. |
Social movements—China—Hong Kong—History. |
Hong Kong (China)—Politics and government.
Classification: LCC HN752.5 L54 2022 (print) | LCC HN752.5 (ebook) |
DDC 303.48/4095125—dc23
LC record available at https://lccn.loc.gov/2021039690
LC ebook record available at https://lccn.loc.gov/2021039691

International edition ISBN: 9780593541494

Printed in the United States of America
1   3   5   7   9   10   8   6   4   2

BOOK DESIGN BY LUCIA BERNARD

To all those who really fucking love Hong Kong

I DON'T THINK I CAN GET THE LAND BACK.

The King of Kowloon

YOUR FURIOUS CHARACTERS ON THE RED POSTBOX
KINDLE IN US A FLAME WE HAVE ALWAYS KNOWN.

"King of Kowloon" by Jennifer Wong

CONTENTS

PART 3: DEFIANCE

AUTHOR'S NOTE

Although I lived in Hong Kong for almost all my childhood and some of my adulthood, I am not a native Hong Konger, and I no longer live in the city. My position on the sidelines liberates me to write more openly than others. However, my freedom must not come at the cost of my sources. Nowadays the act of writing about Hong Kong has become an exercise in subtraction. Though the interviews for this book, unless otherwise stated in the text, were carried out prior to the introduction of the national security legislation in June 2020, the broad and retrospective application of the legislation has compelled me to remove some names and details from the text nevertheless, to protect those with whom I spoke.

This act of stripping away the identities of interviewees is all the more painful because my aim in writing this book was to place Hong Kongers front and center of their own narrative. Yet in this national security era, writing about Hong Kong's distinct identity is land-mined with risk.

Indeed, many of Hong Kong's best writers can no longer find the words, or even the platforms, to express themselves openly. This book owes its existence to all those who spoke to me, both named and unnamed. I hope I am honoring the truth of their words while being mindful of their safety.

INDELIBLE
CITY

PROLOGUE

I was squatting on the roof of a Hong Kong skyscraper, sun blazing on my head, sweat dripping into my eyes, painting expletive-laden Chinese characters onto a protest banner eight stories high and wondering if I had just killed my career in journalism. The air was soupy with heat, and through the haze I could see a satisfying Tetris-scape of rooftops packed so tight they seemed to interlock. I'd come to the rooftop to interview a secret cooperative of guerrilla sign painters who specialized in producing mammoth pro-democracy banners to be slung from Hong Kong's highest peaks. But as I watched, my fingers itched to grab a paint brush and join in.

It was the autumn of 2019, the day before China's National Day, commemorating the seventieth anniversary of the establishment of the People's Republic of China on October 1, 1949. For months, millions of people had marched through Hong Kong's streets, in the biggest and most sustained anti-government protests the territory had ever seen. After 155 years as a British colony, Hong Kong had been returned to China in 1997, in an unprecedented transition of sovereignty. Although Beijing had vowed that Hong Kong could preserve its way of life for fifty years—until 2047—China was now threatening to ram through legislation that would renege on that promise.

The secret band of calligraphers had been busy deploying their team of rock climbers to scale Hong Kong's crags in the dead of night, so that people woke up to gigantic signs exhorting them to "Take to the Streets to Oppose the Evil Law" or "Fight for Hong Kong." The sheer scope of the banners turned the territory itself into a canvas and reinvigorated the protest movement when morale was ebbing. I'd always been fascinated by the audacity of the sign painters, but I had no idea who they were or how to get in touch with them. That morning, someone who knew of my obsession had contacted me out of the blue to invite me to watch them in action. It was an offer I couldn't refuse.

The sunbaked rooftop of this tall building offered both the privacy and the expanse necessary to lay out the huge banners and dry them. There were seven sign painters. I had promised not to divulge any details that might expose their identities, but I was surprised that instead of the young, athletic radicals of my imagination, they were older men and women whose familiarity with one another was evident in the wordless efficiency of their interactions. Working quickly, they unfolded a gigantic bolt of thick black cotton, then used their feet to stamp the material flat on the roof in a brisk, communal dance. They placed rocks along the edges to hold the cloth still. Then an elderly calligrapher began sketching out the characters in white chalk. Moving with a fluid grace, the writer's entire body mirrored the strokes of a calligraphy brush dancing across the fabric as the piece of chalk dipped and curved, tracing the outline of four enormous Chinese characters.

As the final ideogram took shape, I couldn't help but snort with laughter. The words the calligrapher was so carefully inscribing on the banner were 賀佢老母, a sweary and wholly untranslatable pun in Cantonese, the dominant language spoken in Hong Kong and parts of southern China. A literal translation would be "Celebrate their mother!" but this was actually a pun playing on the most popular Cantonese insult: 屌你老母, or "Fuck your mother!" So the actual meaning of the banner was something along the lines of "Fuck your motherfucking National Day celebrations!" In other words, the slogan was calculated to cause maximum offense, by mocking the massive military parade to be held in Beijing and at the same time underscoring that Hong Kongers did not consider themselves part of the People's Republic of China. It was an irreverent slap in the face that was simultaneously laugh-out-loud funny and deadly serious, not least because, if caught, the sign painters could face jail time.

I watched as they grabbed their pots of paint and silently squatted beside the banner to begin filling in the characters, struggling with my desires. For months, my dual identities as a Hong Konger and a journalist had been engaged in a silent contest of wills, as I tried to safeguard my professional neutrality. This was becoming ever harder as the familiar world I'd grown up in, with all its predictable certainties, collapsed around me. On the surface it was still the same city pulsing with energy from the shoals of people surging through the skyscraper-lined streets, the beeping signals at zebra crossings, the LED signs jostling for airspace, the acrid dried-fish reek of a Chinese medicine shop melding with the rich bark-smoke aroma of a stall selling tea-steeped eggs. But the apparatus beneath this sensory cacophony was shifting in ways I could no longer ignore.

The police, instead of being guarantors of security, were behaving like violent thugs who beat and arrested children for wearing a particular color, or for standing in a particular street at a particular time, or for nothing at all. The courts, instead of being neutral arbiters of the law, were handing down political verdicts disqualifying popularly elected legislators from the legislature and imprisoning people for peaceful protests.

The government officials, instead of enacting and administering policy, had disappeared from view and were limiting their interactions with the populace to violence meted out by the police on their behalf. Overnight the world had turned upside down.

The known rules of engagement no longer seemed to apply, and this was also true for the practice of journalism. Far from protecting reporters as civilians, the police were singling us out for attack. They pepper-sprayed us, tear-gassed us, shot burning liquid laced with indelible blue dye from water cannons directly at us, pulled guns on us, beat us, arrested us. We'd begun by wearing fluorescent vests and helmets marked PRESS and 記者, but it soon became horribly obvious that we were effectively putting targets on our heads and torsos.

The sheer density of Hong Kong's maze of apartment blocks, alleyways, and markets meant that few residents were untouched by the government's forceful suppression of the protests. Almost 90 percent of the population had been tear-gassed. It could happen while you waited for a late-night snack of fishball noodles, on a Sunday afternoon stroll along the waterfront, or even while sitting at home, as stinging clouds drifted up from the street, leaching through window frames and air-conditioning vents. One-third of Hong Kong residents showed signs of post-traumatic stress disorder. It sometimes felt like the government was at war with its people.

It felt personal, too. The issue of belonging has always been a complicated one for me, as a half-English, half-Chinese person who was born in England but brought up in Hong Kong. My family had moved to Hong Kong when I was five, so that my Singaporean father could take up a civil service job. As far back as I could remember, this city had been my home. So while I am not a native Hong Konger, I was made by Hong Kong. I was shaped by Hong Kong values, in particular a respect for grinding hard work and stubborn determination. Hong Kongers called it Lion Rock Spirit, after a popular television series about a squatter colony living at the foot of a local landmark, a small mountain topped by a rocky formation resembling a Chinese lion crouching down, poised to leap. To me, Lion Rock Spirit translated into a willingness to fight to protect my values, no matter how powerful the opponent.

During the decade that I had been based in China as a journalist, that compunction drove me to write the stories that I felt needed telling, no matter how politically sensitive they were. It prompted me to leave Beijing in order to write a book about the Communist Party's bloody suppression of the 1989 protest movement in China, and how it had managed to excise those killings from the collective memory. I knew the book would prevent me from returning to China for many years, but I also knew it was a story that should be told. In journalistic terms, protest movements were my bailiwick, but I never in my wildest dreams imagined one would so thoroughly engulf my beloved hometown. Once it did, there was no question in my mind that I had to cover it. I was already living in Hong Kong, on research leave from my job teaching journalism in Melbourne, when the protests broke out. After I went back to work in Australia, I regularly returned to Hong Kong on short reporting trips, until Covid-19 closed our borders.

How to practice ethical journalism under the circumstances? Until this point, I'd unquestioningly followed the accepted journalistic practice of trying to remove myself from the story as far as possible. But could I remove myself from the picture when the picture was already part of me? I'd been grappling with this for months, without any clear answer.

That day on the rooftop, the question answered itself. I knew all the reasons why I should stay sitting on the sidelines, but I also knew that I wasn't going to. Driven by gut instinct, I stood up and walked over to take a paint pot for myself. I knew I was crossing a line, from neutral reporter to voluntary participant in an act of protest, and that in doing so, I was violating the cardinal tenet on which I had based a quarter century of journalistic endeavor. But I also realized at that instant that I didn't care. I didn't agree with everything the protest movement did. I was viscerally opposed to any use of violence, and it still shook me to see protestors throwing bricks at police or hurling petrol bombs, regardless of the tactics the police were using. But since the protests had begun, the idea of accountability seemed to unspool a little more every day. We were all living in the eternal present, where the future was so uncertain that it was unseeable, and the past had receded into irrelevance. And so, I placed my paint pot on the ground and, dipping my brush into the viscous white paint, I became a member of the team.

Filling in the "celebrate" 賀 character felt disappointingly anticlimactic at first. It was basically painting-by-numbers on a grand scale. It wasn't challenging, but the shakiness of my hands meant I had to concentrate so as not to dribble outside the lines. The sun was beating down on the back of my neck, and drops of sweat were falling from my forehead onto the fabric. But as I painted, I entered a kind of meditative daze, zeroing in on my small task to the extent that I forgot I was supposed to be interviewing the others. Quite literally, I was transfixed by the power of the word writ large.

There was something else propelling me, too. For years, I'd been obsessed with a mysterious individual who'd become the most unlikely of local icons. He was a toothless, often shirtless, disabled trash collector with mental health issues. But, through his misshapen, childlike calligraphy, he had become a household name, first reviled, then fêted. His given name was Tsang Tsou-choi, but everyone called him the King of Kowloon. Over the years, Tsang had come to believe that the jutting prong of the Kowloon peninsula had originally belonged to his family and had been stolen from them by the British in the nineteenth century. No one could say for sure why he believed this, but his conviction became a mania, as his imagined dominion extended to Hong Kong Island and the New Territories that make up the rest of Hong Kong.

In the mid-1950s, the King began a furious graffiti campaign accusing the British of stealing his land. His denunciations took the form of tottering towers of crooked Chinese calligraphy in which he painstakingly wrote out his entire lineage, all twenty-one generations of it, sometimes pairing names with the places they had lost, and occasionally topping it all off with expletives like "Fuck the Queen!" He waged his graffiti war first against the colonial British government, and then against China, after Britain returned Hong Kong to Chinese control in 1997.

The King did not bother with paper. Using a wolf-hair brush, he painted directly on the walls and slopes that he believed he'd lost, marking his domain with the art of emperors: Chinese calligraphy. He was exacting in his choice of canvas; he would paint only on Crown land, or, after the change in sovereignty, government land. He gravitated to electricity boxes and pillars, walls and flyover struts. His words played their own magic tricks before a captive audience of haggard commuters and weary retirees; they were there one day, gone the next, washed away or painted over by an army of government cleaners in rubber boots with thin hand towels hanging from the backs of their hats to serve as makeshift sunscreens. But overnight his words were back again, as if they had never disappeared, in a game of textual whack-a-mole played across the entire territory for half a century.

The crazy thing was that it worked, despite the King's execrable penmanship. He'd had only two years of formal schooling, and he advertised that educational deficit in every misshapen, unbalanced character that he wrote. But his shonky, wonky characters laid bare all the flaws and idiosyncrasies a proper calligrapher would have tried to suppress, and that made them memorable. His words were a celebration of originality and human imperfection with a who-gives-a-fuckness about them that was genuinely inspiring. He broke all the rules, repudiating traditional Chinese behavior. This, too, was a facet of Hong Kongness: Hong Kong was an in-between space, a site of transgression, a refuge where behavior not acceptable in mainland China was permitted and even celebrated.

By the time the King died from a heart attack, in 2007, he had made an estimated 55,845 works in public space. Over the years, his blocky characters slowly wrote themselves onto our brains to become a collective memory that was as iconic a marker of Hong Kong identity as its bottle-green snub-nosed Star Ferries or its spiky skyline. For so many, his words served as the first articulation of an uncomfortable instinct they couldn't quite voice themselves. "It's a little bit like our political situation," one commentator observed to me. "The land was owned by British, now owned by China. It's supposed to belong to China, but most Hong Kong people, they don't identify with the Chinese government. In some way they still think that Hong Kong is a colony, a colony of China. So what Tsang Tsou-choi did is something they want to do." The King was speaking for his people.

When he died in 2007, the newspapers erupted in a communal wail. *The King is dead, and everyone is missing him. . . . The King is dead and his people are crying and wailing. . . . The King is dead, his ink treasures were poetic masterpieces. . . . The King is dead and the writer is sad as Hong Kong has lost a legendary figure. . . . The King is dead, who will succeed him?* As his work disappeared from the streets, it appeared on the auction blocks of Sotheby's, surging in price until he was the most valuable artist in Hong Kong.

Some years ago, I'd been seized by the idea of writing a book about the King of Kowloon. It was a notion that I found hard to resist, even though it was obviously a fool's errand. His family had always refused to talk to journalists, and there was almost no concrete information about him. But I stubbornly set off on my quest, trekking out to industrial buildings, public housing estates, and villages in the New Territories to find people who'd known the King. These were places I'd never visited in the four decades that I'd lived on and off in Hong Kong. Along the way, I discovered a multitude of Hong Kongs. The Hong Kong I had grown up in had been a bubble within a bubble, and my pursuit of the King exploded that bubble.

As I painstakingly worked my way through the eccentric cast of characters who had painted with the King, sung about him, written about him, or simply knew him, I found the story slipping away from me. At first my aim had simply been to find out whether his claims to the land had any truth to them. I'd assumed that I would be able to pin down concrete details through my interviews. But all the interviewees disagreed vehemently about almost everything, even the slim handful of biographical data that existed, or whether he was mentally competent. Worse than that, they spent endless hours in interviews sniping at one another. None of my normal journalistic approaches seemed to be working.

Meanwhile, my pursuit of the King took me deeper into Hong Kong's story. To examine his claims to the land, I started looking at the acts of possession and expropriation by the British colonizers. I soon realized that, in order to understand these, I needed to make sense of the complex saga of how Hong Kong had become British in the first place. I hadn't intended to go any further back than that, but everyone who was interested in the King kept talking about the boy emperors of the Song dynasty who'd fled to Hong Kong in the twelfth century. Eventually, my new interest in Hong Kong's precolonial history led me all the way back to the middle Neolithic era, six thousand years ago. The King had somehow taken me back to the beginning.

Along the way, I fell into other untold stories of Hong Kong, creation myths and legends, real and invented histories, tales of rebellion that had been wiped from the record, tales of courage that had never been told. They changed the way I viewed Hong Kong history, which I'd always assumed was an inventory of cut-and-dried facts that fell into a straightforward narrative. Instead, these hidden histories in their kaleidoscopic, multicolor multitudes pushed back against the idea of a singular, authoritative, state-imposed narrative. They put Hong Kongers front and center of their story, in particular reinserting them into the crucial negotiations over the transfer of sovereignty, a chapter in which the most important Hong Kong voices have never before been heard. These hidden histories placed the insurrections of recent years in the context of a far longer narrative of defiance and dispossession. That was the story I ended up writing.

But even as the focus of my interest shifted, I found that the King had burrowed into my consciousness, as a prism through which Hong Kong's story could be viewed. A prism bends and separates white light into a rainbow of colors, and once the massive street protests began in 2019, his story refracted into variegated narrative stripes that illuminated Hong Kong in ways I had not anticipated. Like the story of the protest movement, his was a David and Goliath tale of a doomed rebellion against an overweening power. Like his story, the story of the protest movement has evolved into a story about erasure, about who gets to tell Hong Kong's story. Throughout their history, Hong Kongers have been minimized in, or even completely removed from, the official accounts told by their successive rulers. Hong Kongers have never been able to tell their own story; none, that is, except the poor, sad, old King—"the last free man in Hong Kong," as he was called by writer Fung Man-yee.

As I wrote, the King became, rather than my subject, my unlikely lodestar. Amid the scrolling whirligig of Hong Kong politics, I couldn't help noticing a pattern emerging. When something big happened, I often already knew the main players through my pursuit of the King. When in 2016 an outspoken university lecturer named Chin Wan became the first academic to lose his job for his political views, I remembered that he'd written the first essay in a book about the King. When legislator Tanya Chan was put on trial for her role in the Umbrella Movement, the eleven-week-long 2014 street occupation seeking greater democracy, I already knew her because of our shared interest in the King.

In 2020, when Hong Kong's top satirical TV show, *Headliners*, was canceled for its political content, I messaged my condolences to its host, Tsang Chi-ho; we'd become friends after I interviewed him about a newspaper column he'd written on the King. Sometimes it seemed like the King was guiding me from beyond the grave, breadcrumbing my trail to Hong Kong's most interesting thinkers.

This pattern was no coincidence. To think or write about the King was to consider his preoccupations: territory, sovereignty, and loss. He had publicly raised these issues at a time when no one else dared think about them. The very name he gave himself held within it a rebuke to Hong Kong's colonizers. He was the original sovereign, and Kowloon belonged to him; he was a shaman, a truth-teller, a holy fool.

As the years passed, this book grew harder to write. Its subject matter—sovereignty and identity—became intensely politically sensitive following Beijing's imposition of national security legislation on Hong Kong in June 2020. The way the law is being interpreted appears to view discussions of sovereignty or autonomy as potential secession, meaning that the King himself could nowadays be seen as a threat to national security. But in their continued acts of defiance, no matter how small, Hong Kongers are following the lead of their dead King.

So who today are the Kings of Kowloon? Are they the ancient clans in their walled villages who were the traditional subsoil owners, or the multinational corporations whose towering headquarters transformed the cityscape, or the Communist Party leaders in Beijing who can impose their will on the people of Hong Kong by fiat and force? Or are they the ordinary people who occupied the streets of Kowloon with their bodies, reclaiming the space-time that is their own? As if seen through a prism, the answer depends on the angle of viewing.

PART 1

DOMINION

CHAPTER 1

WORDS

It was during Hong Kong's steamy, explosive summer of 2019 that walls became weapons. Millions of people marched through the streets to protest against the extradition law they feared would mark the end of the territory's way of life. Armed with Sharpies and Post-it Notes, they feathered the walls with sorbet-colored declarations in black Chinese characters: *We love Hong Kong! We are Hong Kong! Hong Kong never give up!* These were not only walls of discontent but also walls of community; over and over, the messages asserted a distinct Hong Kong identity, separate from China.

Soon the notes were proliferating across overhead walkways and through underground tunnels, on shop windows and street signs, railings and billboards, like a swarm released into the wild, to pollinate and colonize the city. They evolved into pavement mosaics made up of scores of A4 photocopies glued end to end across the sidewalk near the government headquarters. Pedestrian walkways and underpasses quickly became impromptu galleries of dissent, with anonymous heartfelt pleas jostling for space. Often they were strategically placed. A black-and-white carpet of pictures of Chinese president Xi Jinping forced commuters to stomp on his face. Black-clad teams were deployed to paper footpaths at jogging speed, for kilometers at a time. Their assembly-line efficiency was mesmerizing to behold: an advance crew ran ahead, spraying glue, followed by a second string who threw down posters in a checkerboard pattern, black backgrounds alternating with white as they cantered past, and bringing up the rear, a final crew who used long umbrellas to tamp the posters down onto the glue as they ran. *Go, Hong Kong! Some people move on, BUT NOT US.* Soon the black-clad protestors had graduated to graffiti slogans spray-painted straight onto roads, highway dividers, and tram shelters. *Fuck the police. Chinazi. If we burn, you fucking burn with us.* Public surfaces became anonymous repositories for people's deepest and most dangerous sentiments.

The protests sprang out of the massive opposition to proposed changes to Hong Kong's extradition laws that would permit the rendition of alleged criminal suspects to China. This would put anyone, no matter their nationality, in danger of having to stand trial under a Communist Party–led legal system rife with abuse and with no presumption of innocence. The new extradition legislation would forcefully undermine the most basic tenets of Hong Kong's cherished status quo. It would endanger the city's judicial independence, its rule of law, and its status as a political refuge, the very things to which Hong Kong attributed its success. The British had not endowed their subjects with full citizenship, the right of abode in Britain, or universal suffrage, but they had inculcated them with civic values, including an almost religious respect for freedom, democracy, and human rights. And Hong Kongers were not going down without a fight.

I was transfixed by this movement building in front of my eyes, and especially by the explosion of subversive Chinese characters running riot across public space, repurposing the city into an evolving, open-air gallery of populist ideas. These displays were called Lennon Walls, after a wall in Prague that had been painted with countercultural, anti-establishment graffiti beginning in the 1980s, shortly after John Lennon's death. Hong Kong's original Lennon Wall had been established in 2014, during the pro-democracy protests of the Umbrella Movement, when people began sticking Post-it Notes on a circular concrete staircase near the government headquarters. I'd visited that wall daily, and I started doing the same this time. But it wasn't long before the Post-it Notes had leaped off the walls to become Lennon Paths, Lennon Footbridges, and Lennon Pavements, and I could no longer keep up.

IN CHINA, the history of the written word dates back some 3,700 years. Some scholars even argue that Chinese script preceded the spoken language. The first instances were pictographs known as *jiaguwen*, or "oracle bone" inscriptions carved with a sharp instrument on tortoise shells or the shoulder blades of oxen, dating to the Shang dynasty, sixteen centuries BCE. The inscriptions concerned all sorts of matters of state— questions about when to plant crops or which days might be auspicious to hold ceremonies or to launch wars. The bones were heated until they cracked, and oracles would divine the answers from the pattern of the cracks. So, from the moment of its inception, the written Chinese word was rooted in political and spiritual authority. Indeed, the original ideogram used for "written character" *zi* 字 is composed of two elements, 子 "child" in a 宀 "building," which together literally mean "new baby in the house." Thus the original meaning of 字 was "to birth" or "to deliver" or "to bring into the world," but that changed over time into "to raise," "to love," "to educate," "to govern," and "to administer." To borrow from the late, great sinologist Simon Leys, in the Chinese beginning, there was the word, and the word was *word*.

In traditional Chinese culture, calligraphy is both the apogee of all art forms and a tool of power. Whereas public squares in Europe are filled with statues of famous people, similar spaces in China contain stelas, or stone slabs, engraved with calligraphy. This holds true in Communist China, too, where the unorthodox rightward-slanting characters of Chairman Mao Zedong still adorn newspaper mastheads and building signs. China's current president, Xi Jinping, has adopted a Mao-style signature, as if appropriating Mao's penmanship might also arrogate some of the Master Calligrapher-Poet's powers. The quality of emperors' brushwork showcased their erudition, aesthetic sensibilities, and poetic capabilities, while giving hints of their leadership style. The appreciation of calligraphy is an art form in itself, since true aficionados do not simply read the text but rather mentally replay the brush's fleeting dance across the page in an act that Leys described as "an imaginative communion with the dynamics of the brushwork."

But the King of Kowloon flew in the face of that tradition, with brushstrokes that screamed his illiteracy. They were everywhere in Hong Kong's public space when I was growing up—they spidered down lampposts and across walls, along curbs and flyovers, flickered at the edge of your vision as you hurtled past in a minibus. The King himself was a fixture of the landscape as well. Hopping on his crutches, with plastic bags swinging from the handles, his crab-like, bow-legged silhouette was so distinctive that, if people saw him in the distance, they would cross the road to avoid him. As he passed, parents would shield their kids' eyes from him and mutter, "*Chi-sin a!* Crazy!" He even became a playground taunt—"You're the King of Kowloon!" was leveled at the slow kids, the weird ones, the poor ones, the outcasts.

The details of Tsang's life are sketchy in the extreme, but it is known that he was born in Guangdong province, in Liantang village in Zhaoqing prefecture. He began school at the age of nine and dropped out two years later. At the age of sixteen, he crossed the border to Hong Kong and worked as a vegetable farmer near Choi Hung and Lion Rock. He was later employed as a laborer at a building-materials company, and then at a trash collection station. In 1956, he married Man Fuk-choi, who had been brought up in San Tin village in the New Territories, home to the Man clan that had settled Hong Kong in the Song dynasty. The couple had eight children, three of whom died in infancy.

No matter how much I asked, no one was able to give me a definitive version of the King's moment of epiphany. Some people said he had gone back to his ancestral village to add his wife's name to family records, and while he was there he had uncovered ancestral documents showing that the Kowloon peninsula had originally belonged to his clan and had been confiscated without compensation after the act of cession. But no one I spoke to had seen these documents. In fact, none had even been to his village. One of his self-appointed regents had attempted the journey but had failed to determine which was the correct Liantang village, among a number in the area.

Another story I heard was that Tsang had been hit by a car around the mid-1950s as he was walking past the Three Mountain Kings Temple in Ngau Chi Wan. When he opened his eyes after the accident, the first sight that flickered into his vision were the words 國 "country" and 王 "king" emblazoned across the lantern outside the temple in thick square strokes. Those two characters became the anchors for the King's slabs of text, looming over all the others. Together in Chinese, they read, 國王, "King of the Country," though he sometimes wrote 國皇, "Emperor of the Country." He became known as the King of Kowloon in English, but in Chinese he was always the "Kowloon Emperor."

The King began writing in public around 1956, and he was initially viewed as a crank and a vandal. In the 1960s, he was said to have smashed the window of a post office with a rock, after which he was sent to the psychiatric ward of the notorious Castle Peak Hospital for eighteen months. On his release, he continued his graffiti campaign, daubing his anger across government property in thick black slashes. His sanity may have been in question, but his methods were highly contextual. "Emperors in China," he said, "have always been calligraphers." In 1970, he first appears in a local newspaper, which mentions his "imperial decrees" across public space. It describes him as living in a small wooden shack on a hillside, which he called his "palace." Outside was a wooden notice-board inscribed with four characters: 國泰民安, "The country is prosperous and its people live in safety." At some point in the 1980s, he had a work accident, possibly when a trash bin crushed his legs, leaving him on crutches.

The die had been cast. Others may have seen him as a disabled, mentally unstable old man who stank to high heaven. But in his mind, he was an emperor, and he lived this reality. Sometimes he even called himself the Emperor of China and England for good measure. He saw everyone else as his subjects, a sentiment to which he sometimes gave voice: "As a King, I can't be in touch with you ordinary people."

Simon Go Man-ching, a photojournalist who became fascinated by the distinctive graffiti he saw appearing everywhere in Hong Kong in the early 1990s, when he was a student at the Polytechnic University, began keeping a record of Tsang's public writings. When a rumor circulated that the King had died, Go spent two days on his trail, tracking him like an urban hunter. Eventually he found the King's address—"living in Tsui Ping estate"—graffitied on a wall. That was how he located Tsang Tsou-choi in his flat on the eighteenth story of a public housing estate in Kwun Tong, an industrial and working-class part of Kowloon facing Hong Kong Island's northern shore.

After that, Go became the first of those self-appointed regents looking in on the King every few weeks, bringing him painting supplies, lunch boxes of roast meat, and cans of Coke. Tsang's own family did not live with him. Some said his wife brought him food every day, but by Tsang's own account, his family had disowned him. "My wife visited me and said I was crazy. She said damaging the post office was a serious crime," he told a film crew. "They said I'd drag them down with me. They said I'd die in prison."

Go saw him as a lonely old man and would humor his wishes, even addressing him as "King." Once when he forgot to bring ink and brushes, Go apologized and jokingly asked whether, as a loyal subject, he should execute himself to atone for his error. The King answered straight-faced, "No need. It's okay." Another fan, photographer Birdy Chu, recalled a taxi ride they took together. As they discussed where to disembark without illegally stopping on any yellow lines, the King regally announced, "I'm the King. I'm the King. I can just be dropped off anywhere." To the King, the normal rules did not apply. To Go, the legitimacy of the King's claims on the land was irrelevant. "I think it's a personal story or history," he said. "To him, it's really important but to me it doesn't mean anything."

The family did not welcome outside attention. Go had once been warned by one of the sons to leave King's apartment immediately or he'd call the police. The curator Lau Kin-wai, who took over as de facto regent, also recalled a son answering the door to his knock by saying, "Go away! He's dead." But while the family could limit contact, they could not stem the King's flood of words even though they were so mortified by his work that they refused to countenance it, and reportedly never received any money from it. They could not stop him from incorporating them in his work, either. The King referred to his wife, Man Fuk-choi, as "the Empress," and he painstakingly wrote out the names of his sons, the dauphins. When his daughters moved overseas—one to the United Kingdom, one to the Netherlands—he sometimes mentioned they were having tea with the Queen of England or the Queen of the Netherlands. Very occasionally he used random English words such as "reach" or "snowman" in his work.

Just before Hong Kong's return to China in 1997, Tsang Tsou-choi had an art exhibition. It was a sensation, a circus, a spectacle, a travesty. The art establishment was scandalized and not a single work sold. The very next day he was out again on the streets, marking his dominion as he always had done.

Over time, the commercial success that had initially eluded his work found him. In 2003, he became the first Hong Konger to represent the territory at the prestigious Venice Biennale. He made cameos in local movies, there were songs sung about him, poems written to him, and his stinky calligraphy-covered T-shirt appeared in the rarefied auction rooms of Sotheby's. His cramped, crooked calligraphy had crawled off the streets onto bedsheets and underpants and tote bags, eventually adorning whisky bottles, T-shirts, Starbucks walls, and sneakers as a commodity in its own right. But the King was always clear about his role. In one of his rare interviews, in 2005, he said, "They should just give me back my throne. I am not an artist—I am simply the King."

His screeds were love letters to both the land and the family that he had lost. Despite their opposition, he went on writing in the streets until 2004. That was the year that he accidentally started a fire in his own apartment, and was sent to live in an old people's home for his safety.

Over the years, the constancy of his message came to reassure Hong Kongers. Our past was contested, our future unclear, but the King of Kowloon was still proclaiming himself our monarch, as he had for half a century, telling a story of dispossession that began to resonate with our own. It might have been written off as a mere game, something to smile about, but the sheer sustained audacity of his defiance lifted the clumsy, misshapen characters into an act of faith repeated day after day, laying claim to our piece of earth and proclaiming dominion over it. As an artist he was Banksy before Banksy, Keith Haring before Keith Haring, but the sheer chutzpah of his claims and the duration of his campaign lifted it into another category altogether. Even David and Goliath didn't approach the asymmetric power differential embodied in one obsessive, mentally and physically challenged pensioner getting out of bed every morning to take on two global powers in succession.

I was fascinated by the legend of the King, in particular because there was so much about his life that was completely unclear. Even those closest to him couldn't say if he was mentally competent. Some said he was schizophrenic, others that he had multiple personality disorder, or delusions. Or that he was totally fine and could play mahjong perfectly, and often did so with his neighbors. Some said he was polite, others said he was incoherent. As a journalist with a penchant for telling untellable stories, this element of mystery appealed to me, as well as his role as a totemic self-made icon. But I also felt a kind of kinship with him that was intensely personal.

I had first studied calligraphy as a student learning Chinese in Beijing in the early 1990s, and I had continued during my first job, as a translator and editor at a state-run publishing house a few years later. I was a small cog in China's publicity machine, and I spent my days "polishing" reams of incomprehensible and risible propaganda, only to find that every mistake I removed was reinstated by my editor, who was terrified by the loss of face implied by the act of correction. The project that summed up my entire time there was the translation into English of the collected works of an eminent, but eminently dull, macroeconomist. I managed to translate only a single chapter, but a friend labored over the rest for months. At the precise moment when the massive tome was complete, the economist fell out of political favor, and the entire project was shelved.

The work was direly dull, but being a state-run work unit, it did not take up much of the day. We had two-hour lunch breaks, during which my colleagues did their vegetable shopping or went to wash in the work unit bathhouse, as well as half-hour table tennis breaks in the morning and afternoon. I needed something to fill my time, so I took up calligraphy and spent my breaks filling flimsy sheets of brown paper with precarious, misshapen characters. It is perhaps no coincidence that "character" has a double meaning in English, signifying both the ideograms of Chinese writing and the range of qualities and defects that create a personality. I loved the meditative simplicity of calligraphy, the idea that the balance and beauty of the words reflected the inner self, though I was slightly disturbed by the import of my own wobbly, unbalanced scrawl.

Once a week, I'd roll up my sheets of brown paper, cram them into my backpack, and cycle over to my teacher's house. He was an elderly, exacting dictator of the old school, and he made it quite clear that he had lowered his standards considerably to accept a *laowai* foreigner like myself as a student. It would be an exaggeration to call him encouraging of my efforts. It was our tacit understanding that he was deigning to allow me to continue attending class even though he had no great hope that I would ever improve.

Calligraphy is about control, in particular dominating the wolf-hair brush and corralling its power. This is far harder than it sounds, requiring the simultaneous deployment of intense mental focus, muscular control, and artistic ability. The art is extraordinarily codified; each character is made up of a series of brushstrokes, which must be made in the correct order. Each stroke has a different name and requires a specific technique.

Take the example of the straight line—*heng*—which to the uninitiated looks like a dash whipped casually across the page. For months, this stroke taunted me with its deceptive simplicity; its single jaunty slash contains a world of unspoken conventions that an outsider would never notice. The calligrapher begins by tilting the brush to give a dapper slant to the left-hand side of the dash. Then the brush is swished across the page, pressure slightly lifted. The trickiest moment comes when navigating the right-hand extremity of the stroke; the writer must flick the tip of the brush around and back in a clockwise movement in order to create a debonair backslash that balances out that side of the *heng*.

Managing the ink presents a separate set of difficulties. It comes in thick, squat, sooty-smelling rectangular sticks, which the calligrapher grinds down with just the right amount of water. Too little water makes the ink thick and sticky, while too much dilutes its ebony tones to a weak gray that bleeds into the tissue-thin paper, turning it into a watery, uncontrollable swamp. Calligraphy is an unforgiving art form. Each element must be perfect in order to create the conditions in which a perfect character can be written. Every mistake is indelible. There can be no do-overs, no second chances, no rescue missions. And weaknesses cannot be hidden or disguised. Its ascetic simplicity is extraordinarily punishing for beginners. I spent weeks—in all honesty, months—trying to master the single *heng* stroke. But my *heng*s lacked panache. They never flowed or flew. The harder I tried, the worse they limped and straggled. As I frog-marched *heng*s across the page, they rebelled by flopping and sagging, dropping and lolling into hesitant, quivery filaments.

Week after week, I could tell from my teacher's expression as he looked at my sheaves of practice paper that I had not performed to his satisfaction. Had I been a Chinese student, I would never have progressed any further, but eventually he took pity on me and allowed me to graduate from the single stroke of number one 一 to number two 二 and then on to number three 三. My excitement at progressing past one *heng* was tempered by the fact that I was still only doing *heng*s, just more of them, which exponentially complicated the challenge. Not only did each stroke have to be perfectly balanced, they also had to work together in harmony.

Calligraphy is in part a meditation, its mental and spiritual aspects building it into a holistic occupation reflecting every facet of the writer's personality. One text from the seventh century lays this out bluntly, stating, "Calligraphy with much strength and rich in sinew is of sagelike quality; that with neither strength nor sinew is sick. Every writer proceeds in accordance with the manifestation of his digestion and respiration of energy." Thus my inability to write a single perfect *heng* represented a full-spectrum failure not just of my artistic ability but also of my character, including my mental focus, moral fiber, and inner strength. I aspired to a nirvana-like state of calm and balance, but my monkey mind and shaky hands betrayed me.

This was, I knew, part of a pattern, as I have an unconscious habit of taking up hobbies that I actively dislike. Over the years, these have included violin playing, birdwatching, parachuting, and, most recently, running, a hobby I both actively despise and have religiously practiced for a full six years. Perhaps, unsurprisingly, I have a habit of failing at my hobbies: I was too tone-deaf to play the violin; I didn't have the patience to watch birds; I was too scared to freefall in parachuting; and when I run, I waddle like an arthritic duck. But I like to think there's something gallant about attempting to conquer a skill to which one is entirely unsuited.

When I took up calligraphy, my father had been quietly elated. His own father, Lim Keng-chew, had been a scholar, and my father had always hoped that one of his three daughters would somehow follow in his father's footsteps. Our grandfather had left his home village of Xiamen in Fujian in the 1880s in disgust at corruption, and moved to Singapore, where he had been a founding member of Sun Yat-sen's Tongmenghui, the movement that overthrew China's last dynasty, the Qing. Our grandfather had helped bankroll the revolution, donating money and shoes from his shoe shop to the troops. He had been a patriarch with four wives—three simultaneously under one roof—and so many children that no one could ever quite manage to construct our family tree. Our father, Lim Poh-chye, was the youngest son of the fourth wife, and had six brothers and one sister of his own, not counting the half brothers and sisters. Family gatherings are epic; the last time I visited Singapore, a small meal for immediate family turned into a sixty-person get-together where the most popular pastime was good-humored bickering about the identity of those family members no one could recognize.

When the Japanese invaded Singapore, my father was forced to burn my grandfather's life's work. The Japanese were targeting intellectuals, and the family needed to rid itself of any evidence of learning. The youngest boy, so tiny he was beyond suspicion or comprehension, was chosen for the task of tending the bonfire. The only piece of my grandfather's work that remains is a single twenty-character poem so complicated that no one has ever been able to decipher exactly what it means. My grandfather's inkstone had even been one of the objects of an unseemly tussle between my father and one of his brothers. Guided by fuzzy half memories of his own father, my father has always cherished a vision of spending his dotage as a traditional scholar surrounded by the Four Treasures of the Study—the inkstone, the ink brush, the brush stand, and the brush pot—penning beautiful characters with a brush that whisks lightly across the rice paper like a water boatman darting along the surface of a river in summer. When I started practicing calligraphy, my father gave me a handsome inkstone bordered with pop-eyed fish leaping through the breaking waves. I suspect we both knew that it would not be all that well used.

Even showing my ugly, lopsided characters to my father—whose own calligraphy was endearingly off-balance and frail—made me blush. Nothing would have induced me to share them with my colleagues or Chinese friends, who would secretly pity me for my illiteracy and wonder why I was not ashamed to show off my failings so publicly. But the King of Kowloon did not suffer from such doubts. He had no regard for the conventions of thousands of years of Chinese culture. He would use the Art of Kings to proclaim his dominion across the territory, regardless of the fact that people found his writing as ugly as the crooked printing of a six-year-old child. My teacher would have tried to turn his blocky square characters—large and small mashed together, sometimes overlapping—into the bland, standardized excellence that Chinese culture celebrates. But a King writes his own rules.

To trumpet his losses publicly rather than hiding his shameful failure was also unusual, perhaps even un-Chinese. This was something I instinctively understood, since my mixed blood also made me un-Chinese, hovering between two cultures like the hungry ghosts flitting between two worlds. My parents had transgressed racial norms to marry, against the wishes of both their families. But they defied their families, and in Hong Kong they defied the roles defined by their respective races. Though ethnically Chinese, my father had managed to snag a position as a colonial civil servant, so he became that most oxymoronic of categories: the Chinese expat. My posh British mother, despite her tone-deaf Cantonese, became one of the first experts on Hong Kong's local cultural heritage. In the in-between zone that Hong Kong represented, both my parents carved out new and sometimes uncomfortable spaces in which to exist.

I grew up in Hong Kong surrounded by a sepia tribe of Eurasians. Many of our fathers worked for the colonial government as administrators or policemen, so we lived in an affluent area known as Mid-Levels, which housed many expats and businessmen, just up the hill from the government headquarters in Central. It was perhaps apt, given Mid-Levels' location halfway up the sharp pinnacle known as the Peak, which was traditionally—and at the beginning of the twentieth century, legally—reserved for European inhabitation. But our small bubble cocooned us from the historical anomaly that we ourselves presented.

We were not exactly locals, and many of us didn't even speak Cantonese, but we never questioned our right to think of ourselves as Hong Kongers. The vast majority of Hong Kong's residents at that time had come from elsewhere, and we saw ourselves as the natural corollaries of Hong Kong's peculiar political proposition, transcending the stale, fixed identities of the past. Our worldview was formed by constant shape-shifting and code-switching. To us, Hong Kong's unusual status, suspended between British and Chinese rule, made it the embodiment of our identity. Every day in our own homes, we were interpreters and intermediaries between the two sides of ourselves. We were hybrids, Chinese-Western concoctions like the *yuan-yang* coffee-tea mixture served in the *cha chaan teng* teahouses, which served fusion versions of European food and so became defiantly homegrown in their commingling.

The work of the King of Kowloon was part of the backdrop to our childhood, a feature of the landscape in the same way as the little shrines punctuating the pavement, the solid red colonial postboxes with their curlicued royal insignia, and the thicket of neon signs vying for air. It was part of our streetscape, and I didn't even think about it; it was just there. Later on, when his characters had vanished, the thought of them evoked a sense of loss that was both diffuse and particular.

The particular regret was straightforward and covetous. I had almost bought a piece of the King's work that I loved but couldn't afford.

It was 1996, a year before Hong Kong's return to Chinese rule, and I was a junior reporter at TVB Pearl, a low-budget local television station that has since become a widely hated government mouthpiece. My salary was derisory, but I was so young that I still felt relatively rich. I had gone to a poky gallery perched on the steep slope leading to Central to meet a friend who worked there, and I'd seen a piece of the King of Kowloon's work hanging on the wall. I immediately wanted it. It was a piece in two halves. One half consisted of a photograph of a gray electricity box covered with the King of Kowloon's calligraphy, standing in front of the gray dome of Hong Kong's Space Museum. The other half was a gray wooden board covered with the King's utterly distinctive calligraphy.

I kept going back to the gallery to look at the piece and dream about buying it. It cost $1,300 (HK$10,000), which was almost a month's salary and clearly out of my price range. The gallerist recognized this immediately and treated me with a mixture of disdain, pomposity, and impatience that should have put me off. But I couldn't keep myself from returning time and again to loiter lovingly in front of the piece. On each visit, the gallery owner would share a new tidbit of discouraging information. The piece might not last, he said with an air of confidentiality, since no one knew how to preserve wooden board and the ink might fade away, so it could be a waste of money. It wasn't really the King's work, either, since the curator Lau Kin-wai had taken the photograph and put the piece together, so technically it was Lau's work rather than the King's, and thus it might not hold its value. I probably could have borrowed money from my parents, who were both wildly eccentric hoarders with collections that ranged from the utterly valueless (hotel keycards, shoe-laces, restaurant matchbooks) to the distinctly valuable (Cultural Revolution stamps, Yixing purple clay teapots, first edition fine art books). They understood the hankering to possess. But for some reason, I never asked them for a loan, and I regret it to this day.

In terms of sheer economics, it was a terrible decision. Although the King didn't sell a single piece from his first exhibition, the value of his work shot up over the years, in part because of its scarcity. In 2009, a similar piece from the same series—not faded in the slightest—sold at Sotheby's for $27,500 (HK$212,500), seven times the presale estimate. Nowadays, it would fetch even more.

The more diffuse regret was harder to articulate. The King's work unlocked emotions that I hadn't known were there. His work rooted me comfortingly in an earlier time, when life was routine and predictable. A time of hope and optimism, when there were things to look forward to. Our city had always been a work in motion, creeping outward as we filled in the sea with massive land reclamations, and upward as we built settlements of shimmering skyscrapers, like pickup sticks that had somehow all landed vertically. It was an act of faith, a steel-and-concrete expression of human endeavor against the odds. Viewed from above, it looked like the city had skittered down the side of a mountain to make a space grab that was horizontal and vertical at the same time. The King's calligraphic appropriations both echoed and transformed our ambitious cityscape.

But in the decades that followed the return to Chinese sovereignty, the city began to feel less and less familiar. Most obvious among the en-croachments, big and small, was the increasing number of tourists from the mainland who filled the streets. Large red Communist-style banners and placards suddenly popped up to mark new public holidays such as China's National Day. After the protests began in June 2019, the city was utterly transformed again, this time into a war zone policed by shielded, booted riot units that looked like villains from a dystopian anime. You could get tear-gassed or arrested or shot while buying a sandwich during your lunch break. By now, the King's work was almost entirely lost from the streets, and the comforting memory of the bygone time of trusting anticipation it evoked was lost to me.

Over the years I worked as a full-time correspondent based in China, a career I juggled with raising two children, and I had no time for anything but the immediate. But on a reporting trip back to Hong Kong in 2011, sitting in my parents' tiny aerie, drinking coffee and reading the newspapers, I spotted an announcement for an ungrammatically titled retrospective called *Memories of King Kowloon*. I cleared out some time between interviews and went.

I'd been expecting to be bowled over, but instead I was struck by an odd sensation of absence. Each room was dark, dramatically backlit. The first contained maps with little glowing orange-red pillars marking where the King's work had been: the eighty locations of the 55,845 pieces of work, using 1,170 liters of ink over the course of fifty-one years of writing. A room labeled "The Treasures of the King" contained his belongings, mounted in temperature-controlled glass cases, his ink-encrusted brushes and leaky Sharpies accorded the sterile respect of religious relics. There was a rusty wall clock, a grubby towel, half-empty pots of writing ink, crushed Coke cans, the detritus of an old man's life elevated to commodity status.

In the third room, the walls were covered with the work he'd done in later life, hanging in white frames. In the nursing home, his ink had been confiscated as smelly and dirty, so he spent his days covering sheets of paper with marker-pen scrawl. The next room was entitled "Original

Works of His Majesty," though on the contrary, it appeared to consist of objects—leather boots, glass jars, T-shirts, plastic toys—that people had brought to him to be painted and curators had pressed into his hands, knowing that the walls that were his natural canvas could not be transported into art galleries or sold.

Then there was a room of glass-covered obelisks, onto which were pinned newspapers with coverage of his 2007 death from a heart attack. Finally, there was a room full of tribute work to him, done by young Hong Kong artists and art students. A gathering of small, squat, fleshy earthen figurines resembling Jabba the Hutt, but with jowls that extended into bosoms. A spermy ink painting, an oil of a doglike creature weeping an enormous tear, then a photograph of an artist bare from the waist up, making a poor copy of the King's work while dangling upside down from the ceiling. As I walked round, I felt bemused, then confused, then cheated. Somehow, amid all these "Memories of King Kowloon," the essence of the artist had vanished. Without the monumental pieces of work that took your breath away with the sheer lunacy of the endeavor, the majesty of his mission was missing.

And that mission had presaged the political movement, in both form and content. The King had taken politics into the street and to the people decades before anyone else. "He was the original Occupier!" exclaimed one young designer to me after the Umbrella Movement, when Hong Kongers occupied some of the city's most important thoroughfares for seventy-nine days to demand more democracy. Again and again over the years, his ideas had trickled into the lifeblood of the city through the medium of calligraphy, percolating through its veins, slowly suffusing its extremities.

Despite the size of his oeuvre, little of the King's work in public space survived his death. Most of it had been cleaned away almost as soon as it was finished, and when he died, there were calls to protect the remaining pieces. But the government was ambivalent about its artistic value, pointedly calling his work "ink writing" rather than "calligraphy," and initially protecting only a pillar at the Star Ferry Pier in Tsimshatsui with a crude plastic screen. Later on, it also encased a lamppost near a children's playground in a plastic box, but calls for a proper audit of the King's remaining work were ignored. In 2017, one of the last extant pieces—writing on an electricity signal box—was whitewashed by an overenthusiastic government contractor. Finally only a tiny handful of fading works remained in good condition in public space, four at last count, with a couple of others weathered beyond all recognition.

Yet even in his disappearance is the King symbolic. For disappearance is the ultimate fear of Hong Kongers. The island, only seven miles from end to end, is destined to be subsumed into a Greater China. There are reams of academic literature about Hong Kong's liminality, its evanescence, its temporality. A borrowed place on borrowed time. Indeed, one of the most famous pieces of writing on Hong Kong is by cultural critic Ackbar Abbas, who back in 1997 theorized that Hong Kong's main characteristic was "a culture of disappearance whose appearance is posited on the immanence of its disappearance."

Disappearance was the fate of the King's work, and it was also the fate of the Post-it walls. Right at the beginning of the protest movement, I came across a carefully copied quote from the film *V for Vendetta* on a Lennon Wall: "While the truncheon may be used in lieu of conversation, words will always retain their power." And so it came to be. Riot police were deployed against the protestors, using first pepper spray, then tear gas, then rubber bullets, then sponge grenades, then water cannons, then water cannons spraying a new chemical-laced indelible blue dye that burned and stung, then a sonic weapon that disoriented people and made them vomit, then, finally and inevitably, live ammunition. The protestors began fighting back with bricks, then catapults, then bows and arrows, then Molotov cocktails and homemade bombs.

It did not take long for the Lennon Walls to come under attack. Soon after the protests began, pro-police protestors dismantled the original wall near the Legislative Council, ripping down the posters and stamping on them. Then dozens of riot police clad in protective gear and wielding shields were deployed to a maze of underground walkways that had been christened Lennon Tunnel in Taipo in the New Territories, to remove Post-it Notes allegedly leaking personal information about police officers. Then a Lennon Wall on a footbridge in Fanling near the border with China proper was set on fire by an arsonist at four o'clock in the morning. Then four hundred suspected gang members wearing identical white T-shirts hijacked the Lennon Tunnel in the dead of night, spending hours covering up the Post-it Notes with stickers of foreign flags, to suggest that hostile foreign forces were driving the protest movement. They left behind funeral wreaths with photographs of outspoken pro-democracy legislators as a not-so-subtle death threat. Then fights began to break out at Lennon Walls, with pro-government supporters accosting people to stop them from putting up their Post-it Notes. Three months into the protests, a mainlander attacked three people at a Lennon Wall in Tseung Kwan O in the New Territories. He asked them their political views, and when they answered, he stabbed them, shouting, "I can't hold it any longer."

In standing up for their ideals, Hong Kongers were putting themselves on the front line of a global battle between liberal democratic values and an increasingly totalitarian Communist regime. That clash began to play out on streets—and walls—across the world, as the Lennon Walls proliferated overseas. They became sites of violent contention in the US, Australia, and Canada, as mainland Chinese—often bearing loudspeakers blasting out their national anthem—faced off against pro–Hong Kong protestors. This tiny dot on the map had managed to unsettle the world's newest superpower with the power of its convictions.

These walls had become a textual outpouring of nationalism for a place that was never meant to be a nation. But that conversation had been opened decades before, by a King who was shunned then embraced by his subjects. Now it was being held in public—with words and weapons—and the stakes could not have been higher.

CHAPTER 2

ANCESTORS

I still have in my possession a gigantic slab of a book that I bought at some point and lugged around the world with me like a totem. *Mapping Hong Kong: A Historical Atlas* is a kind of cartographic storybook that, in collating all the known early maps of Hong Kong, charts its shifting status as it coalesces into being, flitting around the coast of southern China in a variety of guises until it becomes firmly pinned to the map with the arrival of Western surveyors. The first chart, from around 1425, shows a route taken by the Chinese admiral and explorer Zheng He as he and his gigantic fleet ventured far from home, traveling as far as the eastern coast of Africa. The islands are marked by striated boulder-like mountains in the sea. Hong Kong itself is not named, though some familiar spots are marked, including tiny Po Toi Island, where my family used to go to by junk and to eat plates of boiled shrimp and freshly caught steamed fish. Nor is Hong Kong featured on the second map, from 1553, which has carefully hand-drawn waves denoting the sea, and small square forts with flags fluttering over their tiled roofs accompanied by helpful notes ("places inhabited by barbarians" and "barbarian ships mooring").

The name Hong Kong—香港, pronounced *heung gong*—first appears in the atlas on a late sixteenth-century map by Kwok Fei below four sharp rocks rearing up from the sea. This is the earliest known mention of Hong Kong in Chinese records. The map features sturdy double-masted boats bobbing in the waves, likely oceangoing carracks reflecting Portugal's 1557 colonization of Macau. After that, Hong Kong disappears from view. Neither the island nor the name features either in the delicate curlicued lettering of the Earl of Dudley's 1646 map or in a 1723 Chinese map from a woodblock print, where a recognizable coastline is beginning to emerge. As time goes on, the island of Hong Kong periodically heaves into sight, variously named Hung Kong (Red River), Hung Heung Lo (Red Incense Burner), or Hung Heung Lo Shan (Red Incense Burner Hill). One theory regarding the name "Hong Kong" is that it was derived from the island's main export: incense from a tree called *kuan heung*. Thus *heung gong* could mean either Incense Harbor or Fragrant Harbor. In 1760, a map by an East India Company hydrographer calls Hong Kong "Fanchin Chow," a name repeated on Captain Hayter's 1780 hand-colored map alongside a more recognizable alternative—"Fan-chin-chow or He-ong Kong." I find this map charming for its crabbed little notes—"Coast full of Rocks"—and for the parts of it that appear to be entirely make-believe, such as certain coastal features and the decision to give Lantau the alternative name of "Magpyes Island."

Indeed, the Hong Kong of my atlas is itself a fantastical creature, a shifting, slippery entity that, like a sea monster, resurfaces from the cresting waves at different places under different aliases at different times, according to the whim of the cartographer. The very concept of Hong Kong changed under British rule, first referring to the single island in 1842, but eventually stretching to encompass Hong Kong, Kowloon, and the New Territories, as well as 263 outlying islands, by 1898. The atlas in turn inspired an extraordinary book by Dung Kai-cheung, called *Atlas: The Archaeology of an Imaginary City*. Published in Chinese in the year of Hong

Kong's transfer of sovereignty, Dung's book, described as a verbal collection of maps, is part fact, part imagination, somewhat like Captain Hayter's fantastical multicolored map. As Dung writes, "There are enough fictitious Hong Kongs circulating around the world. It doesn't matter so much how real or false these fictions are but how they are made up."

The most common fictitious Hong Kong in the Western world was the version imprinted on my brain as I sat, cross-legged and open-mouthed in my yellow-and-white-checked cotton dress, on the squeaky wooden floor at school, listening to Miss Huntingdon, who was so tall that I felt like I only reached her knees. I don't remember being explicitly taught the story of Hong Kong, but if we had been, this is what Miss Huntingdon would have said: Once upon a time, Hong Kong was a barren rock with no more than a tiny fishing village upon it. Almost no one lived here, because there was almost nothing here at all. Then the British arrived, and that changed everything. The British brought with them schools, hospitals, a police force, law courts, government, and, above all, trade. And so, people began moving to Hong Kong in search of a brighter future, and they helped to build it into Asia's Global City.

This is Britain's imaginary Hong Kong. It was created in 1841 by Lord Palmerston, who before he became prime minister was Britain's foreign secretary. His description of Hong Kong, as "a barren island with nary a house on it," has since been repeated ad nauseam in countless parliamentary debates, books, television programs, and magazine profiles. This narrative deprived Hong Kong of a precolonial history, and Hong Kongers of progenitors: according to this account, they were spawned by a rootless, migratory population who ended up on this stony terra nullius solely for the opportunities created by Britain's Emporium of Trade. As children of the colony, we never thought to question this version of its past. We absorbed the idea that without empire, Hong Kong would have remained a barren rock.

Beijing's narrative has gone similarly unquestioned by legions of Chinese schoolchildren. This version has Hong Kong as Chinese soil from time immemorial until it was snatched away by imperial aggressors who used gunboat diplomacy to enforce an "unequal treaty" that was never seen as valid by the Qing dynasty. That's the context underpinning the story I stumbled across in the textbook my son studied at weekend Chinese school in Melbourne. In fact it was the same textbook, developed by the State Council's Overseas Chinese Affairs Office, that my kids had used when they attended weekend Chinese school in the United States.

In the story, "Visiting Hong Kong," the narrator is a Chinese child visiting her relatives who live in Hong Kong. On the second day of the visit, they drive up the Peak, the island's rocky pinnacle ringed with mansions built by the British settlers who so valued its cooler air that they banned Chinese people from living there. It's now a popular tourist destination, thanks to the slick Peak Tram to its summit, updated from a rickety funicular, and the vertigo-inducing views of the skyscraper-studded harbor. As the family in the story gaze down at the skyline, the child's uncle points out the Convention and Exhibition Centre, saying, "At midnight on July 1, 1997, it was there that the Chinese and British governments held a handover ceremony returning Hong Kong's sovereignty to China." The aunt then explains, "Hong Kong now is a Special Administrative Region of China, which implements One Country, Two Systems, 'Hong Kong people ruling Hong Kong,' a high degree of autonomy. Its first Chief Executive was Tung Chee-hwa. Hong Kong people have confidence that an even better Hong Kong will be constructed." A cousin looks out into the distance through binoculars and points. "Can you see that? There's a Five-Starred Red flag"—the Chinese national flag. Then Uncle drives them down the Peak, and they go shopping. The streets are packed and the atmosphere is bustling. After dinner, they drive to Kowloon and gaze back across the harbor at the twinkling, multicolored lights of Hong Kong reflected in the water. It seems even more beautiful, even more attractive.

At first I was amused by the clunkiness of the story, which fell totally flat with my son at least. Then I realized that this lesson formed part of a sophisticated campaign to seed a particular narrative in Chinese communities around the world from an early age. The omissions are notable. The story never mentions British colonization, which might hint at China's past weakness, but instead turns its gaze to the bright future. The Five-Starred Red flag seems, just by its distant fluttering, to confer fairy-tale protective qualities upon Hong Kong, making it even more prosperous and stable than it has ever been in the past. Hong Kong and its population have been saved from the clutches of the violent and wicked imperialist colonizers.

This was a narrative that I recognized from another book I owned, *An Outline History of Hong Kong*, a compact paperback with tissuey pages that my mother had given me. Its cover shows the same skyline, superimposed with a large, old-fashioned clockface that I had only to look at for my brain to supply the corresponding ticking sound. The very first line sets the tone for the entire book: "Beginning in the 1840s, Hong Kong, a part of Chinese territory since ancient times, became a victim of Britain's persistent aggression against China." The book was written by Liu Shuyong, a historian from the Chinese Academy of Social Sciences who arrived in Hong Kong in 1996 to craft the definitive, state-approved version of Hong Kong's past. This narrative frames Hong Kong as just another Chinese city from time immemorial, which was snatched away from the motherland by force.

This Hong Kong was never a barren rock but rather a repository of Chinese tradition, with thousands of residents in place when the British arrived in the 1840s. The book lays out details of the settlement of the New Territories a thousand years ago, at the time of the Song dynasty, remarking that the territory's oldest Confucian school is also from that era, predating some of the famous colleges in Guangzhou. It also emphasizes Hong Kong's administrative place within ancient Chinese jurisdictions, from the time of the Qin dynasty (221–207 BCE) onward.

There is also a third Hong Kong origin story. This one is told not by one colonial ruler or another but began circulating among Hong Kongers themselves, and does not purport to be anything but myth. It tells of a race of fish-headed mermen called the Lo Ting, or sometimes the Lou Ting or Lu Ting, depending on the method of romanization. The Lo Ting had human bodies from the neck down but fish heads and a shiny carapace of fish scales down their backs that jutted into fish tails. Neither fish nor fowl, they flitted between land and sea, depending on which was safer at the time.

According to one version of this creation myth, the Lo Ting came to Lantau Island—an outlying island that is actually bigger than Hong Kong itself—with Lu Xun, a Guangzhou-based official who staged a rebellion in 411 CE against the Western Jin dynasty with an army of one hundred thousand men. Lu Xun and his army fought up to the Yangtze River, but after being defeated, they fled to Lantau, where they lived in caves. Even Liu Shuyong's official history cites a record from the Tang dynasty (618–907 CE) describing how Lu Xun and his followers "lived like barbarians, feeding on oysters and clams, with the shells of which they built walls for shelter." Popular legend takes it one step further, recounting how they ate so much raw fish that they turned into a species of fish-headed men. These were the indigenous Hong Kongers, the children of a rebel, born of insurrection.

The legends of the Lo Ting were many and varied. Some said they lived in thatched huts on Lantau, tattooing themselves to look like dragons to avoid the God of Water. Others cast them as the ancestors of the Tanka boat people, a Sinicized ethnic group who were so discriminated against that their very name became a derogatory term. There are textual references to the Lo Ting dating back to the Qing dynasty, by southern

Chinese scholar-poets such as Qu Dajun, who lived in Guangzhou in the seventeenth century. He wrote a poem about the Lo Ting, mentioning their yellow-brown eyes and bodies covered with short brown hair. Another poet, Deng Chun, wrote that the Lo Ting lived in caves in Lantau.

As a child growing up in Hong Kong, I never heard of the Lo Ting. My mother's passion for Hong Kong's indigenous cultural heritage meant that she would sometimes drag us out to local celebrations to watch ear-splitting operas on rickety bamboo stages and eat gloopy, unidentifiable food that had been communally cooked in gigantic enamel basins. But the legends celebrated always seemed to be the classical Chinese ones. We'd watch fearsome generals with bushy beards and brocade flags protruding from their backs gliding across the stage, or the mischievous Monkey King, Sun Wukong, tumbling back and forth, blinking and snickering, as the clickers clacked and the cymbals clashed. I had an aunt who was a classically trained Peking Opera singer, and it seemed as if her stiffly formal recitals shared the same cast of characters that we'd seen on those rickety stages. The fish-man was never among them.

Over the years, however, this man-fish hybrid bobbed into my consciousness here and there, and then suddenly the Lo Ting were everywhere. In 2011, the television show *HK Enigmata* did an episode trying to track down the myth of the Lo Ting man. Then a local drama company, Theatre Horizon, did an epic four-year cycle of five Lo Ting plays that traveled to Edinburgh in 2018. There was an online cartoon, and even a big-budget film, *The Mermaid*, by local comedian Stephen Chow.

In 2019, the Hong Kong Art Museum reopened after a much-hyped four-year, multimillion-dollar renovation. Although the museum has a prominent position on the Kowloon waterfront near the Star Ferry Terminal, I went to see it with no great sense of expectation, since I was so often disappointed by Hong Kong's museums. But it was clear from the moment I entered that this experience would be different. The building cleverly showcases Hong Kong's breathtaking skyline, with stools provided so visitors can sit in front of gigantic picture windows to admire the sheer industry at show in the harbor, where tiny fishing boats dodge low, flat barges piled high with sand, as the imposing green ferries doughtily plow their way back and forth between Hong Kong and Kowloon. The museum frames the harbor itself as Hong Kong's most impressive and democratic artwork.

As I went up the escalator, I spied the Lo Ting. He was painted in thick black ink on a wall panel, a slightly hunched figure with his back to me, standing among some tiled, porticoed early colonial buildings as he surveyed the bare hills of precolonized Hong Kong. He was positioned so that he was looking out over the harbor, as if he were in dialogue with modern-day Hong Kong. Though the Lo Ting's fish tail was jaunty, there was something supplicant in his posture. This panel accompanied a series of projections by artist Lam Tung-pang, who layered nineteenth-century etchings onto a video, juxtaposing the downcast Lo Ting with the behatted, unmistakably British figure of an early Victorian, watching through binoculars as the bare hills became dotted with square colonial buildings and Hong Kong manifested itself onto the mountainside. The artist had written, "History is like glasses, giving us perspective, while art is like a mirror, allowing us to see ourselves." In this mirror, Hong Kongers were clearly seeing themselves as the passive, downcast Lo Ting, the forgotten indigenous ancestral counterpoint to the British colonizer in his bowler hat.

These competing mythologies fascinated me, in particular because each was so clearly flawed, shunting the facts aside in the interest of politics. They also made me embarrassed by my own credulity: Had I really swallowed the barren-rock myth without the slightest doubt? I remembered my mother taking us to see the loopy whorls of a geometric rock carving in Big Wave Bay dating back three thousand years, to the Bronze Age. This was clear proof of prehistoric human habitation, yet some kind of cognitive dissonance had allowed me to believe the barren-rock version of history while simultaneously accepting these archaeological sites as real. When I was growing up in Hong Kong, the narrative control of the British empire had been so oft repeated, so overwhelmingly omnipresent, that its myth became fact.

As a writer governed by structure, I was fascinated by these plot holes—such as the rock carvings—that poked through these narratives. I wanted to see the physical evidence that revealed them to be fiction with my own eyes, and I began using weekends to visit archaeological sites. As I strode around them, my jaw jutting forward as my children caviled and sulked, begging to be allowed to stay home to play video games, it was obvious to all of us that I was reprising my own past.

One Saturday I dragged my children to a working-class area of Kowloon called Shamshuipo to visit an ancient tomb, dating from the Eastern Han dynasty sometime between 25 and 220 CE. Somehow I'd imagined this tomb would be in pristine isolation, embedded in nature like a grassy tumulus in the English countryside. I should have realized such grand seclusion would be impossible amid Hong Kong's density, and indeed when we found it, the tomb was incongruously nestled at the very heart of a massive public housing complex, dwarfed by surrounding skyscrapers, though it was next to a pretty garden dotted with pavilions populated by old men appreciating the melodic chirps of their caged songbirds.

At the small museum fronting the tomb, we learned that it had been uncovered by chance in 1955, by workers leveling a slope for the housing estate. The exhibit seemed desultory, with half the wall space devoted to a history of public housing in Shamshuipo. The children were not impressed, and kept warning, "This is going to be disappointing!" But the tomb itself was anything but. We peered through a plastic screen into its cross-shaped chamber to see its orange-tinged bricks rising into a dome at the center. Some bricks were marked with geometric designs, others with stamps showing they had been made in Panyu, in Guangdong province. Even the children were rapt; somehow the diamond-shaped markings and dragons on the bricks made it personal, conjuring a human engaged in a tiny act of art two thousand years ago.

The tomb was noted as the only such burial place ever found in Hong Kong, and no human remains were actually found there. Instead, more than fifty food containers, storage jars, and models of houses made of clay were discovered, similar to those found in Han dynasty tombs in Guangdong, 120 kilometers to the northwest. Archaeologists suspect the contents were produced in Guangdong and brought to Hong Kong, raising questions about who might have been buried there and why. One explanation, given by historian Patrick Hase, was that this had been the burial place of an official from the Nanyue, or Southern Yue, empire. The Yue was a blanket name for non-Han Chinese ethnic groups across a swath of territory, and the Nanyue was one of the Yue states. It was established in 204 BCE and sprawled across the modern equivalent of Guangdong, Guangxi, Yunnan, and parts of Vietnam, as well as Hong Kong and Macau.

The Nanyue emperors established a salt monopoly during their reign (204–111 BCE), which was superseded after the Han conquest by that of Emperor Wu; this began in 119 BCE and continues to this day as the world's longest-running monopoly. In a paper published in 1999, Hase writes that the only Nanyue official stationed in what would become Kowloon City would have been a supervisor charged with safeguarding the empire's salt fields in the area by stopping smuggling and illegal salt production. Interestingly, Hase did not believe that salt production led to civilian Han settlement of that tract of land. On the contrary, he believed it likely that the settlement had been banned, with the valuable salt fields classed as a highly restricted district forbidden to ordinary citizens for almost a thousand years. Chinese historians, too, say the area was guarded by soldiers. Hase even speculates that, based on a later pronouncement, the salt fields might have been worked by convicts and bond slaves.

This speculative reading of the tomb's past—a subjugated local population, deprived of their land and enslaved by an imperial force—reads as startlingly politically sensitive, even more so two decades after Hase's paper was published, and it was not mentioned in the little museum. But the tomb does play a role in Liu Shuyong's party-sponsored narrative. He argues that the tomb's presence provides "strong proof that the Hong Kong area shared a cultural identity with Guangdong, and, like the Guangdong culture, had by then come under the ever-increasing cultural influence of Central China." In other words, the tomb's existence served as confirmation of the Chinese idea of Hong Kong as Chinese from time immemorial.

After leaving the tomb, we sat in a nearby *cha chaan teng* teahouse, drinking hot sweet caramel-colored milky tea and eating sticky Hong Kong–style French toast oozing with peanut butter and swimming in golden syrup as we pondered the mystery of the tomb's missing occupant. I was musing, too, on the two competing interpretations of the tomb, as evidence of imperial conquest and domination or as evidence of Hong Kong's ancient affiliation with China. The two possibilities might coexist, for that matter, with Hong Kong being a place subjugated to China from time immemorial and thus assimilating its culture, though this would cast a very different light on Hong Kong's place in Chinese history. From this one tomb, it was clear just how politically fraught it can be to interpret a past freighted with the historical baggage of dueling empires. It was also clear that, far from ever having been a barren rock, Hong Kong has, from time immemorial, deep soil that guards its secret history closely.

One person who has spent much time digging in that soil is archaeologist Mick Atha, who with his wife, Kennis Yip, has conducted multiple excavations of Hong Kong's past, mainly on the outlying island of

Lamma, a tiny island whose existence on Chinese charts predates the concept of Hong Kong, dating back to 1464, when it was called Pak Lo Mountain or Pok Liu. Instead of focusing on a single period, their method is to concentrate on one geographical site, unearthing layer after layer of its history and drawing upon the results of commercial excavations to piece together a more comprehensive picture of how the landscape has been used through the ages. One wintry morning I went to meet Atha on Lamma, taking the twenty-five-minute ferry ride through the bustling harbor.

In my childhood, we would sometimes take the ferry out to Yung Shue Wan, a village on Lamma island, and do the five-kilometer sun-baked trek over the island's hilly ridge to the smaller pier at Sok Kwu Wan, stopping on the way at a restaurant overlooking the beach to order its famous pigeon with crispy red-brown skin and minced quail folded into lettuce leaves. Atha, an affable Brit from Leeds with a silver crew cut, met me at the pier. As we walked up through the narrow paths of the village lined with open-fronted family-run shops, it struck me that Lamma had changed surprisingly little since my childhood, save for the construction of a gigantic power station. We made slow progress as we dodged small trucks and a mangy dog with a pronounced underbite. Every few meters Atha would stop to greet passersby in choppy Cantonese. Some were local fishermen he'd employed on his excavations, digging vertical sections straight into the soil to expose each layer. "These guys are used to being out on boats, hauling up nets manually," he told me. "They're also keen dragon boat racers, so their upper body strength and the technique they use for straightening a section is virtually the same movement you'd use with a paddle in dragon boat racing." As he talked, he held his hands in front of him, one clenched fist above the other, and sheared them repeatedly to one side to demonstrate the needed motion.

We stopped abruptly in front of a peach-tiled two-story house near a street sign that read, "Sha Po Old Village." The "old" is an understatement: this village was built atop a Middle Neolithic settlement dating back some six thousand years, one of around eight sites of similar age in Hong Kong. Sha Po Tsuen—literally Sand Spit Village—stands on a back beach, or storm beach, full of archaeological remains. Right under the spot where we stood, Neolithic remains of what looked like a six-thousand-year-old picnic site had been discovered: a light scatter of shards of Middle Neolithic red-painted fine ceramic pots, some general-purpose pebble tools, and two unfinished asymmetrical axes, known as adze roughouts, used for working wood. There were no post holes or anything to suggest settlement, but Atha believed the small number of artifacts indicated that Sha Po Tsuen might have been a favored destination for some boat-using fisher-hunter-foragers, perhaps two or three extended families numbering fifteen to twenty-five people in total, who visited intermittently over the years.

After that, the site was not used for more than a thousand years. The next findings were from the Late Neolithic era, around four thousand years ago, and suggested that the site had been in continuous use all the way into the Bronze Age (1500–500 BCE). One interesting discovery was the remains of a complete pot decorated with a diamond-shaped pattern and some shells. "Prehistoric pots generally are quite fragile," Atha said. "If people pulled out a complete Bronze Age pot, it was likely to have been buried on purpose. So this was likely to be a burial site where people had been burying pots as offerings, maybe containing food." The site also provides the best evidence of bronze casting in coastal South China, as splashes of molten bronze had been found on coarseware ceramics.

Evidence of two rows of salt kilns lining the back beach, dating to the Six Dynasties–Tang period (222–907 CE), fit into a bigger picture suggested by the remains of fifty-nine different salt production sites, including more than a hundred salt kilns. This means that Hong Kong was not a sparsely populated fishing village at all in that period, but already a thriving industrial base. As Atha put it, "To sail around the coastline of

Hong Kong, you'd be seeing industrial activity on every back-beach site probably, and smoke rising, and activity on the beach, and boats going away with the salt, war junks patrolling the area. It would have been a very vibrant scene."

In fact, the oldest inscription ever found in Hong Kong—discovered in 1955 by an engineer in Joss House Bay in Sai Kung—is testament to its role as a salt production center. The characters, carved onto an enormous rock in 1274, mark the visit of one Yan Yizhang, an "official who works at this ground." Like the unknown tomb occupant before him, Yan, a native of Kaifeng in Henan, had been sent by the central government to oversee the salt monopoly. His workplace was the gigantic Guanfu Salt Farm, which likely stretched across both sides of the harbor, covering a huge swath of Hong Kong, Kowloon, Lantau, and the New Territories, from Tsing Yi and Tsuen Wan in the west to Tseung Kwan O and Sai Kung in the east.

More of this hidden history was revealed in 2012, when construction for a new subway station at To Kwa Wan uncovered a number of Song dynasty wells, a gully, and pottery shards from Fujian and Zhejiang provinces. Scholars believe these, too, could have been artifacts from the Guanfu Salt Farm. This idea of the area as a major salt producer was crucial to three foundational episodes that place its recent history of insurrection in a far longer historical context.

The first episode happened before 1187, at the fishing village of Tai O in Lantau, whose original inhabitants had mainly been Tanka boat people. Even into the early twentieth century, many of the people of Tai O lived on boats tied together, and still today visitors clog its streets as they Instagram its distinctive stilt houses hovering over the water and the circular, rattan trays of the village's most famous product, a pinkish-gray fermented shrimp paste whose pungent, almost-rotten smell hangs in the air. The village also once had salt pans, but its rebellious residents flouted central authority by producing and harvesting their salt outside the monopoly. Liu Shuyong's official history describes at least two revolts by the residents of Lantau, who chafed against central attempts to impose control. He writes, "After rebels on the island led by Lai You surrendered to the government during the reign of the Southern Song Emperor Gaozong (1107–1187), the younger members of the former rebels were enlisted in the local naval force and the government restrictions on fishing and salt-making relaxed."

By 1197, in the reign of Emperor Ningzong, the islanders were again harvesting salt illegally, and troops were sent from Guangzhou to reassert control, but the Lantau residents were not cowed. They rose up in revolt and fought their way up the Pearl River to the Guangzhou city walls. Navy reinforcements were brought in to brutally crush the rebellion, and historical accounts describe the slaughter of the rebels "without leaving any survivor." The independent, insurgent streak shining through these brief accounts resonates with the legends surrounding Lu Xun and the Lo Ting.

The third key moment came in 1276, when the Song dynasty was overthrown by the fierce Mongols of the Yuan dynasty. The last two boy emperors—Zhao Shi and Zhao Bing, just eight and five when the Mongols took over—fled the Song capital Linan in Zhejiang, and ended up in Hong Kong. Recent research suggests that they most likely took shelter at the office of the Guanfu Salt Farm for five months. They died in exile, Zhao Shi from illness, and Zhao Bing when his loyal military commander put him on his shoulders and jumped off a cliff into the sea. In Kowloon, there is still a place called Sungwongtoi—Song Emperor's Throne—where tiny Zhao Bing was crowned after his brother's death, and it's also the name given to the MTR station built over the site of the Song dynasty wells and the nullah.

The boy emperors' sojourn in Hong Kong was noted in Chinese sources, and even though it was expunged from the British version of Hong Kong's precolonial past, it has shaped customary practices. According to legend, that gloopy dish my mother so loved—*pun choi*, or literally "basin food"—dates back to the days of imperial exile. The villagers, wanting to secretly share their best food with the boy kings, supposedly packed the food into a basin, covering the meat and seafood delicacies on the bottom with cheaper vegetables on top. *Pun choi* is a staple at festivals, eaten communally at round tables placed on the village square at Lunar New Year after the lion dancers have called at every house. Every serving recalls Hong Kong's past as a sanctuary for rebels and fugitives from central power, a place where lost kings are still worshipped through Hong Kongers' favorite activity, eating.

This history of the region's insurrections is slowly being excavated by local archaeologists and historians, digging respectively through shoreline middens and ancient Chinese texts, to reclaim a past that had been wiped clean by the British. It can be read in academic publications, but it has not been widely disseminated, maybe since it fits neither the British nor the Chinese narrative.

The hidden history of Hong Kong's early habitation was, in many ways, not hidden at all. I learned this from Atha, as we continued our tour of Lamma, past a ledge supporting an air conditioner where he'd split his head open by jumping up in excitement at a find. On a sloping hillside populated by two-story houses, a Filipina domestic helper was laboring up the hill dragging two small, grumpy children. This area used to be vegetable fields, Atha said, and back in the 1930s, a Catholic priest and archaeologist, Father Daniel Finn, had noticed that the fields were peppered with circular disks of quartz. These dated from the Bronze Age and appeared to be jewelry of some kind, evidence that a hierarchical society that was capable of both supporting craftspeople and valuing ornamentation had already developed. Later digs on another island, called Ma Wan, found both male and female skeletons with these split quartz rings on either side of their heads, indicating that they were earrings.

The middens, or ancient rubbish dumps, provide evidence that the prehistoric residents of the area ate fish and some shellfish, and some species no longer found in the area, like large wild deer and dugong. Recent analysis of microscopic plant material on stone tools at Xincun on the west side of the Pearl River estuary indicates that inhabitants of the region at that time exploited starchy plants like sago. But there was no conclusive indication of cereal crops being cultivated in Hong Kong at that time. All of this evidence had led Atha to a vision of early Hong Kongers as a seafaring people, not a land-based agrarian society. "My strong theory now is that we need to change our perspective on these coastal people, and stop thinking about them from a land-based person's perspective," he said. "Being land people, we think the islands are inconvenient, faraway, difficult places. But from a boat-using people's point of view, it's a central location. The sea is very much the center of the universe."

That view might not be reflected in *The Hong Kong Story*, an exhibition that opened in 2001 at the Hong Kong Museum of History. It is perhaps symptomatic of the British view of Hong Kong's history that it was not until 1982 that the government decided to build such a museum, to help the "rootless young generation" develop a sense of belonging, according to an international museum consultant working on the project. It took another sixteen years for a permanent location to be opened in Tsimshatsui, not far from the Art Museum. *The Hong Kong Story*, which was six years in the making, billed itself as authoritative.

When I visited in 2018, I made a beeline for the prehistory gallery, which was found by a survey to be the least popular gallery in the whole museum. This was hardly surprising, since the centerpiece consisted of some very tired models of long-haired, mustachioed cavemen adjusting fishing nets weighted down with stones over their wooden fishing boats. Accompanying it was a panel stating, "The ancient Yue people of South China had a distinctive culture that took shape about 3,000 to 4,000 years ago before being gradually assimilated into the Han culture. Ancient Yue culture subsisted chiefly by cultivating cereal crops, fishing and hunting."

These two short sentences do a lot of heavy lifting by omission; in actual fact, archaeologists and historians do not concur that there was a monolithic Yue culture, and there is no consensus that the people of Hong Kong cultivated cereal crops at that time, due to a dearth of solid archaeological evidence. Atha and Yip have argued that there should be an important distinction between two separate populations: the boat-using fisher-hunter-foragers along the coastlines and estuaries of the region, and the settled rice-farming societies in the major river catchments in inland Guangdong. They believe the archaeological evidence indicates the groups had different lifeways, but were in contact and trading with each other. I was beginning to understand just how contentious almost every phase of Hong Kong's history is, all the way back to prehistoric times. "Never, ever believe that archaeology can be apolitical," Atha told me. "Fundamentally, the past is a political topic, and you've got to be careful how you package it and how you present it."

The rest of the exhibit was slick and colorful, featuring local opera singers and towers of fake buns that attempted to replicate the Cheung Chau Bun Festival, when young men used to scale towers made of steamed buns on the stroke of midnight until one year the toppling towers injured dozens of people. The museum's careful presentation of Hong Kong's history was a tightrope act, picking its way carefully between the barren-rock and time-immemorial myths. The narrative foregrounded Hong Kong's growth from a tiny fishing village to an international metropolis, emphasizing its role in the opium trade and its rise as a financial hub, as well as including a section on its fate as an occupied Japanese territory during the Second World War. There were references to the anti-littering Keep Hong Kong Clean campaign, a hurried exhibit on ceremonial costumes worn by British governors, and a single photo showing a million Hong Kongers taking to the streets to support China's pro-democracy protests in 1989.

On my most recent visit, the final exhibit was a temporary show celebrating the fortieth anniversary of China's reform and economic opening titled *Joint Development and Shared Prosperity*. Its aim was transparent: to place Hong Kong firmly within the context of China's opening up. Vitrines containing Cabbage Patch dolls, Teenage Mutant Ninja Turtles, and a gigantic shoe showcased the role of Hong Kong entrepreneurs in building China into the world's second-largest economy. In one corner of the room was a mechanical horse, where a bespectacled middle-aged man was solemnly balanced on a saddle, earnestly trotting and show-jumping his way around a virtual reality ring on a screen in front of him. That exhibit, showcasing the Hong Kong Jockey Club, conveniently ignored the fact that gambling on horse racing is still banned in mainland China.

While there was much about the exhibitions to catch the eye, this Hong Kong story felt like it had been pieced together by a committee operating under very restrictive guidelines. It was the museum equivalent of a press conference in which the speaker keeps returning to two main talking points time and time again, regardless of the question. Without connective tissue, the narrative made little sense. I was used to seeing this kind of slightly nonsensical exhibition in China, but it took me aback to see one in Hong Kong. That chapter of the Hong Kong story, however, is already in the past. In 2020, the entire museum closed for another renovation and remodeling process. Though its version of history was patchy, Hong Kongers flocked to the museum before it closed, chanting protest slogans and obsessively snapping pictures of the galleries. It was a spontaneous demonstration driven by fear of just how their past might once more be reshaped and rewritten once the museum reopens again in 2022.

Any state-sponsored version of history now being crafted will likely support Beijing's next big plan: the Greater Bay Area. The name conjures up mental images of a gigantic beachside expanse, even more relaxed, even more sun-kissed than the original Bay Area in San Francisco.

Beijing's vision for Hong Kong is to fold it into a Silicon Valley–style economic entity arcing across the southern Chinese coast and encompassing Macau and nine other southern Chinese cities. This supermetropolis, including the megacities of Shenzhen and Guangzhou, would become an innovation and economic hub, as well as a single market. To Hong Kongers, it is a blueprint for absorption into Greater China. To Beijing, it would be a reversion to the place held for Hong Kong in China's version of the historical narrative: Hong Kong as just another Chinese city.

One sunny winter afternoon in 2019, I went on a trip with friends to visit Lau Fau Shan, a small fishing village separated from China proper by a bay and famous for its oyster sauce and showy sunsets. It's in a part of Hong Kong bordering China that is still inaccessible by subway, so we had to take a bus from the nearest subway stop. Hurtling down the less-populated country roads past scrubby lots full of junk and overgrown with vines felt like traveling back in time to my childhood.

When we got to Lau Fau Shan, it was a small village of three-story houses threaded with narrow gray alleyways, pungent with the salty tang of plump oysters drying on flat rattan baskets. We feasted on chili-fried crab, scallops laced with delicate glass noodles, and obscenely large oysters, then walked down to the seafront, where a man wearing an army camouflage hat was sitting in a small boat, shucking oysters into a plastic barrel, surrounded by piles of gigantic oyster shells.

Behind him was a jaw-dropping sight. On the other side of Deep Bay, just four kilometers away, were the shiny, glistening skyscrapers of Shekou, a city so brand-spanking new that it looked like a property billboard come to life. Having worked as a foreign correspondent in China, I was used to the warp-speed pace of urban construction there, but still, the appearance of this entirely new city took me by surprise. This area, a suburb of Shenzhen, had formerly been farmland, then industrial docks. In 2015, it was earmarked to be a free-trade zone together with neighboring

Qianhai. Within a few short years it had been entirely transformed into an even more modern simulacrum of Hong Kong, with sinuous, mirrored skyscrapers lining its foreshore as far as the eye could see. In the distance, a sparkling white cable-stayed bridge looped across the bay, linking Hong Kong with Shenzhen.

Looking across Deep Bay, I was reminded of an interview I'd done with the late architect Zaha Hadid a decade and a half before, in the shadow of the Great Wall. It had been a bright, freezing winter's day, and we'd driven out to an upmarket development called the Commune, where Hadid had held court over lunch. She was imperious, brilliant, and terrifying, and she'd decided that she needed to do the interview outside, against the backdrop of the Great Wall, so she could wear her enormous, beautiful sheepskin coat on camera. It was so cold that we could film for only five minutes before we all started shivering. In those five minutes, she referred to China as a tabula rasa for architects, where the ambition of city planners made anything possible. "They want to have more extreme buildings, or buildings which will put them on the map." That was going through my mind as I looked over the water at Shekou and Qianhai. The skyline, including towers designed by Rem Koolhaas's OMA and Norman Foster, looked like a playground for the world's architects.

This moment gazing across Deep Bay represented a turning point for me. Before 1979, when Shenzhen had been the proverbial sleepy fishing village, its people might have gazed on the metropolis of Hong Kong with the same sort of open-mouthed wonder. Now I realized that we Hong Kongers had become the sleepy villagers. Even though this role reversal had been approaching for years, it still required a profound psychological recalibration. Hong Kongers were used to thinking of themselves as more modern, more technologically advanced, richer than mainlanders, but the scene in front of me made clear that the old assumptions might no longer hold true.

The Greater Bay Area scheme was relatively new in policy terms. It had first been mentioned in China's thirteenth Five-Year Plan in December 2016. But the planning for the infrastructural integration had been underway for decades. Hong Kongers tended to be suspicious of these massive steel loops of rail and road designed to gird China ever closer and deplete Hong Kong's coffers. The most controversial was a $10 billion (HK$77 billion) high-speed railway linking West Kowloon with Guangzhou. Right from the start there had been vocal protests over its route, which required the demolition of a village in the New Territories, but these did not stop the project. The railway's opening in September 2018 was accompanied by concerns over the joint-checkpoint arrangement that classified a section of the terminus as a "mainland port" directly under Beijing's jurisdiction, staffed by Chinese customs and immigration officers, following mainland law and patrolled by mainland police. The Hong Kong government had leased that part of the station to China for a token amount of just $128 (HK$996) a year, even though the value of that plot of real estate was stratospheric. Critics argued the checkpoint arrangement turned it into a Chinese enclave, even a modern-day equivalent to the Qing dynasty "treaty ports" that had granted Western powers sovereignty over parcels of land on Chinese soil. To many, the rail link signaled a loss of control over one tiny pocket of Hong Kong.

Another vision of closer integration can be seen in that other Special Administrative Region, Macau, which had been under Portuguese administration since 1557. Macau had returned to China two years after Hong Kong, in 1999, but had become Beijing's favored child for its stability, its lack of any vocal political opposition, and its bulging coffers. A $20 billion (HK$155 billion), thirty-six-kilometer elevated highway—the world's longest sea bridge linking Hong Kong, Macau, and Zhuhai, yet another of these grand infrastructure schemes—opened at the end of 2018. Shortly after, my children and I sped along the bridge to Macau for a weekend. It had been at least twenty years since I last visited, and I still remembered the small, sandy enclave where we'd go to the casino and listen to African music. Gambling had been legalized by the former colonial rulers, the Portuguese, in the 1850s, but the Hong Kong billionaire Stanley Ho had held a monopoly for four decades until 2002. We'd liked walking through his circular Lisboa casino, which looked like a squat white wedding cake with gold piping, watching wizened old men in white vests pulling money out of their socks to place on the roulette wheels.

Since my last visit, everything about Macau had changed. It had taken only four years after the expiry of Stanley Ho's monopoly for Macau to overtake Las Vegas as the casino capital of the world, fueled by visitors from mainland China, where gambling remained forbidden. Now the enclave's geography, its skyline, its social makeup, and its employment opportunities had been reshaped by Chinese money. The massive infrastructure spending was obvious in the gigantic, spotless terminals on either side of the border, their cavernous interiors punctuated by two-way mirrors and surveillance cameras. As we drove away from the terminal, the blood-orange sun was setting showily in a petrochemically induced fluorescent blaze above the brand-new skyline of Zhuhai just across the bay. I couldn't quite orient myself, so I asked the taxi driver what had been on the scrubland before the terminal. "Nothing!" he replied. "Ten years ago, all this was sea! It's new land!" When I looked at the map, I realized that so much land had been reclaimed that Macau's shape had changed.

Now it was the home of casino after casino, fake Italian canal towns and fake Eiffel towers replete with cable cars, fire-breathing dragons, and golden cupolas, all competing in fantastical ostentation. The experience of visiting the Venetian casino, Macau's most popular tourist attraction, visited by half the enclave's tourists, almost undid me. Complete with indoor canals, fake sky, and Chinese gondoliers belting out Mandarin folk songs, the casino is a $2.4 billion copy of the Las Vegas Venetian, which is itself a facsimile of a Venetian town. Mainland tourists were crowded along every inch of the waterfront, hamming it up for photos or tapping and scrolling at their screens as they posted on social media. In the cavernous food hall, competition for tables was so intense that it reminded me of being in the dining carriage of a Chinese train. It turned tourism into a full-body-contact endurance sport.

Venturing out into the real world, we followed the well-trodden tourist route to the ruined facade of St. Paul's Cathedral, where the full pressure of numbers became obvious. In 2019, Macau, with a population of just 667,000, had 39 million visitors, more than 100,000 every day. There were so many tourists at St. Paul's that it was hard to walk. It reminded me of those Chinese tourist parks in the 1990s, where people crowded in to see miniature versions of the world's most famous monuments. The Greater Bay Area strategy envisages Macau as a "world center for tourism and leisure," and it already seemed like a theme park version of itself, with a population co-opted through economic benefits and kept in line with civil disobedience statutes that could be invoked to punish political opposition. It was a reminder that the power of imaginative fiction was not only reserved for the past but could also stretch into the future.

Like Macau's, the future of Hong Kong as just one other mainland city echoes back to Beijing's version of its past, closing that circle. This specific future is being woven into the narrative through free government-sponsored exhibitions offering interactive games to help Hong Kongers understand the concept of the Greater Bay Area and with museum exhibits that use historic artifacts to situate Hong Kong as a way station on China's Maritime Silk Road. This vision is also actively embraced by Hong Kong's Beijing-backed political elite through a proliferation of high-profile fora and symposia on the Greater Bay Area. One senior official even suggested that polling booths for Hong Kong's future legislative elections be set up in China for the convenience of Hong Kong residents living in the Greater Bay Area. Such a move blurs Hong Kong's political boundaries, further fictionalizing the very idea of Hong Kong.

There was something fascinating and unsettling about watching just how far this narrative was being pushed. It was the perfect illustration of Chairman Mao's dictum of making the past serve the present, although in this case the past, the present, and the future were being simultaneously reshaped, driven by the unrest on the ground. Like the Hong Kong of the maps, the very concept of Hong Kong seemed phantasmagorical, like a shimmering chimera that was constantly changing shape depending on the angle of viewing. Dung Kai-cheung, the author of the fantastical *Atlas*, had written that the reality or falsehood of the fictitious Hong Kongs was not as important as how they were made up, and it seemed the same was true of Hong Kong's history. The imposed, colonial narratives of Hong Kong's past, though factually true, might not resonate as much with Hong Kongers as their own, entirely mythical version of their past. It made me wonder how the Hong Kong of the legendary Lo Ting, which had been nowhere during my childhood, had surfaced and taken hold. It turned out that, as with the King of Kowloon, the answer lay in the intervention of an imaginative art curator.

I'd interviewed Oscar Ho Hing-kay several times, first in 1997. By then he was already well-known as an artist and curator whose cerebral shows were driven by a strong sense of ethics. At the time, he'd been thinking about giving the King of Kowloon a gallery show, but had demurred because he believed the King's work would be rendered meaningless if removed from the streets. Instead he'd marked the return to Chinese sovereignty with the first of what would be a trifecta of Lo Ting exhibitions.

The show had been called *Museum 97: History, Community, Identity*, and Ho used it to explore Hong Kongers' responses to that crucial

<aside>60</aside>

moment of transition. He'd asked people to submit their own artifacts representing the next fifty years of Hong Kong history. Their choices—election flyers for Democratic Party legislators and leaflets about the annual vigil on June 4 remembering those who died in China in 1989—showed how obvious the political pressure points were to everyone. One-third of the exhibition was devoted to the legend of the Lo Ting, who attracted Ho because of his "in-betweenness" and rebelliousness. "I was searching for a local mythical figure that represents Hong Kong," Ho wrote to me in an email. "I take myth seriously as it often represents a culture and an identity. If you study the Irish struggle against the British in the early twentieth century, you will find out how important myth is."

He'd dug up historical sources about the Lo Ting, then gone on to bolster them with fiction. He outsourced their backstories to two of Hong Kong's most famous writers, Leung Man-tao and Dung Kai-cheung, the author of the *Atlas* who had been so fascinated by the creation of fictional Hong Kongs. To Ho, the exhibition was a serious attempt to investigate Hong Kong's history and its historiography. "I emphasize a lot that it was not imagination-making for fun, but fabricating myth as metaphors, and metaphors can tell more truth than the official history."

To visualize the Lo Ting, Ho described his vision of the creature to several local artists, giving free rein to their imaginations. He told them that the man-fish hybrid should be completely different from the Western mermaid archetype, and that its amphibian characteristics should be a deliberate repudiation of the agrarian, rice-planting character of China's Yangtze River civilization. Back then, he wrote, "Our ancestors were from the sea, instead of from the land, as a denial of the cultural linkage with China." The Lo Ting would be neither Western nor Chinese, but indigenously, uniquely Hong Kongish. One artistic rendition that emerged was a weeping tadpole with a human face and a rufflike fin down its spine. But the one that stood out was a human-sized statue of a slimy-looking slim-hipped greenish-yellow frog-like creature with a slightly feminine bulge to its belly, a pretty fish head, and webbed hands and feet. I made the mistake of telling Ho that I found the statue a bit creepy, and he wrote back, thin-lipped, "Sorry you find it repulsive, but I actually like it."

His intention had been to encourage numerous depictions and fanciful creations so that no single person could claim ownership over the idea of the Lo Ting. He wrote to me, "There should be no final version of the Lo Ting, but it should be a creation in constant evolution. I want to leave it to the people to elaborate or constrict it. It's a liberation from the tyranny of 'official history.'" The Lo Ting was, in many ways, history, community, and identity all rolled into one human-fish hybrid.

The next year, Ho curated a second Lo Ting exhibition, this time inventing ancient literature, archaeological artifacts, and even a Hong Kong Lo Ting Research Association to bolster the myth. The visual language of the show mimicked Hong Kong's museums, with their white information panels, clinical language, and archaeological artifacts in glass vitrines. But the work itself was deliberately playful, including photos of a fish-shaped burial tomb and a brown fabric fish tail that visitors could strap on to become the Lo Ting. Ho wrote in an email to me, "The exhibition is not just about the local myth and reconstructing a local myth, it is about the rights to interpret history, and the definition of 'real' history and who has the rights to write history. It is also about the fake authority of confirming history of the cultural institution."

Ho followed up with a third exhibition in 1999, this time focusing on the 1197 massacre of the illegal salt panners of Lantau. Again the froggy Lo Ting statue was part of the show, which this time even included a field trip where participants took part in an archaeological dig, looking for Lo Ting artifacts. The ambiguity and confusion was designed, Ho wrote, to challenge visitors. "The exact idea is about challenging: what is real history? In China, they have different history about June 4, and the 1197 massacre is erased from 'history.'"

Once these exhibitions were over, the Lo Ting lay dormant in the collective consciousness for a decade and a half. In the 2010s, as a localist movement celebrating Hong Kong's identity focused on preserving Hong Kong's autonomy and institutions, a new generation of artists and creators seized onto the idea of the Lo Ting and took it in entirely new directions. One acolyte of the Lo Ting was a playwright named Wong Kwok-kui, who had returned to Hong Kong from studying philosophy in Germany in 1997, when he visited Ho's first Lo Ting exhibition. It had percolated at the back of his mind for twenty years, until he was asked by a theater company to create a series of historical plays about Hong Kong. He immediately knew that he wanted to use the Lo Ting as a protagonist to resolve questions about Hong Kong's identity.

The final play was performed in Hong Kong in 2018, but it wasn't until two years later, just after the national security legislation was imposed, that we spoke. Before our conversation, Wong asked if we could avoid talking about politics. I'd been used to hearing this kind of request while working in China, but this was the first time a Hong Konger had ever posed it. The very existence of the national security legislation restricted our conversation like a corset. Wong sometimes left his ideas half-finished, while I purposely avoided asking the follow-up questions that a journalist should ask. For safety's sake, we were both self-censoring, weighing the impact of our words before we spoke. The idea that Hong Kongers had been reduced to this depressed me unutterably.

Wong's cycle of plays reworks Hong Kong history through the eyes of the Lo Ting, who is a figure of pathos. The fish-man is a childlike creature, reminiscent of the creature in Mary Shelley's Frankenstein but without the strength or murderous impulses. He is naive, gullible, and trusting. He is taught to speak by his rulers and then used by them for their own purposes. Toward the middle of the cycle, Wong's Lo Ting becomes so tired of human politics that he amputates his arms and legs to live as a fish once again. By the end of the cycle, Victoria Harbor has dried up, forcing the Lo Ting to return to human form for his own survival.

Wong believed that the two competing narratives—Britain's barren rock and China's time immemorial—had stopped Hong Kongers from seeing reality, so he wanted to use theater as a mirror for Hong Kongers to view their past. It was a textbook example of what the French literary theorist Roland Barthes might have imagined when he wrote, "The best weapon against myth is perhaps to mythify it in its turn, and to produce an artificial myth: and this reconstituted myth will in fact be a mythology."

The poor, defenseless Lo Ting—so gullible, so passive, so ill-used—seemed an odd choice for Hong Kong's mythical founding father. I asked Wong why he had made that choice. He replied, "We need some sort of founding myth like Virgil and how the Romans have Aeneas as their founding father. Because the history of Hong Kong of the last one hundred fifty years is quite vague in our consciousness. We don't have heroes. We don't have war heroes. We don't have great statesmen. We don't have heroic acts. We don't have that storehouse of myths and legends as Chinese history does. So it's really a barren rock in a metaphoric sense." It is one indication of the gritty perversity of Hong Kongers that their self-invented icons are not the conventional warriors or strongmen chosen by proud nations, but rather antiheroes in the form of discriminated-against outsiders and bullied misfits, people who resisted and continued to do so despite the overwhelming forces rallied against them.

Speaking over Zoom, Wong told me, "The Lo Ting is indigenous. He has nothing to do with Chinese civilization. In his eyes, people from the north were the oppressors, agrarian and continental. The Lo Ting is peripheral." More than that, Wong believed the Lo Ting's history—

invented or otherwise—echoed Hong Kong's characteristics, formed in the image of the rebel Lu Xun. "We are the descendants of the oppressed. This island has always been the safe haven, the refuge for those escaping from injustice and tyranny."

In the prologue to the play cycle, the finale is a massacre. Watching a video of this now is unsettling; the stage is full of fish-headed Lo Ting wearing fishermen's pants and wielding umbrellas. As gunshots echo through the air, they jerk and fall to the ground, dropping their umbrellas. I asked Wong gingerly how, given all the violence on the streets in 2019, he viewed his decision to foreground the massacre. He replied, "It's historical fact. There was a rebellion in the salt pans in the Song dynasty. Lantau inhabitants rebelled against the dynasty and were massacred. I cannot envisage what's going to happen now. But that's something that's always happened in Chinese history."

CHAPTER 3

KOWLOON

I was dragging behind my mother as we walked down the hill to Central, on a day so stiflingly hot that we were basted in a slick film of sweat the moment we stepped outside. I was six years old, and wearing my best summer dress and smart sandals for this outing, but I was too hot to behave. I kept whining and complaining until my mother agreed to stop for a drink at a tea shop. No sooner had we sat down at a large round communal table than the elderly Chinese grannies opposite us began throwing tepid tea leaves from their teapot at me. My mother, uncharacteristically flustered, hastily shepherded me out of the teahouse, batting aside my puzzled questions. It was only years later that she told me those wrinkled old women had thrown tea leaves at me because they disapproved of me. They wanted to make me leave because they didn't want to see me.

We were variously called half-castes; the Eurasians; the mix-blood children, *wan hyut yi*; or half-Chinese barbarians, *bun tong faan*. The fact that there still isn't an accepted name for people like me is an indicator of our history, which is one of disappearance. One Eurasian, Joyce Symons, born in 1918, put it most devastatingly: "Eurasians were too different, and in a sense did not exist."

Symons was referring to the vanishing act that Eurasians had helped to perpetrate, erasing themselves from sight and from the bureaucratic record. The early Eurasians tended to "pass" as Chinese by speaking Chinese, wearing Chinese clothes, and keeping the Manchu pigtail prior to the fall of the Qing dynasty. When the category of "Eurasian" was added to the Hong Kong census in 1897, it was claimed by 272 people. Four years later, the number had dwindled slightly, and by 1911 only 42 people identified as Eurasian. None of these figures were anywhere close to accurate; it was simply too difficult to admit to being of mixed background. The other options were hard, too. Many Eurasians were not recognized by their fathers, so using a Western surname could hint at illegitimacy. Yet Eurasians were also often excluded from the clan lineage records that anchored Chinese identity. So they simply made themselves invisible.

My parents had left London, where the postman had asked my father if he was an Eskimo, in the hope that Hong Kong would prove a better place to raise a mixed-race family. My own parents' marriage in the late sixties had been scandalous. When my father left Singapore for Great Britain, his mother had pressed a mahjong set into his hands as a parting gift, along with a warning: "Don't marry an English woman." The British side of the family, who had been hoping my mother would marry a nice army officer—my maternal grandfather was a major general and a veteran of two world wars—was perplexed and disappointed by her decision to marry a younger Chinese man. On the way to the wedding reception at the Army and Navy Club in London, her uncle Claude had leaned over to hiss in her ear, "It won't last, you know." Even my grandmother, who loved us dearly, would sometimes bemoan to us what a pity it was that British blood was being diluted by foreigners.

When they arrived in Hong Kong, my parents were taken aback to discover the deep well of prejudice that still remained against couples like them: Western women with Chinese husbands. The reverse combination was far more common and far less taboo; many of the big, bluff men who'd come out to police the colony had Chinese wives. But Caucasian women who married Chinese men had transgressed the unspoken sexual and racial codes, and were shunned by polite society on both sides of the racial divide. My parents ended up joining a club born of social exclusion, consisting solely of white women with Chinese husbands. The group originally called themselves the Mix-up Club, but the name was hurriedly shortened to the M Club to avoid being mistaken for a cross-cultural swingers' outfit. We often celebrated holidays with the other Mix-ups, the kids running wild while our fathers compared our exam results and our mothers swapped Chinese recipes.

We lived in spacious government quarters in Mid-Levels. Our block even shared a small communal garden with grass, the ultimate status symbol on the densely packed island. Our school was part of a network established by the English Schools Foundation to deliver a thoroughly colonial education to the children of colonial civil servants, as if they had never left the United Kingdom. I had longed to go to school for years. On my first day, in my yellow-and-white-checked cotton dress with my new brown satchel slung triumphantly over my chest, I was delighted to discover that my class was full of mixed-race kids. At last, I felt, I had found my tribe. But the playground pecking order privileged whiteness, and I came to secretly envy the girls with blond hair and blue eyes. I dreamed about changing my surname to my mother's maiden name, and spent hours writing *Louisa de Fonblanque* over and over with my leaky fountain pen.

The same hierarchy ruled the curriculum, which was startlingly Victorian. We started the day reciting the Lord's Prayer, and spent interminable hours copying sentences in curly cursive handwriting and reciting poetry to hone our British accents. Even today, most of us could probably snag a walk-on part on *Downton Abbey*. Our headmistress, Miss Doreen Handyside, could have leaped fully formed from the pages of a Roald Dahl book. A champion golfer, she was spherical in shape, with a head of tightly curled ringlets, and she used her golf swing to great effect to swat naughty little boys on their palms with a ruler. On the few occasions that we learned anything related to China, it was always about some cruel practice like footbinding, concubinage, or the history of rickshaw pullers. Anything British was mentioned in awed tones, but our teachers, who were European, were careful not to overegg the pudding, lest we all decide to move to the United Kingdom en masse. In truth, what we were taught most thoroughly was whiteness, in particular how to sound white and think white. At the same time, our education effectively deracinated us, suspending us in a kind of colonial nonspace designed to ensure that we did not identify too closely with any place.

In 1835, a civil servant in British East India, Thomas Babington Macaulay, wrote a famous memo known as Macaulay's Minute. In it, he argued that select Indians should be given a proper education: "We must at present do our best to form a class who may be interpreters between us and the millions whom we govern—a class of persons Indian in blood and colour, but English in tastes, in opinions, in morals and in intellect." My sepia tribe was the Chinese equivalent of Macaulay's interpreters, a class of persons Chinese in blood and color, but English in tastes, opinions, morals, and intellect. When I think back to how much I wanted to be blond-haired, blue-eyed Louisa de Fonblanque, I realize that the British Crown stamped its dominion not just on our streets and institutions, but also indelibly onto our brains.

To achieve that, it was easier not to teach the troubled history of Hong Kong's acquisition, which encompassed two major wars between world powers and one short, bloody local conflict that had been long since wiped from the collective memory. Hong Kong history was not taught in

Hong Kong schools between the mid-1970s and the 1990s. When Hong Kong's longest-serving governor, Baron MacLehose of Beoch—a fixture of my childhood—was questioned about this in a confidential interview done in the 1990s, he replied, "There were . . . certain historical reserves which *any* ethnic Chinese has about Hong Kong being British." From a British perspective, Hong Kong's acquisition had been so problematic that it was easier simply not to speak of it or to tell Hong Kongers how it happened. That was how our history vanished from the curriculum.

The textbooks that did exist generally consisted of laundry lists of British governors and their achievements. "There are no names, no faces for Chinese," was the assessment of one local historian, Tim Ko Tim-keung. In this way, Hong Kongers had been left out of their own story. This perhaps accurately reflects a history of territorial acquisition, to which the local population represented an encumbrance. The original acts of dominion were driven by flawed individuals who acted in haste or bad faith, or who simply never considered the repercussions of their actions. The underlying themes are like a bitter melody, reprising and swelling over the years: the use and misuse of national honor, and above all, the willful disregard for Hong Kongers. In these high-stakes geopolitical transactions, there had been no mediators, no voices of reason, no off-ramps. The fissures between the English and Chinese language had widened into chasms of incomprehension into which inconvenient facts—bloody military campaigns, entire wars, lives and deaths in the thousands—were swept.

Just as it took generations of cartographers to pin the island of Hong Kong to the map, Hong Kong as an entity was an invention that sprang straight from the brains of its first colonial administrators onto the soil of their new insular possession as they carved it up into lots for sale. Without their colonizing impulses, Hong Kong would not exist in its current form as one of the world's great cities. Its latter-day success makes it easy to forget that its possession by the British was not so much an imperial masterstroke as an accident driven by a confluence of misplaced personal initiative, misunderstanding, and overreach. It was born in fits and starts, century-old acts of piecemeal acquisition that bear revisiting because the city's current plight is rooted in them, their consequences rippling and expanding over the years.

What we know today as Hong Kong was acquired by the British in three separate tranches: Hong Kong island in the 1840s, the Kowloon peninsula in the 1860s, and finally the New Territories abutting mainland China, along with 235 outlying islands, on a ninety-nine-year lease in 1898. The full story of Britain's acquisition of Hong Kong, however, is more complicated, capricious, and cruel than this tidy summary conveys; indeed, it is one of the most shameful episodes in British history. Each of the three phases of acquisition was accompanied by a war; the three tranches of territory that we know as Hong Kong were the spoils of those wars. To understand how Hong Kong ended up where it is, therefore, it is necessary to start at the beginning.

The first two conflicts—long, bloody, and fought between great powers—came to be known as the Opium Wars, because they were occasioned by Britain's effort to protect British traders selling illegal drugs in China. The Opium Wars were hugely controversial at the time. Of the first, William Gladstone, who would become prime minister, said in Parliament: "A war more unjust in its origins, a war more calculated in its progress to cover this country with permanent disgrace, I do not know and I have not read of."

It had its origins in Britain's insatiable thirst for Chinese tea, which had been introduced in the mid-seventeenth century, when the Portuguese princess Catherine of Braganza brought a casket of tea in her trousseau as she came to wed Charles II. The British also wanted to clad themselves in silk gowns and eat off blue-and-white porcelain. But the Qing emperors believed the Middle Kingdom had no need of barbarian goods, save silver and bullion, so they confined British merchants in

China to a single port—Canton—where they could trade only for several months out of the year, through a monopoly guild of Chinese merchants overseen by a famously corrupt official known as the Hoppo. Britain desperately needed a commodity to rebalance this ruinous trade deficit, and it found its answer in opium. Though the opium trade was technically illegal, it was tacitly permitted, since the authorities depended upon entrance duties paid by clippers bringing opium from British India.

The First Opium War was a direct result of the Daoguang Emperor's attempts to stamp out the scourge of opium, though the British spun it as driven by the righteous pursuit of free trade and the defense of national honor. The emperor, an opium addict himself, tasked Commissioner Lin Zexu, a man of legendary integrity, with ending the opium trade. Lin wasted no time. On March 18, 1839, just eight days after arriving in Canton, he demanded that British merchants hand over their cargoes of opium, effectively blockading the foreign traders in their warehouses and holding them hostage until they did so. More than twenty thousand chests of British-owned opium were surrendered and dumped into three huge trenches filled with water. Britain's chief superintendent for trade in China, a mustachioed naval captain named Charles Elliot, had promised traders that the British government would compensate them for their losses. When news of his vow reached London six months later, the cabinet decided the Chinese should be made to pay for destroying British property and leaving the government in a financial hole. They launched a war to efface what they saw as an unjust and humiliating act impugning national honor, dispatching an expeditionary force of four thousand troops and sixteen warships.

The war's mercantilist motive can be seen in a draft treaty sketched out by the foreign minister, Lord Palmerston, in February 1840, which explicitly stated that Great Britain should "forgo the permanent possession of any Island," with the main focus being opening up five Chinese ports to British trade. But the expeditionary force, under the command of Charles Elliot and his cousin, Rear Admiral George Elliot, was later given orders to occupy the island of Chusan (now Zhoushan) off the coast of Zhejiang, as a bargaining chip, then proceed north to the Gulf of Bohai to negotiate a treaty gaining trading concessions from the Chinese.

The battle for Chusan on July 4, 1840, took precisely nine minutes, leaving some 280 Chinese dead and 462 wounded, with no British deaths. The treaty negotiations, however, dragged on for six fruitless months while the Chinese plenipotentiary Qishan stalled for time. Elliot lost patience and on January 7, 1841, launched the Second Battle of Chuenpi at the Humen Strait in the Pearl River delta. The British captured forts on the islands of Taikoktow (now Dajiaotou) and Shakok (now Shajiao) in less than an hour, prompting China's shocked surrender. Accounts by British soldiers described a frightful scene of slaughter, with bodies piled three or four deep, the fort "bespattered with brains," and floating corpses blackening the sea.

Four days later, the first mention of Hong Kong surfaced in negotiations between Elliot and Qishan. I found the original letters in the brutalist concrete rhombus of the British National Archives on the outskirts of London, where anyone can call up the letters of Henry VIII or eleventh-century court judgments written on parchment membranes. I had not thought that I would discover anything new there; I simply wanted to handle the records of the negotiations myself. The letters I was looking for arrived in slim manila envelopes and were written on tissue-thin wheat-colored paper. The first envelope I opened held a letter from Elliot to Qishan dated January 11, 1841, four days after the bloody battle. The Chinese characters were small and neat but had evidently been written at some speed, since some incorrect characters had been crossed out. The document was hard for me to read because it used the formal language of the Qing court, but I immediately noticed something unexpected.

The letter from Captain Elliot states, "The esteemed minister expresses the wish to take Tsimshatsui, Hunghom [both places on Kowloon side] as well as the land opposite Tsimshatsui, namely Hong Kong, in exchange for Shakok." The words "namely Hong Kong" were not in the original text, however, but had been added in the margins between two columns. From its very first mention, Hong Kong was marginal in every sense of the word.

Qishan's reply four days later is far more impressive than Elliot's letter. The document is stamped with three large red seals, and each ideogram is larger, more balanced, and more beautifully written than the crabbed characters of the British scribe. The handwriting exudes erudition and culture in an act of calligraphic one-upmanship that was no doubt completely missed by its recipient. In the letter, Qishan points out that Tsimshatsui and Hong Kong are two separate places. He offers Elliot a choice between the two, but not both.

It took Elliot a single night to decide on Hong Kong. In his reply, written in the same hasty hand, the phrase "a site in Hong Kong" has been changed to "the island of Hong Kong," indicating a last-minute upgrade in British demands, according to Chinese historians.

The choice of Hong Kong, in other words, was almost accidental. Writing in 1895, the colonial civil servant Ernest Eitel describes the cession of Hong Kong as "a surprise to all concerned," reluctantly offered at the last moment by the Chinese plenipotentiary and accepted by the British envoy unwillingly but with little alternative. Reading those three flimsy pages, I was struck by the weight they bear. History would have unfurled quite differently had Elliot chosen Kowloon instead of Hong Kong or had Qishan agreed to cede Hong Kong and Kowloon at the same time.

According to British records, the agreement reached after this correspondence, known as the Convention of Chuenpi, ceded Hong Kong to the British and included a Chinese indemnity of 6 million silver dollars to compensate for the destroyed opium, as well as an agreement to re-open trading ties and start official relations on an equal footing. Just nine days later, on January 25, 1841, Captain Edward Belcher of the HMS *Sulphur* landed at the foot of Taipingshan to lay claim to the land as "the bona fide first possessors." He and his crew drank to the health of Queen Victoria with three cheers. The next day, all the warships in the harbor fired a feu de joie, which thundered around the hillsides to the Peak. They conducted a ceremonial flag-raising at their landing spot, which they called Possession Point. The British history books concur on these points.

Beijing sees this episode very differently. According to China's Marxist historians, this was a seizure by force "while subjecting the Qing government to diplomatic blackmail." There is no doubt that the Convention of Chuenpi was problematic. There were significant differences between the English and Chinese versions, including the crucial point of whether British residence on Hong Kong was temporary or permanent. In his memorials to the emperor, Qishan described the Convention of Chuenpi as "proposed regulations" rather than a done deal, and the convention never received the imperial seal that signaled the Chinese government's official assent. As early as the 1950s, one independent scholar of the Chinese imperial archives, George H. C. Wong, concluded that the British possession of Hong Kong was therefore illegal. In this view, Hong Kong owes its status as a British colony to Elliot's practice of presenting his wishes as faits accomplis.

The reaction to the Convention of Chuenpi was utterly negative on all sides. It took a full ten weeks for the news to reach London, whereupon Hong Kong's first administrator, Elliot, was immediately recalled in disgrace. His failure to open up Chinese ports to trade was seen as reprehensible, and the choice of Hong Kong inexplicable. It was in Lord Palmerston's furious response to him that the infamous line appeared: "A barren rock with nary a house upon it," he wrote. "It will never be a mart for trade." In the same letter, Palmerston himself raised questions about the legality of the agreement, writing, "Even this cession as it is called, seems to me, from the condition with which it is clogged, not to be a cession of the Sovereignty of the Island, which could only be made by the signature of the emperor." The Qing government was equally outraged, recalling Qishan to Peking (now Beijing) in chains and charging him with treasonably alienating Chinese soil. His assets were confiscated and he was exiled to Tibet.

About a week after the ceremonial landing, Hong Kong's residents were summarily informed that their nationality had changed. According to the 1841 census figures, there were 7,450 residents of Hong Kong, including 2,000 boat dwellers. The British occupation of Hong Kong was not recognized and confirmed until more than a year later, when the Treaty of Nanjing was signed on August 29, 1842. It did not officially become a Crown Colony until June 26, 1843, more than two years after the landing. Thus, right from the very start, Hong Kong's identity was conditional and uncertain. Hong Kongers had become British subjects overnight without their knowledge, let alone their agreement, and they continued to exist in a marginal space without clear prospects for the future.

Although the British had no proper authority to do so, they declared that all unoccupied land lots were Crown land. Large swaths of additional land were compulsorily acquired, uprooting communities and nurturing deep-seated hostility toward the new administration. Even where they recognized existing claims on the land, the British made fundamental errors. They failed to understand traditional Chinese landowning practices, whereby small topsoil renters leased land from subsoil owners who paid taxes on the land to the Chinese government. The British instead viewed the subsoil landowners as tax lords taking "irregular squeezes," so they often rejected their claims to the land, instead recognizing the topsoil lessees as the owners. This resulted in subsistence farmers who had rented topsoil rights cheaply suddenly being burdened with punitive land taxes they were unable to pay. At the same time, traditional landowners were suddenly dispossessed, chief among them the powerful Tang clan, who had settled in Kam Tin in the New Territories as early as 973 CE and for centuries had been collecting rent and paying tax to the Chinese government on large swaths of Hong Kong, Kowloon, and the New Territories. The cost of expropriating their land would explode at the end of the century.

The inaugural land sales, held on June 14, 1841, set the scene for a century and a half of frenzied land speculation, whereby the colonial administration controlled land supply to drive up demand, a practice it perfected to devastating effect. In the first land sales, more than thirty lots along the Central shorefront were sold for an average of ninety-six pounds each. Right from the start, the reaction of the crowd was awed disbelief at the prices, followed by a burning desire to bid on the next lot. As one contemporary observer wrote, "The first lot sold was numbered 15 in the list, it was knocked down to Mr. Webster at 20 pounds not only without opposition but he was laughed at for giving so much. The next lot No 14 however fetched 21 pounds." Six weeks after these land sales, Captain Elliot learned of his recall, but by then foundations had already been dug and handsome buildings were being raised.

One week before the land sales, Elliot had declared Hong Kong to be a free port, and open for trade. In this way, the British pressed their advantage, even though their occupation was technically temporary and conditional. Every day, the colony was taking shape with its attendant shops, brothels, opium emporiums and bazaars, a casino, and even a performing orangutan called Gertrude, whose daily luncheon—topped off with wine and a cigar—became a public entertainment. The logic of dominion and imperial expansion, once underway, was unstoppable. For both British and Chinese who flocked there, Hong Kong offered wide-open vistas of opportunity, a tabula rasa where ambitious chancers could reinvent themselves afresh as they constructed a new city.

To the British, ruling meant control and regulation of the local population rather than governance. The first completed building in the new colony was an enormous jail, finished two months after the land sale. In the first city plan, the magistracy and jail loom over the entire settlement, taking up the biggest single plot by far. Hong Kong gained a reputation as a safe harbor for those fleeing trouble on the mainland, attracting all kinds of undesirables, and in the first three decades of its existence as a British colony, more than 8 percent of the population appeared before the local courts. The British preoccupation with justice brought order to the new colony, but it also cemented in British minds a view of the incoming Chinese migrants as deplorable.

London, still vacillating about the cost of keeping an island, had ordered a halt to construction, but Elliot's replacement, a hawkish major general named Henry Pottinger, who was Hong Kong's first governor, argued that the settlement was too advanced to restore it to China without damaging British honor. He later admitted that he had "intentionally exceeded my modified instructions" on the retention of Hong Kong due to its desirability. Pottinger also pressed his military advantage, fighting all the way up the Yangtze River until he threatened to destroy the city of Nanjing. Faced with Britain's military superiority, the Chinese signed the Treaty of Nanjing, ceding Hong Kong to the British in perpetuity. Historical accounts tend to gloss over Chinese casualties, but an 1847 report to the British Parliament noted that 69 British were killed and 451 wounded in the First Opium War, as compared to 18,000 to 20,000 Chinese deaths.

So, right from the start, the two narratives accompanying Hong Kong's cession were markedly different. For Governor Henry Pottinger, Hong Kong was a moneymaker, a "future Great Emporium of Commerce and Wealth." But in Beijing, the Nanjing Treaty was the first "unequal treaty" imposed by gunboat diplomacy, and the loss of Hong Kong marked the start of China's century and a half of humiliation by foreign powers, a matter of national shame that could only be eased with the island's return to its rightful owner.

To this day, Hong Kong's street names reflect an astonishing sleight of hand whereby early colonial administrators stamped their mark on public space while simultaneously expunging the memory of their extraordinarily unpleasant legacies. Johnston Road, which we'd walk down to go to my father's favorite Shanghainese dumpling restaurant, was named after Acting Administrator Alexander Johnston, who in 1842 introduced a curfew banning all Chinese except night watchmen from venturing outside after eleven p.m. on pain of arrest. That curfew was to remain in place for most of the next half century. Bonham Road, which we'd drive down to go to the hospital, was named after Hong Kong's third governor, Sir George Bonham, who believed the study of the Chinese language to be "warping to the mind." Hennessy Road, where I had worked at a stultifying job sitting in a cubicle teaching English to schoolchildren, was named after the eighth governor, John Pope Hennessy, who gave voice to the popular view of Chinese as "dishonest, potentially dangerous, malevolent, entangled in mysterious secret societies, foolish in their religious beliefs and only suitable to be clerks, shroffs, amahs, houseboys and coolies." This knowledge changed the way I thought about Hong Kong, overlaying familiar streets with a cartography of colonial domination and racial prejudice.

The graveyard on a hillside overlooking Happy Valley Racecourse—which itself was built on farmland expropriated from the prosperous village of Wong Nai Chung, leaving the villagers as beggars on their own land—tells its own version of this story. This cemetery, containing around eight thousand graves scattered up the hillside, played an important part in my family life, since my mother spent the best part of a decade there.

My mother is an anomaly. Born Patricia Constance de Fonblanque, a posh English army brat, she became plain Pat Lim after marriage. She had already rebelled against her parents to study history at Cambridge, much to their horror, instead of doing a season as a debutante. When my family moved to Hong Kong, she became fascinated by Hong Kong's local heritage. After writing two cultural heritage guidebooks, she moved on to the graveyard. When she could find no books about it, she decided to write her own.

Thus it was that my siblings and I spent childhood weekends trailing sullenly behind our mother as she barreled past snarling dogs and uncommunicative locals in the New Territories. We were bored by the dusty ancestral halls, where we kicked our feet and slapped at the mosquitoes reconnoitering our legs, as our mother slowly examined endless altars stacked with tiers of ancestral tablets noting the clan's male descendants. We were unmoved by the auspicious trees, oblivious to the hope and heartbreak freighting the thicket of red packets dangling from their branches. We were wildly jealous of our peers who spent their weekends sunbathing on junks or playing tennis at the Ladies Recreation Club, while we sweated through dusty temples with their creepy arhats and nightmare-inducing demons.

But my mother was on a mission. She wanted to extend the notion of cultural heritage so it embraced not only imposing colonial buildings but more vernacular heritage, like earth god shrines and local temples. She wanted to resituate local heritage and history, shifting it away from the colonial ruling class and toward ordinary people by charting how they lived and died. My Chinese father was deeply disapproving, regarding the burial ground with superstitious horror, but my mother assured him she was only intending to write a short pamphlet. By the time she was finished, a decade later, her little leaflet had ballooned into a six-hundred-page tome charting the social history of the graveyard. "I was fascinated by the way Hong Kong had grown up, and nobody knew anything about it," she told me. "All Hong Kong history is here. And Hong Kong people never realized and almost nobody ever visited it."

The centrality of opium to the new colony is reflected in the cemetery's first grave, a simple urn remembering Lieutenant Benjamin Fox, who was killed in the First Opium War in 1841. Governor Pottinger had forbidden opium ships from using Hong Kong's harbor, to try to improve the relationship with China, but his ban lasted only a year, sunk by the exigencies of commerce. From 1845 to 1849, three-quarters of the Indian opium crop passed through Hong Kong. In the cemetery, the influence of the opium trade endures. My mother describes with grim relish the death of the unfortunate Captain Schmidt of the opium clipper *Anonyma*, on August 3, 1850: "He fell lifeless from his chair without a word. At the time he was feeding a favourite paroquet." It took only one year and one day for his successor, Captain John Wills, to succumb to the same fate, shooting himself in the head while temporarily insane.

The British had wanted a trading station free from Chinese jurisdiction, and Hong Kong now flourished as such. The imposing warehouses of opium trading houses such as Jardine Matheson and Dent's lined the waterfront. In the brand-new colony, where social mores were suspended, opium traders became the elite businessmen, and those who worked with them profited greatly. The wealthiest Chinese—men like Loo Aqui and Tam Achoy—came from Tanka boat people, a socially marginalized group who did not enjoy the same rights in China as landed people. But in Hong Kong, they built their own respectability by establishing institutions like the Man Mo Temple and the Tung Wah Hospital, which dispensed justice, welfare, and medical care to the flood of Chinese immigrants. Just as Hong Kong provided a canvas for colonial ambition, it also allowed opportunistic and hardworking migrants, both British and Chinese, to reimagine their lives, though few saw it as a permanent home.

As the new colony took shape along the north shore of the island, the city that emerged was almost exclusively European, with very few Chinese permitted to buy blocks of land. The British built their mansions on the Peak's slopes to take advantage of its cooler clime, leaving the Chinese migrants crowded into a few cramped seafront settlements without proper sanitation or drainage. Living conditions were so poor that the earliest Chinese settlement, Taipingshan, was demolished for public hygiene reasons at the end of the nineteenth century after the bubonic plague raced through it.

The Chinese and British communities remained largely separate amid antipathy so intense that in 1857, a Chinese baker added arsenic to his bread supply in an attempt to kill off the European population. He poisoned some four hundred Europeans, though luckily he added too much arsenic, inducing vomiting instead of death. In 1858, the fourth governor of Hong Kong, Sir John Bowring, wrote, "I do not believe there is a single [British] merchant or Tradesman in Hongkong who speaks, or understands the native dialect, who has seen a Chinaman at his Table, or admitted him to the slightest confidential intimacy." In Bowring's sobering assessment, an absolute abyss separated the governors and the governed: "We rule them in ignorance, and they submit in blindness."

The segregation even persisted into the afterlife. For decades, Chinese were banned from entering the cemetery, let alone being buried there. In the early years of the colony, Hong Kong's Chinese population mainly consisted of migrants fleeing the turbulence of the Taiping Rebellion or floods and famine in China. Though Hong Kong offered a sanctuary for this population, they were "sojourners" who viewed the city as a way station while still keeping their ties to their hometown. There was little sense of a distinct Hong Kong identity.

Early colonial Hong Kong was a dangerous place. Each grave in the cemetery was a potent reminder of its perils: the unfortunate policeman Ernest Goucher, mauled to death by a two-and-a-half-meter-long tiger; the auctioneer Charles Markwick, strangled in bed with the connivance of his servant; or the sea captain Henry Lovett, who died when his mutinying crew attacked him, slashing his abdomen so deeply that his bowels were left hanging out. My mother couldn't help noting that Captain Lovett's British bulldog had defended him during the attack and managed to survive despite suffering great gashes across the nose and hip. The executor of Lovett's will subsequently put the bulldog up for sale, asking fifty dollars for it, a sum which she described as "a lot to pay for a dog, at a time when a gold watch and chain had cost John Wright $23." I recognized this as the same tone she used to chide me for wasting my pocket money.

My mother's adventures in the graveyard were legendary. Sometimes she became so immersed in her research that she ended up being locked into the cemetery by mistake, necessitating panicky escapes over the cemetery wall in the pitch black. One day I met a complete stranger who gleefully told me a story about how my mother had lain down on a gravestone to rest. Some visitors to the cemetery had stumbled over her and, mistaking this silver-haired white woman lying on a slab for a ghost, had run away.

Like all the best myths, this story had its genesis in a real event. One hot summer day, my mother had been leading a tour around the highest reaches of the graveyard when she felt so unwell that she lay down on a gravestone to recover. It was the memorial of Richardson Barry Loxley Leslie, an unfortunate twenty-six-year-old policeman who'd been shot dead responding to a robbery the day after Hong Kong surrendered to Japan in World War II. After fifteen minutes' rest, she had with her customary stoicism gathered herself together and finished the tour. A couple of days later, she went to the doctor, who told her that she'd suffered a potentially fatal coronary event while lying on the grave. We joked that her death in the cemetery would have had a certain poetic justice; she joked it might have boosted book sales.

It was only slowly that I realized that my mother's own family had played roles similar to the British buried in the cemetery. Her people were soldiers and policemen, colonizers who had played peripheral parts in the many chapters of Hong Kong's dominion by fighting for it, administering it, and governing it. My great-great-grandfather, Edward Barrington de Fonblanque, had been part of the British expeditionary force during the Second Opium War, and another relative had been responsible for triggering the Six-Day War of 1899. We had been part of the colonial project all the way up to my father, whose job as a civil servant spanned Hong Kong's transition to Chinese rule in 1997.

Edward Barrington de Fonblanque played a cameo in the war that led to the acquisition of the peninsula of Kowloon, the very spit of land claimed by Tsang Tsou-choi himself. Born in 1821, he was a career soldier whose signature achievement during the Crimean War appeared to have been making bricks without straw, according to his *Times* obituary. He was forced to retire early on half pay after being blamed for an episode when his detachment suffered heatstroke. I had spent many hours deciphering his commonplace books, which contained a surprising amount of scandal for someone living in the buttoned-up Victorian era. In them, he cheerfully confided that infidelity was not the worst crime that a wife could commit. A careful reading revealed a private life so colorful that he narrowly missed being named as a co-respondent in the most scandalous divorce case of the era, that of the infamous Lady Colin Campbell.

At the tail end of 1859, E.B., as he was known, was deployed to Japan to procure three to four thousand horses for the British expeditionary force in China. He did not shine at his mission, as he admits in a book he wrote about his time in Japan and China. He confesses to his deficit of knowledge about either country and his lack of any relevant statistics or any secret sources of information. Like so many other British, in fact, he distrusted those who saw themselves as China experts, writing, "As regards China, the few who, by long residence and earnest study, have acquired some knowledge of that country . . . become so warped in their judgment, and so violent in their predilections or antipathies, as to incapacitate themselves from bearing true testimony." His account is in effect a misery memoir set against the theater of the Second Opium War, to which he was largely peripheral.

In Japan, a country that had been closed to the outside world for two centuries, E.B. needed permission from the shogun for every single transaction. He was in fierce competition for horses with the French—who, though part of the expeditionary force, were hated by the British—and he struggled with cunning Japanese horse-dealers who would lacquer marks onto their horses' teeth to gain a better price. When he finally managed to buy some horses, the Japanese grooms refused to exercise them, since only two-sworded samurai were allowed to ride on horseback. When he sent his horses to China, the ship got turned back by a hurricane. Back at the Japanese port, he discovered that 230 of his 300 hard-won horses had died, as "half maddened with fear and tortured by their hurts as they rolled among the fragments of their boxes, [they] commenced an onslaught upon one another, which death or sheer exhaustion only terminated." When the war finally ended in 1860, he oversaw the auction of a thousand horses in Tianjin for a fraction of their cost.

This war's end came with the cornerstone act underpinning China's century of humiliation: the razing to the ground of the Old Summer Palace in Beijing by British and French troops, who first looted the Qing emperor's rococo retreat. E.B. was in China at the time, but he was not present for the looting, though he spends many paragraphs describing the "golden josses or ingots, or ewers, basins, and vases of the same metals, or pearls and other precious stones, curious for their size or brilliancy, or even of sycee silver." My great-great-grandfather thoroughly disapproved of looting, mainly since he believed that nothing loosened the bonds of discipline and damaged military morale more than the license to plunder.

Just as the acquisition of Hong Kong had been incidental rather than intentional, the annexation of Kowloon was a by-product of the Second

Opium War rather than its aim. A straight line was drawn on the map at what became known as Boundary Street to demarcate the British territory of Kowloon from China on the other side of the border. The British recognized Kowloon's military and strategic value, although they also saw it as a refuge for pirates, robbers, and criminals. As Governor Bowring put it, "To the Chinese, it is not only of no value, but a seat of anarchy and a source of embarrassment."

Once again, the actual cession of the peninsula of Kowloon was a more complicated affair than depicted in history books. By the time the Peking Convention was signed, Kowloon had already been under British control for nine months. Its lease had been negotiated on March 19, 1860, by Harry Parkes, the young consul in Canton whose actions had precipitated the Second Opium War. In his diary, he recorded the astonishingly casual nature of the deal with the acting viceroy in Canton, Lau Tsung-kwan, after what sounded like an alcoholic tiffin with the British generals and their ladyships. He wrote, "In the afternoon to Lau, with my letter in my pocket, and got him to agree to the whole of the scheme whereat I felt jolly in mind though seedy in body." The lease of Kowloon cost just 500 taels of silver, and Parkes held the land in his name for nine months. In retrospect, everything about this episode seems extraordinary; the two parties were at war, and the British were seeking land to train troops to fight the Chinese, and the man they sent to conclude the deal was the very figure responsible for the escalation of that war. And yet Parkes prevailed.

Though my great-great-grandfather viewed the Peking Convention as a good treaty, he was waspish about its prospects. In his book, he wrote, "In spite of the pretensions of our diplomatists, every concession made by the Chinese government has been wrung from them by our soldiers and our sailors, and it remains to be seen what will become their attitude when military pressure shall be removed, and ministers and consuls left to their own devices for maintaining or enforcing treaty obligations." This exact question—of how to ensure that Beijing honors its obligations—has always been at the heart of Hong Kong's plight.

Hong Kong was becoming a cosmopolitan port city, where schools and colleges founded by Christian missionaries offered a Western education. One who took advantage of this was Sun Yat-sen, the father of modern China, who began conspiring to overthrow the Qing dynasty while a medical student in Hong Kong. As a refuge for ideas that could not be discussed in China, Hong Kong offered a different vision of what China could be. Certain Eurasian families were even able to upend social expectations, their fabulous wealth permitting them to break the rules, such as the Hotung family who even managed to live on the Peak, the posh mountaintop neighborhood reserved for Europeans only. Hong Kong was a zone of possibility, a space of transgression.

The Treaty of Nanjing offered the model for other countries to carve China up into spheres of influence, and over the next half century Japan, Russia, Germany, and France also hived off plots of land inside China, known as concessions, where their own citizens could freely live under extraterritorial law. It was against this backdrop that Britain acquired the third, and largest, tranche of land that makes up today's Hong Kong. In April 1898, the British minister in Beijing, Sir Claude MacDonald, began negotiations for a chunk of land for the defense of Hong Kong right up to the Shenzhen River, including as well the more than two hundred outlying islands. This land—known as the New Territories— makes up 92 percent of Hong Kong's present-day landmass. The negotiations took only two months and were concluded on July 1, 1898, with the Second Convention of Peking.

The speed of the negotiations may have been in part due to the slapdash attitude of MacDonald, who began talks without even possessing an up-to-date map of the land. Facing nationalist sentiment, the Chinese were adamant that they would not allow any more permanent cessions, but they were willing to extend more territory on a ninety-nine-year lease in line with other Western concessions in China. MacDonald may have believed such a lease was a permanent cession in disguise. He signed the agreement without addressing the future status of the land, likely because he could not envisage China growing powerful enough to demand its return. MacDonald's assumptions were to have outsized consequences for Hong Kong's residents a century later.

This time, Britain was acquiring a larger and more settled population, namely the "Five Great Clans," some of whom had settled the area a millennium ago. Though they were the traditional landowners, the British saw them as triads and robber clans and did almost nothing to communicate their policies in the nine months before the actual transfer of sovereignty in mid-April 1899. This major misjudgment was one factor that triggered a very short war of resistance against the British in the New Territories.

Another factor was the gargantuan insensitivity of a distant relation of mine by marriage, then Commissioner of Police Sir Francis Henry May—known as Henry May—toward customary practices, in particular the deeply held belief in geomancy, or feng shui. He had been tasked with finding a site for a police headquarters, which would also be used as the venue for the flag-raising ceremony asserting British control over the New Territories. After villagers protested against his first choice on feng shui grounds, he changed the location to the place that became known as Flagstaff Hill. One month before the transfer of sovereignty, May made another bad siting decision, trying to place a police station behind the two clan halls in the village of Ping Shan, the ancestral stronghold of the powerful Tang clan. May's choice of location sent an astonishingly belligerent message to inhabitants: the police station would be "like a rock, crushing" them.

The underlying issue was the assault on local identity. Not without reason, the villagers feared losing their land and their customs. There were also rumors circulating about new British taxes, including a salt tax, which had been the precipitating factor behind two earlier historical re-bellions. The opposition was spearheaded by the Tang clan, who had al-ready lost land twice over, once with the cession of Hong Kong and again when Kowloon was annexed. Their fears were articulated in inflamma-tory placards posted in the New Territories, urging villagers to take up arms to resist the "English barbarians, who are about to enter our bound-aries and take our land." A song sung to the accompaniment of bamboo clappers circulated:

Everything is being systematically changed!
Everyone within the bounds of this territory is to become British!
This nation [Britain] cares nothing for our culture!
Why should the people waste their energies uselessly?

In early April, angry crowds burned down the mat-sheds at Flagstaff Hill and attacked Henry May. Four days later, the governor, Sir Henry Blake, issued a proclamation promising that land usage and customs would remain unchanged. Few believed it. On April 14, the rebel force of New Territories villagers, spearheaded by the Tang clan, launched its first strike by again burning the Flagstaff Hill mat-sheds and occupying a couple of nearby hills, shouting, beating gongs, and firing off bombs and firecrackers. The next day, clashes broke out, which raged even as the flag-raising ceremony was carried out.

By April 19, the Six-Day War was over and the insurgents had sur-rendered. About five hundred villagers had been killed in the hostilities, leaving Kam Tin "awash with blood." This was according to the Tang genealogy, which called the dead "heroic martyrs" and urged that "this people's war of opposition should be commemorated." One list named twenty-nine of the forty-two ringleaders of the uprising as members of the Tang clan. However, there was no loss of life on the British side, and Governor Blake withdrew the military almost immediately. He believed "the rowdies" had been taught a lesson and it was time to "pass a sponge over the events of the past month, and leave them to discover, as they will in a short time, that our rule is not the grinding tyranny that they expected." From the villagers' point of view, this worked; many were willing to put the uprising behind them to move ahead with life under British rule.

This strategy proved successful in wiping the war from the collective memory and from colonial historical records. But the episode is mentioned in Communist Chinese accounts, where it is described as "a glorious page in Hong Kong's history of resistance to foreign aggression," with the villagers seen as patriots determined to preserve national dignity. My mother had taken me to the walled village of Kam Tin, but in my adolescent ennui, I had failed to appreciate its historical importance. The one fact that permeated my teenage sangfroid was that the village was missing its gates. They'd been removed as a symbolic act of retribution by Blake, who had them shipped to his estate in County Cork, Ireland, to use as a garden decoration.

Despite his role in triggering the Six-Day War, my relative Henry May continued to rise up the hierarchy until, in 1912, he became governor of Hong Kong. He was the only governor to be the target of an assassination attempt, which happened the very day he was inaugurated, when a man with a grudge from his police years fired on him. May was unhurt, but the bullet landed in the sedan chair of his wife, Lady Helena May, who was a cousin of my mother's by marriage. May was remembered as the most racist governor of them all, owning a racing pony called Yellow Skin. His predecessor, Sir Frederick Lugard, described Henry May by saying, "I like him very much, he is white right through." May made it illegal for Chinese people to live on the Peak. He stopped mixed-race children from being accepted into Peak schools, writing, "It would be little short of a calamity if an alien, and by European standards, a semicivilized race were allowed to drive the white man from the one area in Hong Kong, in which he can live with his wife and children in a white man's healthy surroundings."

These were the reasons why Hong Kongers did not learn their own history under British rule; the racially based laws and apartheid-like segregation could not be easily explained, nor could the Opium Wars themselves. The sponge that had passed over the Six-Day War was now hovering over large chunks of the past. And the layers of omission were manifold; if Chinese people were largely absent from colonial history books, Chinese women were even more invisible, not to mention the poor old Eurasians who had canceled themselves. A common history provides identity, but Hong Kong's colonial rulers benefited from leaving its people stranded on the metaphorical barren rock, without either a clear British or a clear Chinese identity.

To those watching the protest movement of 2019, it could almost seem that the Six-Day War of 1899 had in a way resurfaced. Both were leaderless, grassroots movements aimed at defending Hong Kongers from an all-powerful colonizing force. Both used popular culture to mobilize support, with the bamboo clapper songs of 1899 prefiguring the protest anthems of 2019. The Lennon Walls that obsessed me were foreshadowed by anonymous notices plastered on public walls more than a century before. They read: "The English barbarians are about to enter our territory, and ruin will come upon our villages and hamlets." The twenty-first-century refrain was simply: "Let Hong Kong be Hong Kong."

Even the visual echoes are striking. The single extant photograph of the Six-Day War features two young men wearing dark cotton clothes and conical straw hats staring directly at the camera, long guns slung over their shoulders. One clue signals that they may have snapped this ceremonial photo in a photographic studio ahead of the impending battle against the British; they're both wearing round white signs pinned to their chests featuring two Chinese characters: *jong yung* 壯勇, or "strong brave," words that are part motivational slogan, part talisman.

That same character *yung* 勇, or "brave," was often heard on Hong Kong's streets in 2019, because frontliners were called *yung mou* 勇武, or "brave warriors." And there's a modern iteration of the photograph as well, showing two contemporary figures attired in present-day protest gear of head-to-foot skintight black clothing, yellow plastic helmets, gas masks, and goggles. They're poised for action, kneeling on a Tsuen Wan street—in territory the 1899 war was fought over—awaiting a police attack. One man grasps a metal pole, the other a brick. It's worth noting that they are far outclassed in weaponry by their counterparts a century before. There's an element of posturing in both photos, but both sets of young men have the same wariness in their eyes, the same stubborn bravado arising from the knowledge that the force they're facing is far superior. They could almost be the same young men transported by a time machine.

The efforts to erase the Six-Day War were remarkably successful. The final communal memory was invoked at the funeral of the rebellion's last leader, Ng Shing-chi, in 1938. A banner recalled his role in the Six-Day War: "Like a valiant mantis trying to stop a cart with its front claws, a matter of strong selflessness, a matter to be admired, this is what the generation before the lease was like." In describing the powerlessness of Hong Kongers against an all-powerful opponent, those words—"like a valiant mantis trying to stop a cart with its front claws"—echo and reprise through the years, as apt in 2019 as they had been more than a century before.

PART 2

DISPOSSESSION

CHAPTER 4

NEW TERRITORIES

It began with a little trip. In September 1982, emerging from the Great Hall of the People in Beijing, where she'd been discussing the future of Hong Kong with Chinese leader Deng Xiaoping, Prime Minister Margaret Thatcher missed her footing and toppled down the steps, landing unceremoniously on her hands and knees. The optics of the British prime minister humbled, kowtowing on all fours before Chairman Mao Zedong's mausoleum, in China's center of political power, reverberated around the world. It caused the Hang Seng Index, the beating pulse of this financial city, to plummet 600 points. The fall was an omen, people in Hong Kong said, of the territory's future. Thatcher had tripped because Deng Xiaoping had run so many rings round her.

In fact, Hong Kongers had no idea quite how badly the meeting had gone. High on her success in the Falklands War just three months earlier, Thatcher had gone in hoping to convince Deng to strike a deal whereby Hong Kong could be returned to China in 1997 but Britain could continue to administer the territory beyond that deadline. Though Hong Kong and Kowloon had been ceded in perpetuity, they were not viable without the New Territories that constituted the overwhelming majority of the landmass. The entire territory was dependent on China for food and water. Thatcher's position stemmed from her argument that only British control would guarantee Hong Kong's stability. Three years earlier, Deng had indicated this wouldn't be possible, and the point had been reiterated the day before the leaders' summit, by Premier Zhao Ziyang, but Thatcher, full of self-confidence, hadn't been listening.

In the high-ceilinged hall, Thatcher's characteristic mix of brassiness and bossiness had not charmed Deng. He wrong-footed her by smoking through the talks and periodically spitting in a white enamel spittoon placed near his feet. She flinched when he spat, and after the meeting, described him as cruel. Deng was obdurate. He insisted that Beijing would take back Hong Kong, Kowloon, and the New Territories in 1997 and warned that it could do so that very day, if it wanted. On the issue of whether Britain's administration could be extended, Deng's answer was a flat no. "We will not be Li Hongzhang," he said, referring to the Qing dynasty official who negotiated some of China's unequal treaties in the nineteenth century. The meeting was disastrous, according to Thatcher's private parliamentary secretary, but few would be told just how badly it had gone, not even the British government's most trusted advisers in Hong Kong.

Their voice—the Hong Kong voice—is the biggest omission in the story of how Hong Kong came to be handed back to China. Just as Britain and China have dueling versions of Hong Kong's past, the two powers also wrote bifurcating narratives about its retrocession. One of the few things those accounts have in common is how they wash over Hong Kong's return to China with barely a mention of Hong Kong's people. Thatcher features Hong Kong in just ten of the 914 pages of her autobiography. John Major, the prime minister who presided over the colony's

1997 return to China, mentions it on five of his 774 pages. The divestment of the last British colony and its millions of inhabitants was barely
a half thought in the great sweep of their lives. Only one of these accounts features a Hong Konger, and he was the first chief executive,
Tung Chee-hwa, who is viewed in Hong Kong as Shanghainese. To the
prime ministers overseeing this grand geopolitical chess game, Hong
Kong people remained nameless and faceless.

I was always interested in the in-between version, the fly-on-the-wall
account from a Hong Kong perspective. But this seemed impossible, as
so many of the main players had died since the negotiations four decades
ago. Then I found my holy grail on a library shelf. It was an archive containing dozens of interviews conducted in the 1980s and 1990s by Hong
Kong political scientist Steve Tsang. He had spoken with Hong Kong's
most important figures at the time, including three British governors
and at least six key Hong Kong advisers, promising that their words
would be kept confidential for thirty years from the last incident described. Now those time limits had expired. The interviews covered sensitive issues including immigration, corruption, and the 1967 riots, when
pro-Chinese leftists in Hong Kong waged a year-long bombing campaign that left fifty-one people dead. Crucially, they also contained the
first inside accounts from those prominent Hong Kong advisers about
how the territory's future had been settled.

The story they told was a revelation, a huge departure from the Chinese and British accounts, which tend to transform the famously testy
negotiations into an orderly, clinical process whose foregone conclusion
was Hong Kong's return to Chinese rule. In fact, it took two years and
twenty-two rounds of these extraordinarily difficult negotiations, which
sometimes came close to collapse. Hong Kongers did not have a seat at
the negotiating table, nor any role except in an advisory capacity. They
were not given the opportunity to vote on the agreement or to change it
in any way. After I read Tsang's archive, I realized that that tone of sober

detachment in the British and Chinese accounts was only made possible by the dearth of Hong Kong voices.

The story that exploded out of those dusty pages throbbed with desperation and anguish, Shakespearean levels of tragedy, heroism, betrayal, and hubris. The papers also lifted the curtain on the prevalence of anti-Chinese racism in the United Kingdom, even at the very top, and its impact on negotiations. Almost as shocking was the unvarnished frankness expressed in the interviews, a raw candor that I found startling, especially in comparison to the official accounts. The agreement to hold the documents for thirty years effectively freed the interviewees from the Official Secrets Act that muzzled them from confiding even in their families. Liberated to speak for the first time, they unburdened themselves to Tsang so candidly that his role sometimes felt more like confessor than interviewer. The words that echoed through their accounts told their own story: *dismayed, angry, upset, scared, devastated.*

Two voices stand out: that of the British governor from 1971 to 1982, Baron MacLehose of Beoch, then Murray MacLehose, and that of his most senior Hong Kong adviser, Sir Sze-yuen Chung, universally known as S.Y. and later as Great Sir. For most of the period in question, S.Y., a short man with a square, pugnacious jaw and rectangular black spectacles, was the senior "Unofficial." In the era before party politics and competitive elections in Hong Kong, the "Unofficials" were the industrialists, bankers, and lawyers appointed by the governor to the Executive Council (Exco) or the Legislative Council (Legco), collectively known by the clunky acronym of UMELCO. The very title of "Unofficial" betrayed the true power of these advisers. However, Exco was the equivalent of a cabinet, and in 1983, then governor Edward Youde observed that no governor had acted against its advice for two decades. But if the British had hoped for an advisory body stacked with docile, biddable yes-men, they had not reckoned with S.Y., who succeeded in transforming the Unofficials into Hong Kong's first unofficial politicians.

In his autobiography, S.Y. accurately describes himself as, "Without my trying, the Chinese in the colony most knowledgeable about what actually transpired from the beginning of negotiations through transition to the establishment of the Special Administrative Region." Middle-class and an engineer by trade, he characterized the other Unofficials as born with silver spoons in their mouths. A hard worker who spent every Sunday reading official papers, S.Y. was stubborn and outspoken, utterly uncorruptible, and thoroughly dedicated to Hong Kong. When he died in 2018 at the age of 101, there was a consensus that he had served Hong Kong well.

As I read the 421 pages of Chung's interviews, which were carried out in 1990 and 1991, I found myself moved by his nervous asides. *The manuscript is not to be seen by anybody, is it? . . . These are the facts, I swear to God. . . . This is confidential and I trust you to respect it. . . . This episode is confidential, but it will be useful twenty-five years from now. . . . If I live and do not leave HK, then this disclosure could lead me into trouble with the Chinese government.* In the middle of an anecdote, he would sometimes seek reassurance: *Thank you for the interview and I hope someone would find it useful.* This anxiety seeded in me a low-level nervousness; what would he have thought if he had realized that his words had been sitting on a library shelf, largely unread and unnoticed, all these years? And should I—possibly Reader Number One—treat these confidences any differently, knowing just how carefully they had been guarded?

But S.Y.'s story, bolstered by other Unofficials' accounts and declassified diplomatic records from the Thatcher archive, restores the Hong Kong voice to the crucial years leading up to the agreement to return the territory to China, known as the Joint Declaration. The stories break through so many conspiracies of silence—silences driven by political necessity and expediency, silences of honor and of betrayal. The account pieced together from the files highlights three moments of crisis for the Unofficials—the gubernatorial trip to China in 1979, the British

Nationality Act in the early 1980s, and finally the visit to Beijing when Thatcher tripped down the stairs in 1982—followed by one long, spiraling descent into despair as the Joint Declaration was signed.

One throughline threaded through the papers was the imperiousness of empire toward its last far-flung colony. In the seventies, Hong Kong faced an influx of an estimated 213,000 Vietnamese fleeing their civil war in rickety wooden junks. Hong Kong was left on its own to set up and fund camps for the boat people. When asked what type of pressure was placed on Hong Kong from London, one Unofficial, the banker Li Fook-wo, simply replied, "I don't think we faced any pressure from Whitehall or Westminster because at that time, to put it crudely, HMG [Her Majesty's Government] never cared for those details."

In 1971, Murray MacLehose, a former war hero, was appointed governor of Hong Kong for his China expertise. From his prior Foreign Office experience, he knew that it was customary to be issued with instructions about British policy regarding any new posting, but he told Tsang that none existed for Hong Kong, and he was told to write his own: "They didn't really have a policy towards Hong Kong. That's the truth of the matter." This was one of the reasons MacLehose agreed to be interviewed. In a declassified 1988 letter to the Foreign Office seeking permission to take part, he fretted that historians would be faced with a dearth of information about Hong Kong. He wrote, "In the seventies there was extraordinarily little official dialogue with London about why things were done in Hong Kong. You might be surprised to hear that a Deputy Under Secretary admonished me, 'Your job is to keep Hong Kong out of the Secretary of State's hair.'" To London, Hong Kong—and its inhabitants—was at best a distraction.

I remember Big Mac, as he was nicknamed, from my childhood, as a six-foot-four-inch no-nonsense Scot in a tan open-neck shirt, towering over his entourage as he strode through the New Territories public housing estates whose construction he'd overseen. These housed 1.6 million of Hong Kong's rapidly growing population, which had been boosted by the Vietnamese boat people and Chinese fleeing the Cultural Revolution who increasingly saw Hong Kong as a permanent home rather than a sojourn. MacLehose saw his mission as "government in a hurry" and adamantly refused to call his outings "walkabouts," as he insisted he was visiting places and talking to people, not simply walking around. By nature, he was a paternalistic authoritarian, whose priority was delivering good government and administrative efficiency.

My abiding memory of the MacLehose era was a warty green-and-red dragon called Laapsaap Chong, or Litterbug, who starred in television commercials gleefully tossing trash over Hong Kong's streets. The spotty red-green dragon was the public face of MacLehose's Keep Hong Kong Clean campaign, which expanded to a series of apocalyptic ads—they haunted my nightmares for years—urging Hong Kongers to stop throwing their beer bottles, television sets, and air conditioners from the windows of their high-rise blocks. The larger significance of the dragon, I learned from the papers, was MacLehose's insistence that such civic campaigns could serve as a substitute for democracy. He told Tsang, "Though history might deny Hong Kong an elected democracy, an effective and more immediate substitute could be 'participation.' . . . As successive campaigns took effect and became established—often doing more or different things to those that were originally envisaged—they demonstrated how 'democratic' a Government could be in how it acted and responded to public requirements without an elected legislature." Governors like MacLehose, who firmly opposed opening the "Pandora's box of drastic constitutional reform" and believed Hong Kong's system could outperform electoral politics, were one key reason why the British did not introduce democratic reform to Hong Kong. In these paternalistic instincts, they were often supported by their local Exco advisers.

When MacLehose arrived in Hong Kong, an overarching silence about Hong Kong's future had reigned for decades. A kind of omertà lingered over the topic, with neither Britain nor China wanting to be the first to raise it. Li Fook-wo described that taboo as being so strong that mentioning 1997 was seen as a "crime." "Nobody ever dared to touch the question," said industrialist and senior Exco member Ann Tse-kai. "China didn't ask the question, so why raise it yourself?"

It was MacLehose who decided it was time to break that code of silence. The ninety-nine-year lease on the New Territories struck by Lord MacDonald with his out-of-date map would run out in 1997. The question that concentrated minds was that of individual leases on farmland, which were issued for fifteen years at a time. By 1979 there was a cushion of just three years before the fifteen-year clock began ticking, and bankers and developers were wondering how to handle the issue. To MacLehose, 1997 represented "an inescapable source of crisis" if it were not addressed and planned for well in advance. It was, he believed, grossly irresponsible, indeed indefensible, to wait for China to raise the subject. He decided it was time to breach the taboo. One key assumption underlined all MacLehose's calculations: that Beijing would not hesitate to intervene in Hong Kong should it be necessary. He firmly believed that Hong Kong's survival depended on avoiding situations that could lead to a confrontation with China. For this reason, the question of an independent Hong Kong was never even considered, let alone discussed, according to MacLehose. He told Tsang, "That is a frightfully important case in which everybody, as it were, combined in a conspiracy of silence about something which they knew they couldn't do anything about."

In March 1979, MacLehose made a historic trip to Beijing, the first ever by a Hong Kong governor. It served as the first official Chinese acknowledgment of British administration over Hong Kong. The governor had formulated a carefully thought-out plan with a small handful of close advisers, including then ambassador in Beijing Sir Percy Cradock; it was not, he maintained, an idea that had been cooked up at the last minute. His strategy was to back into the subject in a roundabout manner by bringing up the individual land leases in the New Territories. He wanted to explore whether China would be open to an agreement whereby Britain could continue to administer the whole of Hong Kong even if sovereignty of the New Territories reverted to China. It was framed as a "leaseback" agreement, or a "management contract," extending British administration regardless of sovereignty. MacLehose hoped to use the technical and commercial matter of blurring the deadline on the land leases as a trial balloon to investigate Beijing's intentions.

When he arrived in Beijing, MacLehose discovered he would be meeting Deng Xiaoping, the cunning Sichuanese vice premier who had survived three purges to become China's paramount leader. On the morning of the meeting, Sir Yuet-keung Kan, who was accompanying him in his capacity as the senior member of Exco, tried to dissuade him from the plan as they walked around the garden of the British embassy in Beijing. But MacLehose was determined to push ahead even though the Chinese Foreign Ministry had preemptively requested he not raise the issue. In the event, he has always maintained that Deng Xiaoping was the first to break the taboo.

In the meeting, Deng told him that Hong Kong was part of China and would be recovered, but Beijing would respect Hong Kong's special status and allow it to continue its capitalist system. When MacLehose tried to bring up his proposal, the response was not promising. It was not clear whether Deng had understood the crucial difference between the individual land leases and the ninety-nine-year lease on the New Territories, which might have been lost through a poor translation conflating the two. When MacLehose tried to bring it up a second time, Deng, through confusion or cunning, would only say that any leases should avoid reference to a British administration since he could not confirm that Hong Kong's political situation would remain unchanged. Its capitalist system would, however, persist, Deng emphasized, and investors should "put their hearts at ease." To MacLehose, this kind of fudging suggested no clear decision had been taken about Hong Kong's future. "It is rather attractive in the light of later events to read into what he said that he had already formed a comprehensive plan—One Country, Two Systems—I bet he hadn't," he told Tsang.

Emerging from the meeting, MacLehose and his team decided to take the official line that Beijing had not changed its basic position, even though he had been dressed down by Chinese foreign minister Huang Hua, who admonished that raising the leases had been unnecessary and inappropriate. In fact, MacLehose's gambit had failed. His strategy was heavily criticized, both for the sidelong approach, which was nuanced and hard to translate, and the fact that he had raised it at the very top level, leaving no space for maneuver. But in an interview with Tsang, MacLehose defended his actions, saying, "What I am absolutely satisfied about is that whether the approach had been made at a different time or through a different channel or at a different level or even through an intermediary, the result would have been the same."

On his return to Hong Kong, MacLehose did not mention the exchange about the leases at all, keeping the secret mainly confined to those who had been in the room. Instead he emphasized Deng's more reassuring message that the investors of Hong Kong could rest easy. The cognitive dissonance underpinning MacLehose's statements echoed the British position for the next couple of years. In public they continued to explore the possibility of prolonging their administration over Hong Kong, even though they knew Deng had signaled the Chinese were not amenable to the idea. One factor was polling showing that between 85 and 93 percent of Hong Kong's population supported the status quo.

The Unofficials continued to be firmly in favor of a continued British presence, in part because they were almost as uninformed as everyone else. With the exception of senior Exco member Y. K. Kan, they were not told, either before or after it happened, about the conversation regarding land leases, since MacLehose was concerned that, should this influential group know the truth, they might sell their assets in Hong Kong, which would devastate confidence in the territory. His primary worry, that a leak might have a "catastrophic" effect on markets, underlined Britain's view of Hong Kong as a mart for trade, an economic entrepôt. MacLehose defended his actions by saying to Tsang, "All sorts of people had to type things, circulate things . . . there was no point in disturbing them [the Unofficials] and it was perfectly legal for me to act without Exco agreement." He also insisted that Y. K. Kan had recommended secrecy to protect the other Exco members. "He said it would put a strain on them because the speculative fears that would be unleashed if the proposal was agreed by the Chinese would have been enormous; similarly if it became known that the proposal was to be made and that the Chinese had rejected it, disappointment would be correspondingly great."

Kan, too, refused to share what had happened with the Exco members, citing confidentiality. When S. Y. Chung wrote asking for details, the letter was never answered. A few months later, Kan asked to be released early as senior member of Exco, and he was replaced by S. Y. Chung. S.Y. was such a familiar face from my childhood that I can still dredge him up from the deepest recesses of my memory. As a child, I'd seen the Unofficials night after night on the evening news. They were elderly Chinese, mainly men, in thick glasses and dark suits, who seemed permanently to be standing before a bank of microphones in airports in different locations—Hong Kong, Beijing, London—their foreheads furrowed, their bodies slanted forward with urgency. S.Y. was almost always in the middle, parrying questions with his jaw thrust forward, his expression somber. After reading the papers, I realized the press conferences always took place outside of or away from the venues where the talks were happening, because they themselves were always on the outside, excluded.

S.Y. emerges as a complicated character. He had one eye firmly fixed on posterity, desperately wanting to be the heroic figure who would serve Hong Kong in its time of need. He even believed he'd been lucky to be placed in that position. To that end, he was willing to accept criticism, and even dealt with death threats and bags of snakes placed outside his house. Some of his views were deeply unpalatable. He firmly opposed a system of universal suffrage and he warned the government that introducing it would cause them to lose control of the legislature. He saw Hong Kong as a company, and he believed the better-off were bigger stakeholders than the poor, so should have a bigger vote. He played a key role in watering down British proposals to introduce more representative government in the mid-1980s.

But even as he took on his new responsibilities as the senior Unofficial, S.Y. was suspicious. He told Tsang, "Now my own feeling was that Y. K. Kan knew something I did not and he was in a hurry to withdraw early." He also hinted that he believed the conspiracy of silence surrounding that fateful meeting was still in force, saying, "History will never know what actually happened." That distrust, and the silence surrounding it, seeped into the Unofficials' interactions with MacLehose, as described by Sir Roger Lobo, a Portuguese businessman who spent thirteen years as an Unofficial. "I remember some occasions when some of us wanted to know if indeed there was something else said [during the Deng meeting] that we were not told, or if there was something that it was not appropriate to say at that time, but should be said now. Nobody would ask the Governor: 'Are you lying to me?' It's difficult."

From that moment onward, the pattern was set: the Unofficials were left out of the loop. Information that was central to their own future was intentionally kept from them, and they often suffered the humiliation of learning major developments from news stories. Their enforced ignorance was not casually done; it was a considered British government strategy, memorialized in diplomatic notes. Since they had not been told of Deng Xiaoping's position, the Unofficials continued to lobby for an extension of British administration for two more years.

They were not served well by their loyalty. The next crisis for the Unofficials was what Chung described as an "external war which we fought against the British government" over the issue of nationality. This disagreement scarred the relationship and sparked an identity crisis that strengthened Hong Kongers' view of themselves as distinct from both Britain and China. It started in 1980, when Britain published a white paper on immigration. This policy document, setting out proposals for future legislation, assigned Hong Kongers the new status of "British Dependent Territories Citizen." To Hong Kongers, this was a second-class citizenship presaging Britain's looming disengagement from Hong Kong. Incredibly, no copies of the paper were made available in Hong Kong. The Unofficials wanted to go to London ahead of the final parliamentary debate, in October 1981, to lobby for an amendment that would give Hong Kongers the status of British Nationals. Having been trained to defer to authority, however, they sought MacLehose's advice. His answer was uncompromising: nationality was a dead issue, the vote had already been decided, and going to London would be a terrible waste of their time.

In the end, two Unofficials, including Li Fook-wo, went to Westminster. According to Li's account, although the British MPs described the legislation as targeting residents from another British colony, Gibraltar, rather than Hong Kong, their reception reflected the pervasive anti-Chinese prejudice. Li described his conversations with MPs. "They all reassured us that it was not the Hong Kong British subject they were after—it was the Gibraltarians and all that—but they did say, 'We don't mind having you people in but I certainly would not like to wake up one day and go to my butcher and my druggist to find that HK Chinese people are running them.'" Ultimately the amendment was defeated by just three votes. To add insult to injury, the Gibraltarians ended up winning right of abode in Great Britain, while Hong Kongers did not. Had they lobbied just a little bit harder, the vote might have gone the other way. The Unofficials had learned a hard lesson: the Hong Kong governor's ultimate loyalty would always be to the Crown.

This was MacLehose's most unhappy moment in Hong Kong, and even years later, the memory of the Unofficials' anger at their abandonment stung. He told Tsang, "They felt they had been betrayed, and this new Bill was a reminder. . . . I had never realized before how strongly they felt. I got this horrible feeling that though I had worked with these people all my time in Hong Kong, I was in the boat and they were not. It was most unnerving." The banality of his epiphany reveals the depth of the chasm between the governor and those he governed.

The Unofficials' distrust of MacLehose was so intense that some wondered if the nationality decision had been part of a secret deal during his 1979 meeting with Deng. Sir Roger Lobo raised this, as he speculated on the factors driving the decision on nationality. He suggested two possibilities: "No confidence on the part of Her Majesty's Government in the Joint Declaration [requiring action to be taken to prevent an influx of Hong Kong Chinese to the UK], or there is an agreement, an understanding between China and Britain that they would hand over the country as an ongoing human factory with good hands to work and produce money, so that the people of Hong Kong will be forced to remain in Hong Kong; with nothing else to do they will continue to be hardworking, prosperous, and will be good for China because China would not wish to take Hong Kong as a shell only." Even then, the Unofficials suspected that Britain cared little for Hong Kongers' well-being, beyond their role as workers in the "ongoing human factory" that was first governor Henry Pottinger's "Great Emporium of Commerce and Wealth."

This pattern—mounting frustration fueled by British obfuscation and withholding of information—was to repeat over and over, escalating through the years. After Thatcher tripped down the stairs of the Great

Hall of the People, the Unofficials were not told about Deng's threats to retake Hong Kong in a single day, or his refusal to contemplate continuing British administration over Hong Kong. They were assured instead that talks had taken place in a friendly atmosphere. By then, Sir Edward Youde had replaced MacLehose as Hong Kong governor, and he sent an official memo advising Thatcher not to mention to Exco some of the starker phrases used by Chinese leaders. She should "give them the impression that she is taking them into her confidence, but she will not wish to go too far." The Unofficials did not learn the details of the meeting until a couple of weeks later, when they, like everyone else, read them in a story in *The Observer* revealing Beijing's blueprint for Hong Kong.

This time they were fuming, especially S.Y., who was stung at being left "inside a drum," in Chinese slang. He complained to the governor, who did not reply to his letter, apparently under orders from Thatcher to stay quiet. When British minister of state Lord Belstead visited Hong Kong in December 1982, Chung gave him an ultimatum, saying that the Unofficials could not help the British if they were treated with such disdain. Finally, in a private meeting with Thatcher, he made a threat: "If her government still could not trust, consult, and inform us, some, including myself, might have to resign."

But he did not resign, and the pattern continued. Indeed, when diplomatic negotiations over Hong Kong's future began in Beijing in October 1982, it was without any Hong Kong representation. The British would not even permit the Unofficials to be present in Beijing while the talks were underway, calling it inappropriate. The Unofficials were in a peculiarly powerless and paradoxical position. To Beijing, they were nonexistent though sometimes sought for their views, while to Britain they were consulted, then ignored. The Unofficials had been conditioned into a kind of enforced Britishness; they were duty bound to Keep the Show Going. Any extreme reaction or public criticism could have provoked a loss of confidence, a bank run, or even mass exodus, so they were locked into reluctant public approbation.

It was clear that the talks were a slow process of Britain giving way to China. The first phase was supposed to set the agenda for formal talks, but even Percy Cradock described them as less negotiations than a tableau, with the Chinese side stuck in the same repetitive loop. Britain was still trying to persuade the Chinese to allow them to continue administering Hong Kong after its return, while the Chinese insisted that sovereignty and administration were inseparable. Cradock, who led the British side, feared that if an agreement couldn't be reached, Beijing would act unilaterally and lock them out of all decision-making. He saw Britain as starting with a weak hand that could only become weaker over time. Faced with this, in March 1983 Cradock organized what he called the "first finesse," securing a form of wording that allowed Thatcher to give ground to the Chinese demands without losing face. She would be "*prepared* to recommend" to Parliament the transfer of sovereignty, if negotiations produced "arrangements acceptable to the Hong Kong people."

"Finesse" is a bridge term, and I could not help noticing the extent to which the language of card playing suffused both the diplomatic memos and the oral accounts, as if the negotiations over Hong Kong's future were little more than a high-stakes game. After Margaret Thatcher's 1982 meeting with Deng, she had reassured the Unofficials that not all the cards were on the Chinese side, but over time the message changed. As Sir Roger Lobo put it, "Whenever the Hong Kong or the British government side said to us, 'We have no cards to play,' we all felt that they were just trying to jump ship: 'We are giving it away because we have only deuces and they have all the aces.' We had to force them to find a solution and not tell us that we had no cards to play: 'Create some cards, invent some situations. That's what negotiation is for. You've got to think and produce some concrete results rather than rub your hands and say, "Very messy, very difficult. We have no cards to play.""

For the Unofficials, who were supposed to be representing the Hong Kong people, this was a moment of intense frustration and anxiety. They had finally been granted access to confidential documents at the start of the year, and a secure room had been set up in Hong Kong for them to read the official papers, but they suspected they weren't being given access to the full contents of the negotiations. When they tried to pressure Cradock to take a harder line, his signature move was to rub his long, thin hands together and say hesitantly, "Oh, this will be very messy." It did not inspire confidence.

Cradock's first finesse opened the way to a second phase of talks starting in July 1983, as the two delegations began meeting to hash out the details of Hong Kong's return to China. Again Hong Kong was not represented at the table. That same month, a twelve-point plan for Hong Kong's future was presented to a group of surprised Hong Kong secondary school students visiting Beijing. The way the blueprint was revealed was a gesture of contempt for the official talks. In September, Deng Xiaoping laid down a one-year deadline, warning that if an agreement could not be reached, Beijing would act unilaterally. In November, Beijing publicly released a new, alluring slogan: "Hong Kong People Ruling Hong Kong." China was progressively cutting the British out of decision-making, realizing Cradock's fears. Over the summer, he played his second finesse, acknowledging that Britain would be willing to explore whether Hong Kong's prosperity could persist in the absence of continued British administration. This was a major climbdown for the British, an acknowledgment that they were giving up on the idea of a presence in Hong Kong beyond 1997.

Speaking frankly to Tsang, Roger Lobo described "moments during the period of negotiations when we felt our case was not being properly handled." The Unofficials sometimes strategized about how to put pressure on the negotiators, the prime minister, or the foreign minister to act. With no ethnic Chinese on the British negotiating team, S. Y. Chung feared they might be missing the nuances of spoken Mandarin. Then there was the bigger problem: he feared the Foreign Office mandarins simply failed to understand the down-and-dirty nature of haggling with the Chinese. Chung spilled his frustration to Tsang: "When I come to England and go shopping I must adopt the British mentality—I do not bargain, you cannot bargain in Harrods—but when you come to Chinese territory and go shopping, if you do not bargain you are paying too much, you will be overcharged. You must realize the Chinese mentality expects you to bargain, and you must have that kind of mentality when you negotiate with the Chinese. They are making opening bids, not the final offer."

Thatcher was keenly aware that Hong Kongers were being sidelined. Her view, set down in an official memo, was, "If she were the Chinese in Hong Kong, she would be becoming worried that the Hong Kong Chinese were not involved in the negotiations." But, pragmatically, too, she identified the issue that was vital for her interests: how to get the people of Hong Kong to accept any agreement. In this, the role of the Unofficials was central.

By December 1983, Britain had officially dropped any hope of continuing to administer Hong Kong, and the Unofficials were informed. When the announcement was made, the silence in the room was broken by sobbing from two councillors, one of whom was Rita Fan, who later on transferred her loyalties so thoroughly that she was nicknamed "the Wicked Witch of the East" for her pro-Beijing sympathies. Cradock insisted the British had retreated in good order from what had been an untenable position. But there was an unbridgeable distance between what the Unofficials wanted and what the British were delivering. "We were still young at heart, so to speak; we wanted to fight and get the last drop out of the case," said Li Fook-wo. "To our minds they seemed to have already come to the conclusion that they should accommodate the Chinese. In other words, they were . . . I wouldn't put it as rudely as to say that they were a little scared of the Chinese, but anyway I think that was our impression."

The start of 1984 was characterized by a mood of panicky gloom, as Hong Kongers began to look for escape routes. Sir Roger Lobo, who sat on both Exco and Legco, recalled being mobbed wherever he went by people asking if he was about to leave Hong Kong. Though he knew Hong Kong was to be handed back, he wasn't allowed to share the news, and that silence weighed upon him. "I could not even tell my wife or children, and in fact at home we never talked about politics, never talked about future," he told Tsang. "We were going into a very depressed situation. I was put in the desperate position of not being able to tell the people that they wouldn't even have a chance to glance at their future."

The Unofficials were beyond dejected. The agreement being hammered out was the Joint Declaration, which would allow Hong Kong to be handed back to China in 1997 with its capitalist system intact, and a pledge that its way of life should continue for fifty years unchanged. But there were no mechanisms to monitor or ensure Chinese compliance, and the agreement rested on Beijing's acting in good faith. When in January 1984 the Unofficials told Thatcher that continuing confidence required safeguards to ensure Beijing's compliance with the agreement, she gave a frosty response: "The Chinese could walk into Hong Kong at present but had not done so. We had to negotiate with the cards that we possessed."

By March, S.Y. was calling the Chinese stance the last nail in the coffin. Utter despair pervades the diplomatic cable sent by Governor Youde, relaying S.Y.'s words: "We had gained nothing from the process of negotiation and had been forced in constant retreat. . . . No worthwhile assurances had been obtained and the Chinese concept of an agreement was worthless.... The house we were now building was not only roofless but had no foundations." To the Unofficials, it seemed like Britain wanted to wash its hands of Hong Kong as quickly as possible. On April 6, 1984, still pushing for safeguards, the Unofficials even reminded Thatcher of her own assessment of the Chinese, as one diplomatic memo from their meeting noted: "[NAME REDACTED] recalled that at the first meeting in 1982 Mrs Thatcher had said the Chinese were Marxist/Leninist and could not be trusted." The only reassurance Thatcher could give was that she suspected that China would not wish to lose face in the world by violating any agreement.

However, the declassified records show that Thatcher secretly shared their doubts. This is clear from a single remark appended to a confidential telegram from Foreign Secretary Geoffrey Howe describing testy negotiations in Beijing. It had been sent less than ten days after the meeting where the Unofficials had reminded Thatcher of her own doubts about Chinese trustworthiness. Thatcher's response reveals a startling and chilling admission. She had scrawled in blue ink across the top of the cable, "It seems the Unofficials were right in their judgement of the Chinese." And yet Thatcher pressed ahead with negotiations, without adding any safeguards to monitor or require Chinese compliance, as requested by the Unofficials.

On April 20, 1984, Hong Kongers received the most momentous news of their lives: Howe, speaking in Legco, told them they would be handed back to China in 1997. By then, most Hong Kongers already realized no other options existed, but the finality of the announcement made it real. Even government officials, sitting just feet away from the foreign secretary, sobbed as he spoke. His speech bypassed the fact that no external guarantees had yet been negotiated to ensure Beijing would stick to its promises, simply noting that several points of substance were still being discussed. It also ignored the conditions set out in Cradock's first finesse, which stated that any arrangements for the territory would have to be acceptable to the Hong Kong people. Hong Kongers were never given the chance to vote on their future or even a clear consultation process. The Unofficials had been placed in the uncomfortable position of proxies whose public silence could be taken for assent. But all that was about to change.

This moment emboldened the Unofficials, who had agonized about their own complicity in an agreement they found unsatisfactory. Finally liberated from their silence, they launched into full-throated campaigning mode, taking their concerns public. In an unusually courageous move, they issued a thousand-word statement in May, raising questions about what Britain would do if Beijing did not comply with its treaty obligations, what would happen to those holding the British Dependent Territory Citizen passports, and what would happen if Hong Kongers did not accept the agreement. They were publicly drawing attention to the weaknesses in the agreement by raising the questions Britain did not want to tackle openly, fearing they might anger Beijing and complicate the negotiations. Even before the twelve Unofficials left to lobby the British Parliament ahead of its debate on Hong Kong, Governor Youde tried to lean on Chung to withdraw the statement. He refused.

By the time the Unofficials arrived in London, a whispering campaign to discredit them was underway, driven by the Foreign Office. The government spin doctors drew on racist fearmongering with their suggestion that the Unofficials' actual aim was to seek British nationality for millions of Hong Kongers. This made for a frosty atmosphere when the Unofficials met British MPs. Even Howe chided them, saying that since they were not elected, it was hard to claim that their views were representative.

To Chung, this criticism—coming from the same authority that had appointed him to represent the Hong Kong view—was unforgivable. A decade and a half later, he told Tsang, "I shall never forget the words of the MPs who criticised us saying that the Unofficial members of the two

Councils were not elected so how could they represent Hong Kong? I said to them that I agreed with them; we never claimed to represent Hong Kong. We only claimed to reflect the views of Hong Kong people because we are Hong Kong people ourselves and know our people's feelings better than you do. I said to them: 'How can you claim that you can negotiate for us? You have no mandate from us either; I never elected you. If we cannot reflect the views of Hong Kong people, you have no right to represent us in Beijing in the first place.' That I will never forget. I will never forgive them."

Worse still, MacLehose, who was by now sitting in the House of Lords and whom they counted on the most for support, betrayed them in the most humiliating fashion: he chastised the Unofficials publicly for doubting the integrity of the British government. He recounted to Tsang his memory of that moment: "They were obviously losing the confidence of the people sitting round me. This group was saying: 'Come on, Murray, why are they taking this line? . . . They're overstating their case. We hadn't thought of HK people like this. You'd better do something.' So I intervened and said: 'You're putting your case very badly,' or something like that." It was a move he bitterly regretted, and he told Tsang he'd been "unforgivably stupid," but the damage was irreparable.

It was a crisis point for the Unofficials, who had reached a new nadir of misery, since a session of China's National People's Congress allowed them to be denounced simultaneously by London and Beijing. Chung's answer was to turn to the people of Hong Kong for vindication, warning them, "If you don't speak up now, you may not have another chance to do so." In the next few days, the Unofficials received more than eight thousand letters and telegrams, almost all endorsing their views unconditionally. It was a vindication for the unelected Unofficials, proving their claim that, in outlining their concerns with the agreement foisted upon them, they were reflecting the views of Hong Kong people. The messages showed just how closely Hong Kongers had been watching events in London. One read, "Kindly ask Lord MacLehose to jump into a lake."

When the Unofficials attended a dinner with Howe, Chung arranged for each member of the delegation to stand up and read out ten telegrams, clearly enunciating every word of support. By the time the third member had started, Howe could no longer bear it. "Enough!" he conceded. "You don't have to go on. You do reflect the true views of the Hong Kong people." The acknowledgment was, S.Y. later told friends, the highlight of all his trips to London.

It was a pyrrhic victory, since by then S.Y. increasingly believed the British were not exerting their maximum effort in negotiating Hong Kong's future. He said, "They, and in particular the Prime Minister and the Foreign Secretary, had so many things on their plate.... To us Hong Kong was the only subject at that time, but to them it was only one of many and therefore I believe there is a danger that they said, 'Although we may not get the best bargain, let's close the deal, close the file, and call it a day. There are other things to deal with.' I think that was rather unfortunate although unavoidable."

S.Y.'s humiliation was not yet complete. Since May 1983, he and two other Unofficials had been meeting in secret every month with Beijing's representative in Hong Kong, Xu Jiatun, and reporting the contents of the meetings back to the governor. In June 1984, they were invited to Beijing. S.Y. had been determined that they should be received in an official capacity as Unofficials, but at the very last moment they were informed that they could only visit as private citizens since Beijing did not recognize Exco or Legco. They did, however, receive an audience with Deng Xiaoping.

Right from the start, Deng laid out his position firmly, telling them there was no role for them in negotiations over Hong Kong's future. He said, "You know the Sino-British talks well. Britain and China will settle

Hong Kong's future without any interference. There have been references to a 'three-legged stool.' There are no three legs, only two."

For Sir S.Y., this was a decisive moment. For the sake of posterity, he decided he would press ahead with what he had come to say. He was worried that this tiny, powerful figure was surrounded by yes-men and sycophants, and did not understand the concerns of Hong Kongers. In his autobiography, S.Y. remembers the words he chose: "There are three main worries. First, people are worried that instead of genuinely being administered by the people of Hong Kong, the future government of the Special Administrative Region (HKSAR) would actually be governed from Beijing. Second, people fear that the middle and lower level cadres who are responsible for the implementation of China's policy over the HKSAR may not be able to accept the capitalist systems and lifestyle of Hong Kong. Third, while people have faith in Chairman Deng and the present leadership, people are concerned that the future policy of China may change and future leaders may revert to extreme left policies." In retrospect, S.Y.'s words were darkly prophetic. Thirty-five years later, each of those three worries has come true.

Deng did not welcome such bluntness, and his answer targeted S.Y. personally. "Generally speaking, you said Hong Kong people don't have confidence. Actually it is your opinion. It is you who have no faith in the People's Republic of China." Shortly afterward, Deng ended the meeting, declaring he needed to rest. The Unofficials had, yet again, been very publicly rebuffed. All-caps headlines greeted them on their return to Hong Kong: HUMILIATION! DENG TURNS ON UMELCO THREE. Beijing's and London's interests had finally aligned, with the shared goal being to sign an agreement quickly. Once again, Hong Kongers were sidelined.

Things were about to get worse still for Chung. On his return to Hong Kong, he was told by police that he was the target of an assassination threat. The information had come from the Hong Kong branch of the New China News Agency. The police asked whether Chung had any scorned lovers or financial disputes that might have precipitated the threat, but he was sure that, given its source, the threat was designed to intimidate him into silence as the political negotiations on Hong Kong's future picked up speed. He told Tsang, "I actually took precautions for six months until the Joint Declaration was signed and sealed. I thought it was over then because I should not be able to influence the matter any more; the die was cast." A month after returning from Beijing, S. Y. Chung pushed for a referendum to measure whether Hong Kong people would accept the Joint Declaration. This proposal was rejected by then governor Edward Youde.

By then, Deng's one-year deadline was ticking down. In August 1984, when there was just a month left, the Chinese were so determined to finish on Deng's schedule that they suddenly became more amenable. To the disappointment of the Unofficials, the British did not use this softening to gain concessions. Chung criticized the negotiating haste to Tsang, saying, "When the Chinese wanted to complete the negotiations . . . they refused to talk about the details, and we ended up with a Joint Declaration that could be interpreted in many ways and that led to the present difficulty in the political system."

The biggest sticking point was the matter of elections of the chief executive. The agreement simply said, "The chief executive will be appointed by the Central People's Government on the basis of the results of elections or consultations to be held locally." It made no mention of democratic elections and gave no timeline for democracy. Chung feared this omission would haunt Hong Kong, telling Tsang, "We [Exco] insisted that it [the legislature] must be fully elected but without describing how the Executive Council would be formed, how the Chief Executive was to be appointed or elected. At the moment this is one of the major problems. Even today the Chinese have not been able to resolve the problem." This fear was prophetic.

At just over one thousand words long, the Joint Declaration—this document on which Hong Kong's future was hung—was shorter than an undergraduate thesis. By the time it was signed on September 26, 1984, to a celebratory lunch of pigeon eggs and stewed abalone in the Great Hall of the People, there had been forty thousand cables sent by British officials. This document stipulated that Hong Kong would be handed back to Chinese rule on July 1, 1997, and a "One Country, Two Systems" principle would be used to govern it. Hong Kong's capitalist system and way of life would be unchanged for fifty years, until 2047, and all this would be written into the Basic Law, which would become Hong Kong's mini-constitution. Hong Kong would have a high degree of autonomy to make its own policies, except for foreign affairs and defense, and all rights and freedoms enjoyed in Hong Kong would remain. The document was greeted enthusiastically across the political spectrum. The pro-Beijing *Wenweipo* said it created "a bright future for Hong Kong people," and even one of its harshest critics, journalist Derek Davies, called it a "masterpiece of drafting."

But the Unofficials thought it to be dangerously imperfect. Speaking confidentially, Chung bluntly admitted, "No one was happy; I was not happy." The British, too, were blunt about the limits of their ability. When Howe was asked what would happen if Hong Kongers did not like the agreement, he said, "The choice throughout this exercise has been between getting a bad agreement, getting a good agreement [and] getting no agreement at all." The underlying message to Hong Kongers was clear: Like it or lump it.

On my first reading of the archive, I saw Chung as a one-man Greek chorus caught between two great powers, powerless and despised by both. In his autobiography he describes the singularly unenviable position that the Unofficials were placed in: "To some in the United Kingdom we were 'running dogs' and 'collaborators,' and to the Chinese, we were 'quislings' and 'traitors.'" I could see so clearly how hard the

Unofficials had fought to get involved in the formulation of policy, and how often they had been ignored. I could also, in retrospect, see how accurate the advice they gave was, and how Chung had pinpointed the problems at every step of the way. So I was stunned when I read in his memoir that he felt the only period when the Unofficials had not been ignored was between 1982 and 1984. To me, those were the years the Unofficials were kept in the dark, betrayed, insulted, and publicly shamed. To him, it was the high-water mark of their participation.

The Unofficials, despite recognizing the powerlessness of their position, forged ahead. They spoke up, even knowing that the changing diplomatic calculus aligned Beijing and London against them and that political expediency required their silence. When they raised their voices, they were ignored, belittled, and humiliated by both the British and the Chinese. The image of the valiant mantis trying to stop a cart with its front claws came to mind, for this was another story of the small man standing up to great powers.

From a negotiating perspective, the Unofficials' impact on the Joint Declaration was limited, though some commentators believe that they forced Britain to fight harder for Hong Kong. But their success—which was perhaps not visible to them—was in their very public performance as Hong Kongers. With every press conference, they sent a clear message: Here we are, the Hong Kongers, and although we have no power, we have a voice. The pile of letters and telegrams they read out loud to Geoffrey Howe demonstrated the tangible existence of the Hong Kong people as a political community. Their repeated demands for democracy, accountability, and transparency served to embarrass the British and irk the Chinese, both of whom were hoping to sweep the whole issue of Hong Kong under the carpet. They were holding world powers to their word. It might have been an act of political naivete, but it was also an expression of hope in the kind of society the Unofficials imagined Hong Kong could be.

By the late 1980s, S.Y. feared that he would be seen as a traitor. "It was not easy for us because, basically we are Chinese, and we were advising the British government on how best to fight the Chinese," he told Tsang. He had stuck his neck out for Hong Kong, at times risking his life as well as his pride. Chung was afraid that he would be seen as having sided with a foreign power against China, and that anxiety may have guided his later actions. He had been steadfast in his loyalty to Hong Kong, but there was no place for that in the great power negotiations. There was, literally, no middle ground on which to stand.

By the time I finished reading the files again, I had changed my mind about S. Y. Chung's role. He was not so much a Greek chorus as a tragic hero of Shakespearean proportions. His hubris, it seemed to me, was his regard for honor. He had thought that he could earn honor by serving Hong Kong in the face of two different masters. His sense of honor had made him tell unpalatable truths to powerful people. It was his pursuit of honor that caused him to accept literal honors from both the British and the Chinese in later life, and that duplication undercut the value of each. In his mind, behaving in the most honorable fashion possible was the only course of action. But can a person, no matter how influential, be honorable when those they serve do not behave honorably? The untold, unofficial story that unspooled from those dusty, forgotten files is not that of an honorable retreat, which was the dominant narrative in the British press in the run-up to 1997. Instead it is a story of political expediency, denial, and betrayal of a people that sowed the seeds for the unraveling of one of the world's greatest cities.

CHAPTER 5

HONG KONG GOVERNMENT

It was October 1, China's National Day, 2019, and the Hong Kong police were marching through the harborfront streets grabbing and arresting anyone dressed in black. I'd been following behind them, but their aggression had an uncontrollable edge that scared me. I was walking away when I spotted some English-language graffiti spray-painted in baby pink on the blue MTR station wall that stopped me in my tracks: "Now Hong Kong people are to run Hong Kong. That is the promise. And that is the unshakeable destiny."

I recognized those words instantly. They were the final lines of the parting speech that the last British governor of Hong Kong, Chris Patten, had given on June 30, 1997, as he prepared to return Hong Kong to Chinese sovereignty. They cast me back into a different era, that of pre-handover Hong Kong, when I was just starting out in journalism. As the most junior reporter in the newsroom, I was always assigned the least important stories; my very first, which gave me more satisfaction than just about anything I've done since, was about fake Ferrero Rocher chocolates. But as the 1997 deadline approached, with an accelerating drumbeat that was the soundtrack to life in Hong Kong, we journalists were front-row observers to an extraordinary political experiment: the divestment of a colony from one sovereign power to another.

The question of how much democracy Hong Kong would get fell to the Basic Law Drafting Committee, which was formed in 1985 and charged with the task of fleshing out the framework of the Joint Declaration. As the Chinese had demanded, it consisted solely of Chinese and Hong Kongers. Thirty-six were officials and scholars from the mainland. The Hong Kong contingent of twenty-three included tycoons, publishers, scholars, and two prominent Democrats, lawyer Martin Lee and unionist Szeto Wah, who left—along with two others—in protest at Beijing's 1989 crackdown. A million Hong Kongers had taken to the streets in support of the pro-democracy movement in China, and the bloody killings prompted a wave of emigration ahead of the return to China.

The committee finished its task in 1990, producing the Basic Law, or mini-constitution, that would be enacted when Hong Kong returned to China in 1997. This document was extremely vague on the subject of democracy. It stipulated that the method for selecting the chief executive should be specified "in the light of the actual situation . . . and in accordance with the principle of gradual and orderly progress." The ultimate aim was selection by universal suffrage of a chief executive who was to be nominated by a broadly representative committee in accordance with democratic procedures, but the law did not give any more details of how the nomination would happen, how big the committee would be, or how it might be formed. Similarly, when it came to Legco, the law stipulated it should ultimately be elected by universal suffrage but crucially provided no timeline.

When he was interviewed by Steve Tsang just before Patten's arrival, Great Sir—S. Y. Chung—had been clear-eyed about how dangerous this oversight was. He told Tsang he did not know how the stalemate over political reform would be resolved: "The Chinese cannot resolve it; the political system is still a major problem and the major worry I have is that with all the attention paid to keeping the other systems unchanged, if we cannot devise the right political system, then Hong Kong may not survive. If Hong Kong cannot survive, the Chinese will interfere." Yet again, his warning was prophetic.

That was the background for Chris Patten's arrival in 1992, bringing with it a whirlwind of political change. He'd been offered the governorship as a consolation prize after winning the 1992 general election for the Tories in his capacity as chairman of the Conservative Party, but losing his own constituency along the way. It seemed as if handing off Hong Kong to him was a kind of thank-you note from Prime Minister John Major. Patten was the first—and only—politician to serve as governor of Hong Kong, deviating from the long line of pragmatic Foreign Office mandarins. It was a surprising appointment, and Hong Kongers initially had reservations. But Patten was determined to set a different tone right from the start. He refused to wear the traditional colonial governor's garb, partly because he feared the ostrich-plumed hat made him look ridiculous. He put his political skills to good use with energetic outings around the colony, kissing babies and consuming vast quantities of the territory's famous egg tarts. His prodigious appetite quickly won him the affectionate nickname of Fei Pang, or Fat Pang, using a phonetic Chinese rendering of his surname. He soon became the most popular leader Hong Kong had ever had, one who would not be surpassed by his successors.

Patten faced an impossibly tricky challenge: how to increase democracy to shield Britain against accusations that it had left Hong Kong without universal suffrage, while avoiding a breakdown in ties with Beijing. The British had signally failed to bring democracy to Hong Kong for more than a century. World War II had derailed an earlier effort by Governor Mark Young. Since then, British governors had been content, like MacLehose, to prioritize effective governance, strong social services, and a veneer of consultation over widening the democratic mandate.

By the time Patten arrived, Hong Kong's electoral system was a confusing mishmash designed to ensure that the legislature was always controlled by pro-government forces. Legco members were chosen three different ways: the governor directly appointed one group; the second group were directly elected through popular elections held according to geographical constituencies; and the final and most contentious group were called functional constituencies. The latter were electoral groupings decided by a single profession, so a handful of licensed accountants or real estate agents would select a single practitioner to represent their sector. While the directly elected seats were dominated by forces aligned with the Democratic Party, the functional constituencies by design tended to return pro-government, pro-China candidates. They were, according to Patten, an abomination designed by someone "who must have had a good working knowledge of the worst abuses of British eighteenth-century parliamentary history, and had presumably concluded that such a system would appeal to the business barons of Hong Kong."

But Patten's hands were tied by the Joint Declaration and the Basic Law, which limited any electoral reform. After close study of the documents, he believed he had found wiggle room in the detail of how functional constituencies should be formed. His plan was to vastly expand the functional constituencies by introducing nine new superconstituencies, such as "Finance, Insurance, Real Estate and Business Services," which embraced large swaths of the population who'd not previously been able to vote in functional sectors. Though Patten repeatedly described his reforms as "embarrassingly moderate," their effect was to widen the functional constituency voter base by a factor of five, to 2.7 million out of a population of around 6 million. The outcome was still far from true universal suffrage, but it did make the electorate more representative.

Beijing was, predictably, outraged. It unleashed an escalating stream of vituperative insults at Patten—the prostitute, the tango dancer, and the sinner for a thousand years—which provided much joy to newsroom headline writers. It also made public a stream of secret diplomatic correspondence between the foreign ministers Qian Qichen and Douglas Hurd in 1991. The letters, seven in all, stipulated that the Legco in place in 1995 could "ride on a through train" through the handover, with the same legislators serving until the next election in 1999, only if electoral arrangements were maintained as stipulated. Patten, scrambling for cover, claimed he had not been shown these agreements and that his reforms did not contravene them in any case. But Beijing saw Patten's actions as a triple violation: of these letters, the Joint Declaration, and the Basic Law. Should he press ahead, Beijing warned, he would derail the legislative through train.

Patten had braced himself for a hostile reaction, but he was nevertheless unsettled by its intensity. On top of Beijing's invective, he was also wounded by sniping from influential internal foes, including former governors David Wilson and Murray MacLehose, who argued that confrontation was not in Hong Kong's long-term interest. But he stuck to his plan, backed up by Prime Minister John Major. His underlying assumption was that China's economic reforms would inexorably lead to political liberalization, bending the arc in his favor over time. "I don't think you can open up the Chinese economy and keep an absolutely tight grip on political structures," he told his biographer Jonathan Dimbleby. He believed that if Hong Kong could prove its worth to Beijing, it would be safe. Those closer to Beijing had a far bleaker assessment. "It's really a myth to think that they will not kill the goose that lays the golden egg," Vincent Lo Hong-shui, chairman of the property conglomerate Shui On and of the General Chamber of Commerce, told Dimbleby. "Today I would say, we need China more than they need us."

After months of stalled negotiations, Patten decided to press ahead unilaterally. The 1995 Legislative Council elections were held according to his reforms, producing the first fully elected legislature in Hong Kong's history. Those allied to the Democratic Party, known as the pan-Democratic camp, came out victorious, with the largest bloc of seats: nineteen out of sixty seats, including sixteen of the twenty directly elected seats. After this, Beijing acted on its threat and began replacing the through train with a shadow legislature—known as the Provisional Legislature—which met across the border in Shenzhen. That group of sixty politicians, handpicked by a Selection Committee, would take the place of the elected legislature after the change in sovereignty. The Democratic camp boycotted the shadow body, but some pro-China politicians straddled both the elected and the shadow legislatures.

It's hard to overstate the lasting blow dealt to Hong Kongers' trust by the derailment of the through train. Although the lawmakers enjoyed only very limited powers, such as the ability to veto bills or to decide when to introduce them, the replacement of a vaguely representative body with one top-heavy with pro-China politicians ensured short-term compliance but also initiated an irreparable rupture between the people and those supposed to represent them.

For me, those handover years were the start of my career in journalism. I had returned from Beijing in 1995 to be present for the return to Chinese sovereignty. At the time, the English-language press in Hong Kong was still awash in hard-bitten, hard-drinking hacks from Fleet Street. I got my first opportunity at the *Eastern Express*, a newish newspaper that, unbeknownst to me, was already in its death throes. The stories I was assigned were mundane space-fillers, such as medical scare stories or warnings about faulty water heaters, that fell beneath the notice of the other reporters. I didn't care. I loved every minute, especially the unbridled ambition of my trash-talking colleagues and the endless nights of drinking, which often ended in outrageous alcohol-hazed dramas when someone set their trousers on fire or got ill-advised, poorly executed tattoos they could barely remember having gotten the next day.

When I look back, I'm astonished by our arrogance in believing we were equipped to report on Hong Kong. Though there were local Cantonese-speaking reporters, the news desk was heavily populated by young, aggressive expats who spoke only English. In those pre-internet days, when we wanted to research a story, we'd order up English-language clippings from the newspaper library. Even though our sister paper, the Chinese-language *Oriental Daily News*, was in the same building, there seemed to be little communication between the two publications. Several months after I joined, my editor asked me to move with her to the business desk, and I resolved to turn down her offer. When I woke up the next morning, I discovered that the *Eastern Express* had become a business paper, so I decided to move with her after all. Six weeks later, it closed down altogether, and I was jobless.

That was when I moved into television, finding a job at TVB, which was based in Television City in Clearwater Bay, a studio set up by the legendary Shaw Brothers that still produced some of Hong Kong's best entertainment. I didn't love television the same way I loved newspaper journalism, but I enjoyed the surreal encounters in Television City, such as eating lunch in the canteen next to actors dressed as Pigsy or Tripitaka from the television adaptation of the classic saga *Journey to the West*. Once a year, the whole place filled with leggy miniskirted beauties as TV City hosted the annual Miss Hong Kong contest.

As Hong Kong's return to Chinese sovereignty approached, we were in an odd position, as local news reporters at a moment when the local news we were reporting also happened to be the biggest story in the world. We were ill-equipped for the role, and our shortcomings became increasingly clear. We were bigfooted by famous journalists from London who snatched A-list interviews from under our noses and dominated press conferences with their posturing. We had hours of airtime to fill, and we tended to attack them in two-minute chunks that dealt with the procedural issues in all their minutiae but never tackled the foundational questions surrounding the change of sovereignty. What would we have said anyway? Hong Kong's future had never been up for discussion. It had been presented as a fait accompli to the people of Hong Kong, who had no choice but to accept it.

In the spring leading up to the transition of power, one face popping up in newspapers and on television screens with increasing regularity was the mad old King of Kowloon. For decades, no one had taken him seriously, but 1997 was the year that his status changed forever. In April, to the surprise and dismay of most of the art establishment, he was given a solo exhibition at one of the territory's most prestigious venues, the Hong Kong Arts Centre, jointly sponsored by the Hong Kong Arts Development Council and the Goethe Institute. It was probably the most scandalous exhibition in living memory in Hong Kong. The city's traditional calligraphers were aghast that Tsang Tsou-choi, with his ugly, infantile writing, was not only given a formal exhibition but also received government funding for it. "He's psychotic," Wan Ching-lee, a professor of fine arts at the University of Hong Kong, told *The Washington Post*. "I don't see any artistic value."

The show was organized by the curator Lau Kin-wai, who had a taste for showmanship and an influential daily column in *Hong Kong Economic Journal*. Lau was a bon vivant who favored flowery, brightly colored silk shirts and stylish hats. He'd spent a year preparing for the art show by providing Tsang Tsou-choi with ink and brushes, trundling around after him photographing his work, and on occasion even helping him strap sandals onto his fetid, unwashed feet. For the show, Lau decided to reconceptualize the King's work, since his normal canvas—the city itself—could not be moved into an art gallery. So he brought smaller, more saleable items to the King to paint, such as paper lanterns, glass bottles, a copper thermos, and even an umbrella, an object that later seemed prophetic. Lau knew he would face a storm of criticism for tampering with Tsang's art practice, but he believed these objects allowed Tsang to "link his calligraphy with reality." He tried to preempt any criticism by addressing the controversy head-on in the catalog, writing, "I don't mind the slander of others. I interjected myself into his work and helped him realize that he still has unexplored potential that he was unaware of."

In conversations today, Lau describes the King as a naive artist, comparing his work to Grandma Moses's and Picasso's. But in the catalog, he tried to place his work firmly within the canon of classical calligraphy, writing, "Compared to the Li style of the Han dynasty, perhaps only the 'head of the silkworm and tail of the swallow' rhythm is missing. However, [Tsang's] strokes are moderate, incisive and swift, with a hefty body." Lau even described characters the King had written on a utility box in Tsui Ping Road as "especially sophisticated, providing viewers the joy of seeing new blossoms on a decayed branch."

The catalog itself was designed by a young architectural designer, Kacey Wong, who sifted through hundreds of photos of the King's work to compile the slim, imperial-yellow pamphlet. Wong noticed that the King was unerring in his choice of space, picking only surfaces owned by the government for his messages. This led Wong to an epiphany about the King's work, which he told me when I first interviewed him in 2015: "It's all about my sense of belonging, my home, my identity. And this land is identity, this home is being stolen. That includes the past, and the future."

The exhibition opening produced exactly the kind of scene that Lau had hoped for. Young avant-garde artists settled in to copy the King's work, as their own act of protest. A critic named Long Tin stalked the gallery striking a gong and denouncing Lau Kin-wai for exploiting Tsang. The art world was overcome by paroxysms of indignation. The curator Oscar Ho, who believed that removing Tsang's work from the streets rendered it meaningless, was so outraged by the show that two decades later, the memory of it still made him fume. "I'm still so annoyed by it," he told me when I met him in 2015. Ho was suffering from voice problems by then, and the more he fumed, the more his hoarse voice rebelled, cracking and scritching painfully. "He was mentally retarded. He wasn't even competent. If someone treated him nice and asked him to do things, he would do it. So there are several problems here—not just artistic ones, but ethical ones."

Ho dismissed the idea that the King's work had any calligraphic merit as "a bunch of nonsense." He believed its meaning derived from the particular political context, but that Lau had crossed a line by providing him objects to paint on. He also accused Lau of conflating the roles of curator, collector, agent, and art critic, so that he was promoting the King while also commenting on his work and actively collecting it. "That's a brutal violation of professional ethics," Ho stated flatly. "In fact, in the States, it's a criminal offense." But Lau Kin-wai did not care, and decades later he was still triumphant when he recollected the show. "The exhibition was controversial," he told me, smiling. "That was something I like to do. I like something controversial."

The press turned out in force, hoping to see the show's eccentric star basking in his newfound infamy. They were not disappointed. The King was in his element, the sun at the center of the universe, beaming as he received obeisance from his subjects. As Lau Kin-wai held forth at one end of the room on the artistic significance of Tsang's calligraphy, at the other end of the room the King was mumbling incoherently to himself. As the press yelled questions about his art, he proclaimed himself owner of all property on view and shouted "Fuck off!" at questioners. Many of his answers were monosyllabic grunts, although when he was asked whether he thought he could regain his family holdings, he replied, speaking in a full sentence, that he did not think he could get the land back. On that much, at least, he was clear, but the impossibility of success did not stop him from continuing with his quixotic mission.

The exhibition resulted in the sale of not a single piece on display. But its undeniable triumph was to ignite a discussion about the very nature of art. The King's work was now appearing in newspapers, giving it a new permanency, and it was to get another fillip just ten days before Hong Kong's return to Chinese rule, during the last Fashion Week under British rule. The centerpiece show by Hong Kong's first superstar designer, William Tang Tat-chi, was a homage to the King of Kowloon. At the end of 1996, Tang had been part of a Hong Kong cultural festival in Berlin, alongside the prominent poet and critic Leung Ping-kwan. For that, he'd created a capsule streetwear collection using a new Canon textile printer. He'd printed a photograph of the King of Kowloon's calligraphy straight onto the fabric, and he'd been struck with the result. He'd decided it was so successful that he'd thrown out the entire collection he'd been working on and started again from scratch.

The entire 1997 show was a tribute to the King. Sashaying through an archway covered with massive projections of the King's characters, the models were clad in streetwise, eccentric, extraordinary creations of whimsy also covered with his distinctive calligraphy. The finale was the pièce de résistance: a concrete-colored, graffiti-covered asymmetric creation slung over the model's shoulder. Tang had found the fabric so beautiful that he couldn't bring himself to cut it, so the dress had a twenty-meter-long train, stretching almost the full length of the catwalk. The calligraphy covering it had a visual cacophony that replicated Hong Kong's street energy and density, characters tumbling into one another in their urgency. The dress was slit to the waist, paired with shiny black trousers that conjured trash bags. This model did not sashay—she strode, her face steely with determination. This was not just fashion: it was a statement of identity.

It was a defining moment, the start of a visual Hong Kong aesthetic that summed up the island's sense of itself: modern, hybrid, streetwise, confident, and utterly distinctive. When I met Tang in 2019, he was tall and astonishingly boyish looking for sixty, dressed totally in black. When I asked him to sum up the impact of the collection, he smiled. It was, he asserted, the most—really the only—memorable collection in Hong Kong's fashion history.

The King's calligraphy had reminded the designer of the ancestral tablets listing generations of Tangs in his family's clan hall. Tang had grown up spending his weekends in a traditional village house in Ping Shan in the New Territories. It was there that he had learned to draw, using the broken terra-cotta tiles from the roofs instead of crayons to sketch on the flat open terraces where villagers laid their crops to dry. To him, the King's calligraphy invoked the tablets by exposing death and loss, personal tragedies that would traditionally be corralled within private records, not shared with the world. Tang found the King's public display discomfiting, but he also knew the lopsided words spoke to him in a way he could articulate only through fashion.

For Hong Kongers, the engagement of William Tang with the King of Kowloon's work sent a message with deep historical resonances. Tang is a descendant of the powerful Tang clan, which had settled in Hong Kong in 973 CE. They were the original landowners who had been dispossessed and who had provided the ringleaders of the 1899 Six-Day War opposing the British takeover of the New Territories. "My family—the Tangs—have been here for one thousand years," Tang told me. "*We should be the King of Kowloon.*" His appropriation of Tsang's calligraphy could be read as one dispossessed king paying tribute to another, although he insisted to me that this had not been his intention. "People were laughing about the collection. They said, 'Is the idea that you are using the King of Kowloon to talk about your family?' I said, 'Don't make it that complicated. I'm not that kind of person.'"

Tang's collection created another sensation, garnering headlines and spawning more outrage. By turning the King's screed into clothing, Tang was reanimating the texts and, intentionally or not, imbuing them with another layer of political significance. His use of the King of Kowloon's characters carried an extra potency because the indelible images spoke of themes that had traditionally remained unspoken: a history of mass dispossession, the stinging humiliation of a once powerful clan, an old man's subversive act of calligraphic reclamation, and a defiant, yet coded message to those in the know that none of this record had been forgotten.

In this way, the King's concerns, which were narrow and personal, became a cipher for a moment in time. The newspapers concurred, with the *Apple Daily* concluding that the King of Kowloon collection expressed the mood surrounding the 1997 handover. When I asked Tang to explain the significance of the collection, he struggled to put it into words. It was only when he was describing the train of that final dress that he finally found the metaphor he was looking for. "It was exactly like the handover," he said. "It's a long story. It's like the Cantonese saying *yut put bo gam cheung*—as long as a roll of fabric. That means the story is so complicated, it's very difficult to explain."

THE DAY OF HONG KONG'S return to Chinese sovereignty, I was sitting at my desk at TVB, where I'd recently moved to the local reporting desk, watching Patten on a small monitor. We worked in a cavernous newsroom so arctic that we often wore coats and scarves over our smart little TV suits. Its chill that day was deepened by the atmosphere of impending gloom.

I was supposed to be in Beijing for the handover, covering events and reaction there. I should have been delighted at the airtime opportunities this assignment would have afforded me, the chance to do hourly live shots beside the massive countdown clock in Tiananmen Square, but I was terrified. I was famously bad at live television, and the only live shot I'd ever done—wobbling uncertainly on top of a ladder at the annual Lunar New Year market as I looked in the wrong direction—was such a disaster that it had become the subject of much mirth in the newsroom. I was scared of messing up in front of so many people on this of all nights, but the real reason I didn't want to go was that I couldn't bear not being in Hong Kong for this extraordinary moment in its history. I knew it wasn't very professional to prioritize my own desires, but I didn't care. I made up a lame excuse and, perhaps remembering my woeful live shot, the station sent someone else to Beijing. Having gotten my wish, I'd hoped to be out and about in Hong Kong, but instead I was assigned to remain in the fridge-like bowels of TV City. It didn't matter. I was on Hong Kong soil.

The day had been one long farewell as Great Britain divested itself of its last major colony with all the pomp a fading empire could summon up. The formal withdrawal began at 4:30 p.m. sharp, as Chris Patten made his ceremonial exit from Government House. A lone bugler standing on the roof of Government House played the Last Post as the Union flag was lowered for the last time. The band struck up "God Save the Queen" as the flag was handed off to Patten. Then a group of Hong Kong bagpipers clad in tartan trews struck up the distinctive reedy tones of "Highland Cathedral," as the drizzle spackling the shoulders of Patten's dark blue suit thickened to a spatter.

As Patten made his ceremonial exit from Government House, the King of Kowloon was not far away, continuing his crusade against the British right until the final moments of their rule. Heedless of his newfound fame, the King was working on the walls of an underpass close by, deep in concentration. Through a certain lens, he was presenting a very clear picture of what it meant to be a Hong Konger in that moment: a person dispossessed and with no rights.

By the time Patten arrived at HMS *Tamar*, the British naval base, for the official British farewell ceremony—which my father, as a senior civil servant, was also attending—the rain had become a downpour.

The sight of the imposing square tower, named after the ship that had originally served as a naval base until it was replaced by buildings, always reminded me of the one time I'd been inside. I was seventeen years old, and a friend and I were smuggled in by two handsome British officers we'd picked up in a taxi queue when we were meant to be heading home. They took us up to the kitchens of the officers' mess at the top of the building and, as if by magic, managed to procure champagne and strawberries from a gigantic fridge. It was past midnight, and looking down from these commanding heights to the ships' lights twinkling in the harbor far below, I was struck, in a sudden, drunken moment of clarity, by how far removed these posh British boys were from ordinary Hong Kongers. I'd never really thought of the British as colonizers before, but now I saw how much closer their lifestyle was to that of my great-great-grandfather more than a century before. It was an odd moment, encountering the waning empire embodied in these young men, knowing their entire experience of Hong Kong would eventually be reduced to a few amusing dinner party anecdotes. (This memory is always tempered by the subsequent scene when we arrived home at four in the morning to find my mother waiting for us at the dining room table, grim-faced with anger.)

Now these barracks were about to be handed over to the People's Liberation Army. But first, the British farewell ceremony, which, with blithe disregard for Hong Kong's summer typhoons, had been planned for the outdoors, to accommodate the maximum number of guests. The rain was coming down in torrents, and the VIPs cowered miserably under their umbrellas. Patten, blinking through the fat drops, launched into his farewell speech: "For Hong Kongers as a whole, today is cause for celebration, not sorrow."

It certainly did not feel that way in our newsroom. The atmosphere around most of our field transmissions was a jittery tension. Ours was a shonky operation, and days when we had live shots were invariably marked by a degree of panic, as things often went dramatically wrong. Once, the entire computer system had failed a few minutes before airtime, and the anchors had to ad-lib their way through the whole newscast. When we went live to mark the death of ninety-three-year-old Deng Xiaoping, a mistake on the autocue led my colleague to announce, straight-faced, "Deng Xiaoping has died. He was thirty-nine years old."

This night, however, the mood in the vast newsroom, almost empty with so many reporters out in the field, was a glum silence. Even the tape editors—notorious for their loudness, impatience, and irritability—were quiet. It wasn't so much that they mourned the departure of the British; many believed that Hong Kong's future was as part of China. But we all shared a kind of dumb numbness, a sheer disbelief that an entire island could simply be handed over; such a trade in human lives seemed like an anachronism from another era. The sense of passivity was underscored by the almost complete absence of Hong Kongers from the grand spectacles playing out on our screens. The key roles that night were dominated by visiting dignitaries: Prince Charles for the United Kingdom and President Jiang Zemin for China, with Chris Patten and his weeping blond miniskirted daughters playing important supporting roles. The Hong Kong people were mere spectators to their own fate.

Indeed, most Hong Kongers struggled to articulate their attitudes toward the handover. There were a few street demonstrations, but most described a complicated and contradictory mix of apprehension, excitement, pride, sorrow, and preemptive nostalgia. The centerpiece event was the midnight ceremony, held inside the Convention and Exhibition Centre, a cavernous purpose-built hangar with metal wings that soared over the Wanchai Harbor, symbolizing a bird about to take flight. The ceremony itself presented a gargantuan protocol headache, solved by ensuring that the Chinese and British delegations entered the hall at exactly the same moment, with neither side taking precedence. This extreme attention to etiquette produced a tableau with a painful symbolism that apparently went unnoticed until it was too late.

The Chinese delegation occupied the left side of the stage. They were mostly elderly men in identikit dark suits with red ties, fronted by the People's Liberation Army, Navy, and Air Force. The British took the right-hand side of the stage, complete with bearskin-toting grenadier guards and an honor guard of Black Watch kitted out in kilts, sporrans, and gaiters. Marooned by herself in the no-man's-land between the two delegations was the diminutive figure of Hong Kong's chief secretary, Anson Chan Fang On-sang. As the most senior civil servant, she was also the most prominent Hong Konger on the stage. Known for her sartorial elegance, Chan wore a gloriously eye-catching red cheongsam, the traditional Chinese dress, which leaped out from the sea of sober suits.

In this most symbolic of ceremonies, Chan unwittingly personified Hong Kong's plight: stranded between two great powers, the passive and neglected center of attention with no clear role to play. The awkwardness was intensified by Chan's own history. As an extremely popular and able administrator who was Patten's second in command, she should by all rights have been Hong Kong's first local chief executive. But she'd been blackballed by Beijing, which feared her closeness to the British. She dealt with the awkwardness with smiling grace. Her position was noted in the aftermath, even by Sir S. Y. Chung, who was clearly not a fan from his description of Chan as "simpering and shimmering . . . seated in a spot, alone like a throne, at the exact middle point between the British and Chinese platforms." The oversight was not, however, noticed by the incoming chief executive, Tung Chee-hwa, until it was pointed out to him by Singaporean prime minister Goh Chok-tong.

The ceremony began with a ritual salute, followed by a speech by Prince Charles. His attitude, summed up in an account he later wrote, was of "exasperated sadness." He offered thanks, admiration, affection, and good wishes to the people of Hong Kong and closed his speech with the words, "We shall not forget you, and we shall watch with the closest interest as you embark on this new era of your remarkable history." With those carefully chosen words, Great Britain effectively washed its hands of its last major colony. There were no guarantees, no monitoring, no oversight, just a vague promise that Great Britain would watch from afar, putting its faith in a government that had just eight years before turned its army on its own people.

At 11:59 p.m., the Union flag was lowered for the last time. The ten silent seconds that followed were, people later joked, the only moments that Hong Kong truly existed. Then, on the stroke of midnight, the red Chinese flag with its five yellow stars glided up the flagpole to the strains of the Chinese national anthem. Alongside it, a smaller flag was hoisted featuring a stylized depiction of Hong Kong's emblem, a white *Bauhinia blakeana* flower set against a red background. Another moment of unwitting symbolism: the *Bauhinia blakeana* is a sterile hybrid that cannot reproduce naturally. Hong Kong's flagpole was lower than the Chinese one; the requirement that the national flag take prominence over Hong Kong's wherever they fly was already enshrined in law.

From the deep freeze of TV City's control room, I watched as the descending and ascending flags repeated and refracted across the banks of screens. Preoccupied with my mental to-do list, I noted the artificial breeze that made the flags flutter jauntily for photos, even though they were indoors. I had imagined that the scene might be similar to a rocket launch, with cheering, clapping, or even sighing in the control room. But the tense silence was broken only by the director muttering instructions into the mics. Everyone simply got on with their jobs.

Then it was the turn of Chinese president Jiang Zemin to speak. It was a moment that Prince Charles would describe vividly, in a written account for friends that was leaked in a massive breach of protocol. He wrote, "After my speech the President detached himself from the group of appalling old waxworks who accompanied him. . . . He then gave the kind of 'propaganda' speech which was loudly cheered by the bussed-in party faithful." The Prince's brusque dismissiveness highlights the gulf in understanding between the two sides. Jiang's speech was rooted in Communist rhetoric, and his speaking style was of the stagey yet wooden variety favored by party apparatchiks. But his message was unequivocal: "The return of Hong Kong to the motherland after going through a century of vicissitudes indicates that from now on, the Hong Kong compatriots have become the true masters of this Chinese land, and that Hong Kong has entered a new era of development." Jiang was underlining the righting of a century and a half of Chinese humiliation at the hands of Western powers by finally negating the unequal treaties.

By twelve minutes past midnight, it was all over, and Hong Kong had returned to Chinese sovereignty. All that remained was for the new Beijing-backed elite to be sworn in. First up was the new chief executive, a shipping tycoon called Tung Chee-hwa, whose family had fled Shanghai for Hong Kong when the Communist Party took power in 1949.

At midnight, the Democrats were holding their own ceremony, making sweaty speeches on the balcony of the Legco building to mark their last few moments in office before they were replaced by the China-backed shadow legislators. Their scrappy, urgent farewells were a stark contrast to the well-rehearsed scenes playing out in the Convention Centre. The Democratic Party chairman, Martin Lee, took the microphone and, speaking in English, said, "We are Chinese. We are proud to be Chinese and that Hong Kong is no longer ruled by Britain. But we ask ourselves this question: Why must we pay such a high price to become Chinese again?" He finished with a solemn pledge. "We hereby give to the world a promise: We promise to our people that we will fight all the way. We will continue to be your voice. We will continue to be the voice of Hong Kong." He could not have known what that pledge would cost him.

WHEN I HEADED BACK into the newsroom the next morning, I found the building almost entirely deserted. No one seemed to have any idea what we were meant to be covering. We had planned the lead-up to the handover with minute-by-minute military precision, stationing staff all around the territory, including at the border. But we had neglected to plan for Chinese rule. I was hurriedly dispatched to the Convention Centre with my own cameraman—a luxury almost unheard-of for English-language reporters—with vague orders to capture whatever was happening. When I arrived, I immediately noted the absence of any other reporters. The tall white celebrity journalists we had been jostling with the day before were nowhere to be seen. Likely they were back in their hotel rooms now, packing to leave. For them, the story was over. It had finished with Patten and his photogenic daughters sailing out on HMY *Britannia*.

The Convention Centre was full of Chinese officials attending cere-monial functions, and I spotted Deng Xiaoping's son Deng Pufang in his wheelchair. I chased him, trying to elicit a comment on what his fa-ther would have thought, until I was told to leave him alone. To be hon-est, there was little demand. The only reason I had been sent out was that the senior reporters had been burned out by hour after hour of live shots the night before. But our failure to think forward also reflected our in-ability to grapple with what was happening. In our thinking, there was no day after. It was as if our minds—and our news agendas—had been colonized into believing that the departure of the British would be the end of our story. In our inability to think beyond the British, we had failed to prepare ourselves for the new era.

That night I joined my family to watch the magnificent Chinese fire-works display over the harbor. My uncle Poh-seng was there, delighted with himself, as he had scooped up an enormous collection of sugar packets and paper napkins from the Royal Hong Kong Golf Club as souvenirs for all the family in Singapore. They were historic, he kept saying, as they were the last sugar packets and napkins to bear the "Royal" designation.

When I saw my younger sister, I was shocked to see that her face was swollen from crying. She was inconsolable. Jo had been born in Hong Kong and lived there her whole life. She'd spent the entire handover night in a bar with a school friend, sobbing. The moment I saw her puffy face, I realized that I'd been so immersed in coordinating live shots and monitoring running orders that I'd forgotten to feel anything. In truth, I'd hidden so far behind my reportorial detachment that I didn't even really know what I felt. As a child of colony, I'd seen firsthand how efficiently the stolid British-trained civil servants had run Hong Kong, and I was sad for the passing of an era, but I also accepted there was no other option except returning to China. I was pragmatic. Colonies were an anachronism, and maybe Hong Kong could find its place as a role model for a rapidly changing China. There was no such emotional equivocation for my sister. That night represented the end of the familiar world that had grounded her, and she mourned its passing.

In the days that followed, the return to Chinese sovereignty started to feel like something of an anticlimax. Life continued as before, with fewer changes than we had expected. The People's Liberation Army kept out of sight in their barracks, and although elected legislators were replaced with appointed ones, the net impact seemed remarkably small, especially after those provisional legislators were duly replaced by newly elected ones, including many of the Democratic Party lawmakers who had been thrown off the through train. People continued to hold protests, and I went on filing lame television reports about newly built bridges and dangerous water heaters. For a while, it seemed as if the four-word formula of One Country, Two Systems compact might actually hold. But the biggest problem—the exact meaning of that tricky three-word phrase "constituted by elections"—was kicked farther and farther down the road. By deferring the crisis for two decades, the Hong Kong government continued to nurture hope and desire, ensuring that when the crisis came, it would be explosive.

By 2019, Chris Patten's era seemed like a lifetime away. But Hong Kongers hadn't forgotten, as the protest graffiti quoting his parting speech testified. A month after I spotted his words scrawled on a Hong Kong wall, I had the chance to interview Patten himself, as he was visiting the University of Melbourne to deliver an oration on political leadership. He was now Baron Patten of Barnes, and the chancellor of Oxford University. Stooped and silver haired, he had become a titled grandee whom the Australians treated with an embarrassing degree of deference. But Patten sounded exactly the same, speaking with that familiar breadth of intellect backed up by warm humor. I shadowed him from a distance over several days, watching as he gave glib speeches and made amusing after-dinner remarks. Although retired from politics, he was still a politician through and through, and he knew how to play a crowd. I was granted a tight half hour for an interview. Despite all the years I'd spent watching him from a distance, it was the first time I'd ever spoken to him. I knew that his press handling was so deft that my biggest challenge would be getting anything new from him.

As he sat down, my worries were confirmed. He was smooth and confident, launching into his favorite anecdotes and talking about de Tocqueville, dipping and rolling away from my questions with the intellectual acuity that I knew so well. He'd been talking for eight minutes when I decided to interrupt. This was my only chance, and I couldn't miss it by being too polite. I wanted to know what he would have done differently, if he were to have his time again. He replied that he wished he'd moved faster on electoral reform: "What I wish I'd done was not to spend so much time arguing with people who weren't going to change. And I think it would have been better if we'd established in discussions rather quicker that the Chinese weren't going to move, and then gone and made arrangements."

Who, I asked him, were those people who weren't going to change: the Chinese or those influential British critics like Percy Cradock? Mainly Beijing, he answered, though he went on to talk waspishly about Cradock, saying, "It's another aspect to the British Hong Kong story, the extent to which the policy was driven by officials with only the most vestigial, shadowy input from ministers. The Cradocks and others, they didn't listen to people in Hong Kong. They knew what Hong Kong required, and what Hong Kong, they thought, required was whatever would be acceptable with China for a quiet life."

Would it have made any difference, I asked him, if more attention had been paid to the Hong Kong advisers like S. Y. Chung? "I think it might have done, actually," he replied. "Whenever anybody behaved as though Hong Kong should be more central to the issues, or the interests of Hong Kong should be addressed more openly, the Percy Cradocks and so on moved in very rapidly to squash the idea."

What I really wanted was to find out what he thought of the Unofficials' suspicions about a secret deal between MacLehose and Deng Xiaoping in 1979, to hand Hong Kong back as a kind of human factory. If there had been such a deal, Patten was possibly the only other person who might know about it. Could there have been anything behind these suspicions, I asked him. Patten looked me straight in the eye. "I don't think there was," he said, firmly. "I mean, it would be all more explicable and in a way more defensible if there had been." As for the shift in loyalty that some Unofficials made to Beijing, he showed unexpected sympathy. "They thought that Britain would hang them out to dry. I'm not sure they were wrong."

There was one more thing I had to do. I took out my phone and pulled up the photograph showing the graffiti quoting his parting speech. He squinted and adjusted his glasses. The letters on my phone screen were so small that I wasn't sure if he could read them, so I leaped in. "It's the words from your leaving speech, I don't know if you can read it. It says—"

He interrupted me curtly. "I know the words very well."

"'Now Hong Kong people are to run Hong Kong,'" I went on.

He joined in with me, "'That is the destiny—'"

I corrected him. "'That is the *unshakable* destiny.'"

He shook his head. "It's been shaken, unfortunately."

I pressed on. "How does it make you feel, seeing that photograph?"

Suddenly the flood of words stopped. He was silent, and he lowered his head right down to the table for a long moment before he answered. "Bad. Bad. Bad. *Bad*." Then he gathered himself up and was off again, talking about the challenge that China's behavior posed to the international community.

I'd seen that gesture before, during a single intensely personal moment during those pomp-laden handover ceremonies two decades earlier. After Patten had delivered those parting words, and after he turned his back on the rain-drenched microphone, and after he had taken his seat between Prince Charles and Prime Minister Tony Blair, and after the crowds had roared in the rain, and after Patten had stood up to raise his hands to shush the clapping, and after the crowds had quieted, the elegiac chords of Elgar's "Nimrod" softened into the expectant silence. The composer's stirring dignity did its work on Patten; he bowed his head down almost to his knees, visibly undone by emotion. The symbolism of that moment when the cameras panned away and the crowds stopped watching evoked a less-remembered part of Patten's speech that night. "History is not just a matter of dates," he'd said. "What makes history is what comes before, and what comes after the dates that we all remember."

CHAPTER 6

KING

In the first few years after the handover, just as Deng Xiaoping had promised, the horses still raced, the stock market sizzled, and the nightclub dancers continued to writhe and grind through the night. As their symbols of decadent capitalism flourished, Hong Kongers relaxed warily into their new reality. The immediate post-handover period was, politically speaking, staid and reassuring, a period of apparent stasis broken only by the Asian financial crisis and the SARS outbreak. It was only later that it would prove to be a mirage of calm, and that the cost of inaction would be exacted, with interest.

The first post-handover chief executive, Tung Chee-hwa, was a shipping tycoon who took a chairman-of-the-board approach to running Hong Kong. According to the official account, he was chosen in late 1996 by a four-hundred-strong Selection Committee of Hong Kongers, but everyone knew that actually he'd been anointed a year earlier, when Chinese president Jiang Zemin—also a Shanghainese—sought him out, deliberately crossing a room in front of television cameras to shake hands with him. In fact, there had been a still earlier approach, through Sir Run Shaw, the Shanghainese founder of my former employer, TVB. As Tung later described in a newspaper interview, "He sat down and spoke to me in Shanghainese. He said, 'Heh, I think you are going to be CE.' I said, 'What? Come on, you are kidding. I am so busy with my business. I don't know anything about that stuff.'" Language was key; Shanghainese is not the tongue of Hong Kong. Through Tung Chee-hwa, Beijing was—like London before it—governing by indirect rule, using local elites as a proxy.

Overnight, the style of government changed. The desperate urgency and high-stakes politics of the Patten years were over, as were the rowdy walkabouts and impromptu pressers. Tung Chee-hwa always seemed out of his depth, a figurehead businessman in an unfamiliar world who appeared only to deliver stilted pre-scripted remarks at ceremonies. In the newsroom, I was back to the interminable rotation of faulty home appliances, approaching typhoons, and property prices. It felt like we'd fallen off the map.

In 1998, I moved to London to work at the BBC World Service, where I spent five years until I got posted to Beijing as a junior correspondent. For the next decade, charting China's economic and political rise for the BBC and then NPR, I again had that sense of being on the front line of a historic shift. I loved living in China for its dynamism, its limitless possibility, and above all its proximity to Hong Kong. I went back every few months, sometimes for work but mostly just to go home. There wasn't all that much news from Hong Kong; smallish annual protest marches on the July 1 anniversary of its return served both as an indicator of public anger toward the government and paradoxically to underline the fact that Beijing continued to abide by its pledge of "One Country, Two Systems."

It took five full years for Tung's reckoning to arrive. The catalyst was known in Hong Kong simply by the shorthand "Article 23." This was an article of the Basic Law requiring the Hong Kong government to enact national security laws prohibiting treason, secession, sedition, and subversion against the Central People's Government, as well as preventing foreign political influence. Although their enactment was obligatory at some point, the Basic Law set no time frame. In 2003 its passage had been steered by an ambitious, wildly unpopular, pro-Beijing politician named Regina Ip Lau Suk-yee, who served as secretary of security in charge of public security, safety, and immigration. Such posts had been held by politically neutral civil servants under the British, but Tung introduced a system whereby political appointees took on these ministerial roles. Ip, who spanned this change, had characteristically been the first government minister to declare her political stance. On Valentine's Day 2003, the government tabled the bill proposing the changes to the legislature.

There was an uproar. Lawyers were worried about the lack of clarity in the definitions of the crimes. Journalists were dismayed that the official secrets ordinance would be expanded, while nongovernmental organizations and religious groups feared they could be targeted. After five rounds of amendments, the bill was still described by a prominent legal expert as "a very threatening piece of legislation."

Ip upbraided Hong Kongers in her schoolmarmish manner, telling them that Beijing was showing its trust in the Special Administrative Region by allowing it to enact laws by itself. Hong Kongers, she emphasized, should be grateful for this trust: "We are not introducing Mainland law into Hong Kong. We are developing our own approach. Can you imagine California or Connecticut enacting their own laws against treasonous acts or foreign organizations bent on the overthrow of the US government?" Despite the vocal criticism of the measure, the posthandover administration, proving to have inherited the paternalism of its colonial predecessor, apparently did not recognize the depth of public opposition.

The issue had become a lightning rod for civic engagement, birthing the forces that would end up transforming politics in post-handover Hong Kong. A group of prominent lawyers began a concern group, which later morphed into the Civic Party, and a body called the Civil Human Rights Front coalesced as its mobilizing arm, bringing people out into the streets to demonstrate. A decade and a half later, it would organize the massive street protests that brought the city to a standstill.

On July 1, 2003, the front page of Hong Kong's most popular paper, the pro-democracy *Apple Daily*, carried a simple exhortation: "Take to the streets! See you there!" Folded into the paper was a ready-made protest poster that depicted the chief executive as a giant perplexed baby, being swept out with a broom.

Hong Kongers heeded the call. Half a million of them—8 percent of the population—came out to protest, wearing black T-shirts to symbolize the death of their freedoms. There were so many people that it took six hours for the marchers, under a bobbing sea of umbrellas that offered protection from the burning summer sun, to edge its way along the traditional protest route from Victoria Park in Causeway Bay. The two-mile-long march wended its way down a wide thoroughfare lined with skyscrapers to the Central business district, alongside clanging trams. Protestors carried Tung's effigy, top-heavy with his distinctive oversized bald head and eyes heavy-lidded with fatigue. "We deserve better," went one popular slogan. Another was "Down with Tung Chee-hwa!" One gigantic banner summed up the day in two words: "People power."

It was a stunning rebuff for the government, and it torpedoed the bill, leading to its indefinite withdrawal. The political risk was simply too high. So Article 23, along with the demands for democracy, was simply kicked into the future. Once again, the people had spoken, and once again, the administration wasn't listening. It was a dangerous dynamic, Democratic legislator Albert Chan Wai-yip warned, putting the government on notice: "If they are not listening this time, the next demonstration will be more hostile, the anger has been demonstrated. There may be riots in the future."

At the time, the 2003 protest seemed more like an outlier than an augury. But in the years to come, it would prove to be a journey in a time machine, a chronicle of a future foretold, as spasms of discontent shook the government's self-confidence ever more frequently. The causes were disparate, but they all revolved around one core issue: identity.

Tung Chee-hwa was mortally damaged by the Article 23 debacle, although it took another two years for him to resign, citing ill health. He was replaced by his deputy, Donald Tsang Yam-kuen, the homegrown British-trained chief secretary of the administration, who was famous for always wearing a bow tie. In his retirement, Tung came to be nicknamed the Kingmaker, for his top-level involvement in local politics, and in 2005 he became a vice chairman of the Chinese People's Political Consultative Conference, an advisory body. Still, many Hong Kongers, myself among them, viewed him as a cuddly, avuncular figure, ineffectual but harmless, thwarted by a population who did not behave like employees. The information I unearthed in my work as a journalist more than a decade later changed the way I thought about him in his political afterlife.

In 2018, I was working on a Long Read piece for *The Guardian*, delving into China's outreach campaign to the global media. It was a piece I'd stumbled into, after David Wolf, the editor I'd been working with, kept pushing me to write a far more ambitious, global treatment than I'd originally intended. In the course of my reporting, I discovered that in 2008 Tung had used his shipping fortune to set up a foundation called the China–United States Exchange Foundation (CUSEF), which played a pivotal role in marketing China to the US. I spent weeks down a regulatory rabbit hole with my colleague Julia Bergin, examining filings made in the US under the Foreign Agents Registration Act that mapped some of CUSEF's activities. We discovered that Tung's foundation had funded all-expense-paid trips to China for at least 127 American journalists from forty different outlets in less than a decade, as well as funding trips for policymakers, business leaders, and academics, and bankrolling policy research at several US institutions. CUSEF had also paid large retainers to several American lobbyists to place Tung's Beijing-friendly op-eds in American newspapers, to cultivate a stable of "third-party supporters" in the US, and to review US high school textbook content on Tibet. A single lobbyist, Brown Lloyd James, or BLJ, was being paid almost $250,000 a year to place an average of three articles per week favorable to China in US publications like *The Wall Street Journal.*

We even acquired jaw-dropping private memos written by a BLJ executive to Tung Chee-hwa, suggesting two outlandish strategies to reshape public opinion toward China in the US. One was a plan to get a play mounted on Broadway—to the tune of $2–3 million (HK$15–23 million)—called *The Phone Call*, featuring a family with members living in New York and Beijing, which would culminate in a live video link using the stage "as a diplomatic platform." The second, even more preposterous idea—with a price tag of $8–10 million (HK$62–77 million)—was the construction of a Chinese town called Gung-Ho in Detroit. Gung-Ho would be populated by American and Chinese college graduates and professionals, and would showcase Chinese technology like natural gas–burning buses and the WeChat app. The entire project, the executive proposed, could also be charted in a reality TV show that would be "a living metaphor for the promise of the US-China relationship."

When we got in touch with CUSEF to check the status of Gung-Ho, the response was a bland statement asserting CUSEF's status as "an independent, nonprofit and non-governmental foundation committed to the belief that a positive and peaceful relationship between the strongest developed nation and the most populous, fast-developing nation is essential for global well-being." It was then that I realized that Tung had leveraged his leadership of Hong Kong into a new role: as the acceptable, business-friendly, globalized face of China's Communist Party. He was using that respectability to market China to the West.

The economic aspect of Tung's story was instructive, too: his shipping company, Orient Overseas, had been bailed out of bankruptcy in the 1980s, with Chinese banks offering half of the $120 million (HK$923 million) funding. By 2017, it was the world's seventh-largest shipping firm. Then it was acquired by China's state-run shipping company, COSCO. The Hong Kong press described it as a $6.3 billion (HK$49 billion) godfather deal that couldn't be refused, an agreement that simultaneously created the third-biggest shipping giant in the world and delivered another Hong Kong firm into mainland hands. But while Tung's company was headquartered in Hong Kong, he had never been a native son, and his loyalty had always been to Beijing. In retrospect, his term marked Beijing's first failure to live up to its promise to allow "Hong Kong people to rule Hong Kong."

Meanwhile, as predicted by S. Y. Chung, Hong Kong failed to make any real progress toward democratic reform. Though the Basic Law said the ultimate aim was elections "by universal suffrage," those three words turned out to span a world of options. Beijing exerted its control by dominating the "broadly representative nominating committee" that picked candidates for chief executive. In 2004, China's top legal body, the National People's Congress Standing Committee, ruled that an eight-hundred-person Selection Committee would pick candidates for the top job in 2007, effectively ruling out any change before 2012. Then in 2007, the same body vetoed direct elections in 2012, broadening the Selection Committee to 1,200 people and again kicking the can down the road. This time, the body issued a resolution mentioning specific dates but falling short of any firm commitments: it said the chief executive "may be" elected by universal suffrage in 2017, after which the legislature "may be" chosen by universal suffrage, in a reference to the 2020 election. To Hong Kongers, who had no choice but to trust in Beijing's sincerity, these became talismanic dates.

At the same time, this political struggle helped to define what it meant to be a Hong Konger. Just as Hong Kong itself had once been an amorphous idea waiting to be pinned down on a map, Hong Kongers' identity had always been plural, more like a constellation of evolving and overlapping self-images rather than one fixed point of light. For so long, Hong Kongers had been told that they were purely economic actors. But they were political animals, too, who would show their dissatisfaction when their core values were threatened, whether that be supporting the 1989 pro-democracy protests in China or the 2003 campaign against Article 23. However, defining those values turned out to be tricky, even as an academic exercise. One political scientist described to me the difficulties that a group of scholars encountered when they focused on this very issue in the aftermath of the Article 23 protests. "We asked the question: What are we? What are we trying to defend? And then we started the discussion about Hong Kong core values. To be honest, we couldn't really figure out what are the key pillars of Hong Kong identity, and what exactly are the values we cherish the most."

The group came to the tentative conclusion that Hong Kongness was defined by a Weberian sense of meritocracy, whereby hard work would be rewarded with success, as well as a respect for Britain's institutional legacy, such as the rule of law and professionalism. It was no coincidence that these values were exactly what China was missing. But the Hong Kong and Chinese identities could still overlap and elide. In those years, many Hong Kongers had business and family in China. They crossed the border regularly, and saw themselves as both Hong Kongers and Chinese, or Hong Kong Chinese. It was an aspirational identity underpinned by the hope that Hong Kong could serve as a model for what China could become. The Beijing Olympics in 2008 served as the high-water mark for Hong Kong's Chinese identity. Hong Kong's first gold medal winner—Lee Lai-shan, who won for windsurfing in 1996—was an Olympic torchbearer, and there was a glow of pride in being part of a nation that had pulled off such a spectacular games, though this was still underpinned by an ever-present undercurrent of unease.

Still, the Hong Kong mindset is markedly, recognizably different from that of mainlanders. I asked Chip Tsao, who is known by his pen name To Kit, to help define it. After a quarter century of writing, Tsao was arguably the most influential columnist in Hong Kong, sometimes getting four hundred thousand clicks a day when he wrote for the pro-democracy *Apple Daily* newspaper. He credited his popularity to his undergraduate degree in English literature from Warwick University in the UK, "Thanks to my English literature training, I manage to use understatement, sarcasm, and irony to hide some outrageous messages."

As I sat on a gigantic squeaky white leather sofa in Tsao's spacious flat in Pokfulam, listening to a loud green parrot squawking on the balcony, he sprinkled his responses with Federico Fellini, William Wordsworth, George Orwell, and the history of the Southern Yue dynasty. Like so many Hong Kongers, he traversed the intellectual traditions of both East and West with ease. To Tsao, language is the crucial determinant of the Hong Kong mindset. "Nowadays all [mainland] Chinese in their minds are still submissive to an emperor," he said to me, dismissively. "They're interested in being governed by a benign emperor rather than embracing democracy. But the Cantonese genes are a bit different. We don't go submissive all of the time, because of the language we speak."

Language is a key identity marker for Hong Kongers, who speak Cantonese rather than the standardized Mandarin—known as *putonghua*, or "common language"—introduced by China's Communist rulers in 1956. Though Cantonese is often viewed as a dialect, it's incomprehensible to Mandarin speakers. Some linguists see it as closer to classical Chinese than Mandarin, deploying archaic participles, ancient sounds, and traditional complex characters rather than the simplified ones used on the mainland. Unlike standardized Mandarin, Cantonese is gloriously irregular, its rules of pronunciation so casual that some words can be pronounced with either an initial *n* or *l* sound, used interchangeably. Cantonese didn't even get a romanization system until the 1950s, a full century after Mandarin was romanized by Thomas Wade. To this day, there's still no consensus about which of two romanization systems should be used or even how many tones Cantonese has; the range is five to eleven, depending on whom you ask.

Although Cantonese is used by 97 percent of the population of Hong Kong, the Education Bureau claimed as recently as 1994 that it was not an official language. Internationally it is even less recognized, with library software automatically sinicizing Cantonese names into Mandarin Pinyin. This bureaucratic erasure is also political, since its effect is to transform Hong Kongers into mainlanders, altering their identity without their consent or even knowledge. Indeed, the simple act of speaking Cantonese as a native tongue effectively makes Hong Kongers semantic subalterns, second-class linguistic citizens.

"What would it mean for Hong Kong to write itself in its own language?" ruminated the cultural critic Rey Chow. This question has always been anxiety-inducing for me, since Hong Kong's language is not my own. Though I speak Mandarin fluently, my Cantonese is shamefully basic. We never spoke it at home since my father, who spoke different languages with each of his mothers, ended up speaking the language of school, English, as his first tongue. My tone-deaf mother speaks execrable Cantonese the same way she speaks French: with a posh British accent and the unflinching determination that she will command understanding through force of will alone.

Throughout my school years, I witnessed the use of Cantonese evoking a distaste, a disgust even, that echoed the casual racism suffusing Hong Kong society at that time. A science teacher needled a classmate named Francis Pan, "What are you—Peter Pan? Or Frying Pan, perhaps?" We didn't study Cantonese until secondary school, and then only for two years. We thought of Cantonese class as the least important on our schedule, and used the sessions to torment our poor sweet teacher to the point of tears. I left school still wanting to learn Cantonese, so I began taking classes in my spare time, and I've continued sporadically over the years. My various surreal experiences studying Cantonese brutally highlight its subordinate status, especially when set against the increasing standardization of Mandarin teaching.

I embarked on my first Cantonese course as a teenager on my mother's recommendation, as she had enjoyed the class. In retrospect, this should have been a massive red flag. The school was somewhere in the New Territories, which in those days seemed a world away. The teacher did not bother with textbooks, but instead directed us like the conductor of an orchestra. Sitting in rows, we warbled, *"Sik faan, sik min, sik min BAAU! . . . Eat rice, eat noodles, eat BREAD!"* hitting the high tones in unison as our teacher punched the sky. That was the sole sentence I retained from those many weeks of rote chanting.

I switched focus to Mandarin for many years, and when I went back to studying Cantonese—this time in Melbourne—I discovered that the state-backed Confucius Institutes had established a stranglehold on Chinese language teaching, crowding out other language providers. The only place where I could learn Cantonese insisted on its own bizarre pedagogy that required all classes be taught against a background of elevator music. The school refused to teach tones or Chinese characters to beginners, and instead demanded that we keep our eyes shut while repeating new words, the insipid music supposedly an aid to memorization. I survived about a year, helped by an enthusiastic young teacher who acted out skits in funny voices, but eventually I couldn't bear the Muzak anymore.

In Hong Kong, I tried attending evening classes with an international group of students, where our teacher, a cheerful, exhausted man called Mr. Wu, gently schooled us in the ways of Hong Kong people. "Hobby—*ngoi hou*," he'd intone, with a wry chuckle. "Hong Kong people don't have hobbies. We get up early. We work all day. We work all night. Then we come home and sleep. And then we get up and start again. Weekend—*jaomut*—let's use it to make a sentence. Mine is, 'I am working all weekend. I work every weekend.'" Here was the renowned Lion Rock Spirit, the key to Hong Kongers' vision of themselves. The name derives from a popular soap opera depicting life in a squatter settlement under the shadow of a famous lion-shaped mountain, and denotes a kind of hardscrabble work ethic that values pure perseverance and the ability to bootstrap one's way up in the world. Simply put, Lion Rock Spirit is the ability to work extraordinarily hard for a better life, no matter the obstacles; harnessing the Weberian sense of meritocracy that the political scientist had mentioned.

This concept was second nature in my favorite Cantonese class of all, one designed for Mandarin speakers in Hong Kong. All the other students were young, single, upwardly mobile mainlanders—bankers, engineers, IT workers—and the class felt like a massive dating club, as we spent each session flirting madly and ineptly. The women loved teasing the best-looking young man in the class, interrogating him for his address and personal details until he flushed all the way to the tips of his ears, then pointing this out to uproarious laughter.

This group could already communicate with their colleagues in Mandarin and English, but they wanted to be able to talk to Hong Kongers in their own tongue. One student even lived across the border in Shenzhen but traveled to Hong Kong twice a week for class. "No one speaks Cantonese in Shenzhen anymore!" she said. This was exactly what Hong Kongers feared: that Cantonese speakers would be swamped by Mandarin speakers, and their language rendered obsolete. It was already happening. When I was a child, we never heard Mandarin on the streets, but increasingly there were parts of Hong Kong where Mandarin had become the lingua franca. Around the time of the 2003 protest, Beijing signed a free trade agreement with Hong Kong that allowed more mainlanders to visit in order to kickstart Hong Kong's economy. This, along with an agreement to permit 150 mainlanders a day to move to Hong Kong, had contributed to a demographic shift whose effects could already be heard as well as felt.

My fellow students were part of that one-way flow. In the classroom, we *wah*-ed and *lor*-ed, inviting each other to dinner and acting out elaborate skits involving losing our wallets at the vegetable market. As we did so, we became more expansive, less buttoned-up. The tiny explosions of emotion in the language—the violent declamatory force and wonderful lewdness of Cantonese—helped break down barriers. As the weeks passed, I noticed that in the pause between sessions we had begun talking about sensitive topics that mainlanders generally avoid. I wondered whether just speaking Cantonese was a small act of linguistic defiance for the regimented mainlanders. Or maybe they were learning to think like Hong Kongers.

Hong Kong had traditionally been a place of refuge and free thinking. It was a sanctuary for Chinese dissidents and revolutionaries, a place where taboo topics could be discussed and forbidden books sold in tiny bookshops tucked up narrow staircases. Hong Kong's freedoms became more concrete for me toward the end of my time in China, when I began writing a book about the Communist Party's success in erasing the collective memory of the bloody suppression of the 1989 Tiananmen Movement. Back in Beijing, I could not speak about my book at home or in the office, since I assumed they were bugged. I didn't mention it on the phone or in emails. I worked on a computer that I kept offline and locked in a safe in my bedroom when I wasn't writing. Every so often, I carried hard drives of material to Hong Kong for safety, and it was only there that I could speak to my editor in New York. Indeed, Hong Kong had always been the only place on Chinese soil to hold an annual June 4 vigil in memory of the 1989 killings.

To me, even the air in Hong Kong felt freer. Whenever I crossed the border from the mainland, I felt a sense of lightness, a physical lifting of my soul. On one visit, I met a young mainland student at the Tiananmen Museum who summed up how the city made him feel: it was, he said, a place where you "dare to speak out, dare to do stuff, dare to criticise, and dare to think." I'd never tried to put the difference between Hong Kong and the mainland into words before, but I realized I felt exactly the same.

One person who took full advantage of those freedoms, and whose star was continuing to rise, was the self-declared King of Kowloon. Neither his solo show nor the return of sovereignty changed the King; he continued to paint every day on the city's walls and flyovers. Even in post-handover Hong Kong, his assertions of sovereignty, which could be considered sedition in China, were shrugged off as eccentricity. He was often stopped by the police—who would then become the target of his incoherent rage—and occasionally fined for criminal damage, but while his writings were routinely cleaned away, he himself was generally left alone.

In 1997, his work was included in the international traveling exhibition *Cities on the Move*, an attempt by superstar curators Hans Ulrich Obrist and Hou Hanru to showcase the warp-speed change sweeping East Asian cities. To Hou, the King's work was part of a radical search for the city's social and cultural identity through endless negotiations with its colonial past and neocolonial present. More than that, he believed it exposed the "oppressed collective unconsciousness of Hong Kong's population, which is eternally haunted by the deep crisis of their souls, having been colonized by multiple hegemonic powers in the past and present. Obrist simply saw him as "a poet whose page was public space." But the Hong Kong government's cultural bodies refused to fund his travel to Europe for the exhibition, arguing he was neither a calligrapher nor an artist.

Two years later, the King was part of another show, *The Power of the Word*, organized by one of Hong Kong's best-known curators, Johnson Chang Tzong-zung. Much to the King's delight, Chang paired his work with Chairman Mao's calligraphy, elevating his status. Dressed in a traditional Chinese jacket and delivering cutting insights in a plummy British accent, Chang made for a memorable interview. He saw Tsang as a true pioneer, predating Keith Haring's graffiti by at least a decade. "For Western art history, he would have been the first graffiti artist."

To Chang, the King's graffiti reclaimed sites of power for the written word. In reading the texts, he noted they were essentially composed of territorial claims, leading him to wonder if the King was fantasizing a grand ancestral lineage to legitimize his claims. When I asked him to sum up the importance of the King's work, Chang replied, with characteristic grandeur, "It is really about civilizational loss, the loss of the structure of the world, basically." In his view, the King slyly subverted the traditional claims to temporal, cultural, and secular power exerted by public writing. By virtue of an ancestral lineage such as he possessed, he should have been a Somebody, an important official or a learned scholar. But Tsang's grand statement was the Reveal: he was a Nobody. The idea that this symbolized civilizational loss seemed somewhat far-fetched to me, but when I expressed my doubts, Chang retorted, "Modernity is about stripping the people of their cultural lineage. This is the main feature of modernity." The exhibition traveled to Taiwan and the US, but Chang did not take the King. When I asked why, his answer was withering: "He smelled so repellent! I can't imagine taking him anywhere!"

As the King's fame grew, retainers and envoys came to pay tribute at his squalid, fetid eighteenth-floor apartment in the housing estate. Almost all the wall space, as well as the thin, grubby white curtains, was covered with dense skyscrapers of his text. The characters, big and small, sometimes overlapped one another, and the effect was claustrophobic, as if the words themselves were closing in on visitors. The flat emanated a stench of rotting flesh and home-cooked sausage so strong that one Japanese television reporter had to run out to vomit in the corridor. The living room was furnished with a couple of chairs and a table, and the floor was a sea of balled-up pieces of calligraphy, running with cockroaches. Those who visited were often traumatized by the experience, and the King compounded their plight with his hospitality, cheerfully serving them glasses of water bobbing with unidentified vegetable matter.

In 2000, the King's public persona underwent another change, after he starred in an advertisement that reinvented him as a lovable mascot for the city. The commercial was for a cleaning fluid called Swipe, and it became so iconic that it featured in the 2018 *Very HK Very HK* exhibition. The ad is like a tiny documentary, starting with cheerful, humorous music as the camera pans across a calligraphy-covered table to a calligraphy-covered teapot. "My ancestors came 2,700 years ago to Kowloon City," says the King's breathy, hesitant voice. The camera pans over a word-covered concrete bridge, followed by scenes of the King painting on Plexiglas, then on a flyover strut. "I clean whatever I write, on everything and every place. Kowloon City. Fortress Hill." The King is seen washing away his work with Swipe as he says, "Everything is clean. Hong Kong is clean. Sau Mau Ping. Choi Hung. Tsui Lok Building. Cleaning until everything is spotless. Clean the Kitchen. Clean the Toilet." He has a little smile on his face, and he looks like he's having a whale of a time. "Even a space shuttle can be cleaned," he says. "Blue Swipe Cleaner cleans your house, no matter how big it is." In the final shot, he beams toothily, seated in sheepskin-lined yellow robes on a golden throne with a scepter in his hand, the white marble grandeur of the Peninsula Hotel looming behind him. "It's good to clean your house. I suppose your house will never be as big as mine."

The subtext was understandable to all Hong Kongers. "His home is the entire Hong Kong!" said director Alfred Hau, who shot the commercial. Hau, a tall, handsome fifty-something dressed head to toe in black with a minimalist black Y-3 anorak, beamed as he remembered making the ad nearly two decades earlier. We met in the high-ceilinged concrete-floored warehouse headquarters of his company, Off-Lo-Hi, which was named after the temperature controls on an air conditioner.

Hau remembered the King as good-natured but confused. He could repeat his lines, but would add his own unintelligible mutterings to the end of each, which had to be edited out. He could follow instructions, although it wasn't clear whether he understood what he was doing or what Swipe even was. He balked when the crew asked him to write on teapots, tables, and chairs, since his practice was to write only upon government property. Eventually he agreed, but when the King began to paint on the Plexiglas, he wouldn't stop, even though only a patch of calligraphy the size of a piece of printer paper was all that was needed for the shoot. The whole crew had to wait while he covered the entire door-sized panel from top to bottom. Then he refused to film anymore until he could paint a second panel as well.

The commercial proved a surprising hit, and, according to Hau, it transformed perceptions of the King. "It's the first time they really have a close encounter with the King. Usually people see him around the street, nobody goes to talk to him because people think he's crazy. But this is the only time they get to know a character better. He's like a celebrity now. He's on television." People began to refer to the King as "Choi Suk," or Uncle Choi, which over time became Grandpa Choi. He had become a member of the family. But the ad was accompanied by a mini scandal. The Inland Revenue discovered that the King had been paid around $1,000 (HK$7,760) and stopped his social security payments, arguing he was no longer unemployed. This sparked even more news coverage.

When we met, Hau still had those two panels daubed with the King's calligraphy casually propped against the wall, within his line of vision from his desk. "I have no idea why I was keeping this!" he told me, as if it still surprised him. Aware that the King's work had become extremely valuable, he had fully intended to sell the panels. "Sotheby's has asked me to name my price," he told me, lowering his voice confidentially. But he didn't need the money, and he had been held back by an impulse he couldn't quite identify. He had even been inspired to learn calligraphy himself, and now when he looked at the panels he saw them as an expression of something unique and pure. He was thinking of lending them to a museum where they could be shared with as many people as possible. "I think it is part of Hong Kong," he told me. "I just think it's a piece of memories within all of us. My generation, we all have a piece of him in our mind."

I'd become familiar with this kind of reaction. Whenever I interviewed someone about the King, I seemed to plumb a secret well of passion that surprised even the interviewee. Just thinking about him seemed to transport people to some point in their past, back to the Hong Kong of their childhoods, the boom years of the 1980s, or even the tumult of the Patten years. Whichever alternative universe they landed in still had a wide-open horizon in which anything was possible and there was hope in the future.

One factor that made the King so comforting was the sheer constancy of his behavior even as the world changed around him. His content was unerring and repetitive: an assertion of sovereignty that was also a wail of anguish for his loss and the failure of his duty to his ancestors. But over time, people began to pick up and amplify his message. In 2001, the rap group MP4 penned a song to him that opened, "I'm the King of Kowloon. Kowloon and the New Territories are mine." The band rapped about the government's inability to tackle the King and ended the song with a recitation of locations that spoke to the King's ubiquity. "Yauma-tei, can't wash it away! Mongkok, can't wash it away!!"

Suddenly the King of Kowloon seemed to be everywhere. He starred in a documentary about himself. He made an improbable appearance in a Louis Vuitton ad for handbags, and his shuffling, hunched silhouette became a fixture in locally shot movies. In the 2001 film *Hollywood Hong Kong*, the director, Fruit Chan, who'd shot to prominence with a handover trilogy exploring Hong Kong identity, featured the King himself along with his calligraphy, which framed a maze of squats and even appeared daubed onto some of the pigs owned by the obese butcher who is one of the film's main characters. The King, who relished being the center of attention, appeared in other films as well, including *The Queen of Kowloon* by director Clarence Fok. Cinema suited a monarch's exercise of power, which thrives on both visibility and limited contact with his subjects.

Among the King's steady stream of courtiers was a young artist and rapper named Chan Kwong-yan, who had just graduated from art school in Paris. Chan, who became famous as MC Yan, was Hong Kong's first rapper, as well as one of its earliest street artists. He was a localist before localism even existed, and his first band was called NT, after the New Territories. At that time, he wore his hair in one long pigtail down his back, leading the King to mistake him for a being from ancient China. But Chan had sought out the King with a very specific purpose: to study the craft of graffiti. He wanted to tag on the streets of Hong Kong, but he didn't know how to navigate the pitfalls of such a densely populated city.

Some walls belonged to powerful local gangs known as triads, and the police were so efficient that MC Yan had twice been charged with vandalism and once for assault. He wanted to figure out how the King had managed to write so much graffiti for so long without attracting police attention. After tagging with the King, MC Yan came to the conclusion that perhaps the King's insanity was the ultimate streetcraft, since it served as a form of self-protection. After all, Tsang broke the law in broad daylight every single day of his life and almost always got away with it.

In 1996, MC Yan became one of the frontmen of LMF—Lazy Mutha Fucka—a hip-hop group from working-class backgrounds that was signed by Warner Music. In songs larded with bilingual profanity, they rapped about social alienation, political incompetence, and Hong Kong identity. They devoted one song to local kung fu hero Bruce Lee. "He taught us we are not the 'Sick Man of Asia.' Though having yellow skin, we can still be ourselves," they rapped, exhorting Hong Kongers not to copy others or look down on themselves.

I first met MC Yan in 2014, by which time he was in his forties and a devotee of Tibetan Nyingmapa Buddhism. He was late to our meeting because he'd been releasing fish into the sea as part of a Buddhist ritual. A diminutive figure with a scraggy salt-and-pepper beard and gray ponytail, he was dressed in baggy maroon fishermen's pants and a maroon T-shirt. He was accompanied by his beloved pug, Gudiii, who was, he informed me, not just a Buddhist but the reincarnation of a Tibetan monk who had been punished by being reborn as a dog. I asked how he could tell. He replied that Gudiii ate Tibetan medicine every day, had never been ill, and excelled at animal release ceremonies. "He never barks unless he really has something to say," MC Yan told me, without a hint of irony. "He's a commander. He feels superior. He never hangs out with dogs, only humans." I glanced at the dog surreptitiously to see whether he displayed any visible signs of holiness. To me he just looked puggily annoyed, though he seemed to relax after MC Yan lit up a large spliff.

MC Yan had his own distinctive take on the King. "He tagged before people were tagging," he said. "He really had that mind of occupying space. He thinks this is what is happening in Hong Kong. Hong Kong was being occupied." In 2001, MC Yan brought the French graffiti artist who operates under the pseudonym "Invader" to the court of the King. Invader was also occupying Hong Kong space, visiting repeatedly to install tiles of dozens of pixelated video game–inspired characters on buildings and walls. During the visit, the King ripped a page from his wall calendar and wrote on it, then offered it to Invader. In return, Invader spontaneously installed a squatting red-and-yellow space invader on the wall of the King's house, and MC Yan tagged the wall as well. Reflecting on their bond, Invader wrote in an email to me, "We both play with the architectural elements of the city to write our work, we invade the architecture, maybe also the idea of obsession and persistence." There was another commonality, too: disappearance. Like the King of Kowloon, much of Invader's work has vanished, removed by collectors or government departments.

In 2003, the King made history, becoming the first Hong Kong artist to show at the prestigious Venice Biennale. This was curated by Hou Hanru, who included the King's calligraphy in what he called a Zone of Urgency, "created out of urgent demands instead of regular planning." By 2004, the King's work was auctioned for the first time at Sotheby's, with a wooden board he painted selling for $7,050 (HK$55,000). It was becoming harder for the King, who was already on crutches, to get around. Much of his work was clustered around bus stops on his favorite cross-harbor route. In 2004, a relapse of his leg injury sent him to hospital. That was also the year he set his apartment on fire while cooking and was moved into the nursing home in Kwun Tong.

So began the King's vanishing act. He could no longer paint on the streets. Inside the nursing home, he was banned from using sticky black traditional calligraphy ink because of the mess and smell. The King was distraught. When he couldn't write, he was unable to sleep. By now he had a new regent, Joel Chung Ying-chai, who had taken over some of the tasks formerly done by the curator Lau Kin-wai. Chung was a slim young advertising executive and collector who brought him markers and paper. The King continued writing the same characters, but his bold declarations of sovereignty were shrinking into emaciated, quavering lines. His ideograms were becoming misshapen and confused, the lines looping unpredictably around each other. Sometimes he forgot how to write familiar characters and had to ask Chung for help.

Even as his world shrank, the characters continued to leap off the pristine sheets of paper. He was hospitalized three times for ailments in 2007, and his medical records were covered with heartfelt messages to his doctors—"Many thanks! Many thanks!" His writing jumped onto the striped hand towels looped over his bedstead and the tempting cream-colored bedside cabinet, on which he scrawled "Emperor's Palace." His third hospitalization, on June 28, was for pulmonary edema from smoking. It seemed like a routine admission, like the earlier two. When Joel Chung visited him in hospital, he found him sitting up in a chair, wearing green-and-gray-checked pajamas. Chung had brought some yellow canvases and a lemon-yellow model of a terra-cotta warrior for a charity auction. The King wrote happily on them, but his characters were meandering and falling out of alignment. Nonetheless he was in fine form, laughing and joking. But as he painted, he commented, "Hey! I'm not the King anymore! I'm not doing it. I'm not!" Chung was confused. "You're not the King?" The answer was good-natured but firm. "I'm not doing it. I'm not the King! Let someone else do it!"

Afterward, Chung realized that Tsang had signed the back of the terra-cotta warrior not with his usual "King of Kowloon" but with a scrawled "Tsang Tsou-choi." It was the last time Chung saw him, and he would come to think of this as the moment when the King of Kowloon abdicated his throne.

On July 15, 2007, at three o'clock in the morning, the King died of a massive heart attack. It took more than ten days for news of his death to break, but when it did, all hell broke loose. Newspapers issued urgent alerts across their wire services, and Joel Chung's phone did not stop ringing for two full days. Lau Kin-wai was so hounded for information by reporters that he wrote a newspaper article taking the media to task for being out of control. "For days, the media have been trying to find out when his funeral will be," he wrote. "It's understandable, but it's unbearable. Have they thought about the feelings of the family?" The King's death was reported in newspapers across the political spectrum, even the Communist-sympathizing *Wenweipo*. The *Apple Daily* printed a full-color commemorative edition with a wraparound front page announcing "The King Is Dead!" Even the choice of vocabulary was distinctive, using a form of Chinese characters—駕崩—reserved for the death of a monarch. This lamentation echoed across the front pages in one shocked wail of mourning. *The King is dead. His writing remains on flyovers and walls. . . . The King of Kowloon is dead. Everyone is writing about him. . . . The King is dead. In his lifetime, Grandpa Choi challenged the British queen and was actually a political figure seeking justice. . . . The King is dead, his relics remain. But how many are left? . . . The King of Kowloon Tsang Tsou-choi is dead. The "ink treasures" of the street left by the old man are very few. . . . Now the King of Kowloon is dead, we must act to preserve Hong Kong people's collective memories.*

The use of imperial honorifics, even in sarcasm, was not just a rhetorical flourish. By dying, Tsang had finally gained the recognition he had yearned for in life. The level and intensity of the coverage invoked the Mandate of Heaven, a concept that traditionally governed sovereign power in China. It was believed that the emperor's ability to rule was predicated on the support of the people. As the philosopher Mengzi wrote, heaven sees with the eyes of the people and hears through the ears of the people. Thus an unpopular ruler who loses the support of the people forgoes the Mandate of Heaven. Chief Executive Tung Chee-hwa's precipitous fall from grace was one example; his approval rating dropped from 64.5 percent in 1997 by almost half around the time of the Article

23 protest in 2003. His successor, Donald Tsang, who ended up being imprisoned for corruption, had experienced an even more precipitous descent. Hong Kongers desperately wanted to believe in their leaders, but each time, it seemed, they were disappointed.

The King, however, was another story: he had become only more beloved. The newspaper coverage was not so much positive as fawning. His misshapen words were lauded as 墨寶, or "ink treasures." He was compared to Van Gogh, Picasso, Banksy, Jean-Michel Basquiat, Keith Haring, and Yayoi Kusama. Even descriptions of him as a silly old man or a madman elevated him to an unlikely Everyman. The newspaper *Ming Pao* drew parallels with the "beggar emperor," the Hongwu Emperor, who had been the first sovereign under the Ming dynasty (1368–1398) and spent some of his early life as a mendicant.

One influential columnist wrote that the King of Kowloon should have been given an OBE for his services to the empire. Tsang was called "the most honourable emperor in history," in contrast to Hong Kong's formal leaders. Chief executives and colonial governors past and present were found wanting the King's strength and endurance. One columnist wrote, "Donald Tsang can be Chief Executive for five years. Tsang Tsouchoi was Hong Kong People's King of Kowloon for his whole life. The Tsang dynasty weathered wind and rain for half a century." There were pieces invoking the King of Kowloon as an embodiment of Lion Rock Spirit, praising his unwavering passion and his daily routine of leaving the house at seven every morning. He was "not living above others but among the despised and ordinary people" and "a moral teacher, who lives a frugal life, without the least itching desire for Gucci, Prada, and shark-fin soup."

It was perhaps MC Yan who best summed up the King's importance when he said to a reporter, "No matter if he's a true or fake [king], he was very sure of his own identity, unlike Hong Kong people who don't know if they're from the East or the West." The King's work had become a defining memory of Hong Kongness, and he himself was an exemplar of a distinct Hong Kong identity. The economy and constancy of his public statements—only ever asserting his ancestry and sovereignty over his land—stood in stark contrast to the mealymouthed statements of successive chief executives who, by their very job description, had been unable to speak either for themselves or for the people of Hong Kong. In stark contrast, the King of Kowloon was a self-governing entity, the last free man in Hong Kong.

His funeral turned out to be its own kind of circus. The media staked out the Universal Funeral Home in Hung Hom with all the enthusiasm of hyenas sensing a kill. Unusually, the memorial hall was desolate, cold, and empty. There was no coffin, no body, no mourners, not even a photograph of the deceased. The two lonely funeral wreaths on display were both from members of the media; one from photojournalist Simon Go and the second from a magazine. The only mourner who turned up, albeit briefly, was Joel Chung. The press pack was baffled and disconsolate, cheated of their spectacle.

The scene didn't feel like a real funeral because it wasn't; it was a decoy. Just 150 meters away from where the media were gathered, at the Kam Fook Shau Funeral Parlor, the publicity-shy family held their own private service, and then the body was sent to the Wo Hop Shek cemetery. Not even Joel Chung and Lau Kin-wai, the King's closest art world collaborators, were invited. When the press discovered what had happened, they described the fake memorial as an "Empty City Strategem," invoking the classic battle strategy used to throw an enemy off-balance. The King's famously private family, who had never issued a public statement, had in death closed ranks entirely. In mourning him behind closed doors, they were reclaiming Tsang Tsou-choi as husband and father, stripping him of the regal status he had spent his life pursuing.

Weeks after his death, the little yellow terra-cotta warrior to which he'd signed his name was put to auction. It was just thirty centimeters high, and the reserve price for the piece had been $128 (HK$1,000). It ended up fetching one hundred times more than the reserve price, selling for $12,932 (HK$101,000). The papers were full of reports about how the auction result validated the King's artistic status. But even as his significance grew, his work was disappearing from the streets. He had become a representative of Hong Kong's collective loss. His legacy, like his artwork, was paradoxically everywhere and nowhere at all. It meant all things to some people, and nothing at all to others.

The timing of his death coincided with a moment of collective introspection, arriving just after the tenth anniversary of Hong Kong's return to Chinese rule. If the Article 23 protest four years before had been a political earthquake, other forces were brewing that would turn out to be almost as consequential. The first inkling of these came toward the end of 2006, when the government announced it would demolish the historic Star Ferry Pier to make way for a highway. This news sparked such a wave of nostalgic sadness that an estimated 150,000 people rode the Star Ferry on its final day operating from the old pier. Thirteen protestors even tried to retake the terminal building and were arrested by police. This marked the start of a heritage preservation movement that over the years evolved into a localist movement intent on preserving Hong Kong's identity and autonomy.

By mid-2007, the focus had switched to another waterfront pier in Central, the fifty-three-year-old Queen's Pier, which was to be demolished to make way for a land reclamation project. This jetty had historical significance as the site of first landfall for some of the British governors, but it played a more mundane part in the fabric of everyday life as a place where office workers ate sandwiches at lunchtime, wedding parties posed for photos, and concertgoers strolled after City Hall recitals. Its demolition became a cause célèbre, with seventeen groups jointly petitioning to save it, and the government-appointed Antiquities Advisory Board recommending its preservation as a structure of outstanding merit. As the demolition date approached, artists and activists occupied the pier for ten days, staging performances, a sit-in, and a 118-hour hunger strike. But the government refused to give way, arguing that preservation would harm Hong Kong's competitiveness. When the newly appointed secretary for development, Carrie Lam Cheng Yuet-ngor, arrived at the pier, she was met with jeers and boos. The dynamics of this confrontation—the government's intransigence in the face of the popular perception that the administration was prioritizing business interests over the people—set the tone for all that was to come.

On August 1, just two weeks after the King's death, the pier was demolished. Many newspapers noted the simultaneous disappearance of the King and the Queen's Pier as the loss of two icons. The prominent commentator Lee Yee wrote, "Hong Kong people remember the King of Kowloon and want to keep the Queen['s Pier] not because they are nostalgic about colonial times, but because they see the grandeur of government buildings in China and the tenth anniversary ceremony, and they want to keep things that are convenient, simple, comfortable, and on an intimate scale." The activist Joshua Wong was a ten-year-old schoolboy at the time, but in his autobiography he summed up the importance of the fight over the two piers: "They were about defending our fledgling identity. Those spurts of resistance and anger were only the tip of the iceberg. The rise of the new Hong Konger had begun."

The new Hong Kongers found their initial training ground in a number of campaigns revolving around protecting the city's distinctive cultural heritage, from colonial buildings left behind by the British to public housing estates and traditional clan halls like those I'd been dragged around as a sulky child. Over the next few years, the activists mobilized with protests and sit-ins. They lobbied for Wedding Card Street in Wanchai, which was demolished for a shopping mall in 2007, and Choi Yuen village in the New Territories, which was knocked down in 2009 to make way for a high-speed rail link to China. Gradually a campaign to protect Hong Kong's local culture from mainland influence was taking shape. The activists had also learned from the Article 23 protest that radical action could achieve results, whereas working through the system often achieved little. Each of the four legislative elections during this period was a reminder of that truth: Patten's expansion of the functional constituencies was rolled back, and although the pan-Democrats consistently polled better in the popular vote, they were constrained by a system that was gerrymandered by design.

The new Hong Kongers defined themselves against the mainland migrants who were increasingly taking up school places and hospital beds. By 2012, 28 million mainland tourists were crossing the border every year to buy Louis Vuitton handbags and Nike trainers, sparking outraged headlines when a couple were caught defecating in the street and eating in the subway. A number of safety scandals on the mainland had led to the growth of "parallel trading," when mainlanders bulk-bought products they couldn't get across the border, causing shortages and rationing. Hong Kongers were beginning to feel overrun in their own city.

I felt this one day when I went to do an interview in Sha Tin New Town Plaza. This gigantic shopping center is more like an indoor city, and it was packed with mainlanders on day trips, clutching gigantic shopping bags. There was a long queue for the hard-shell suitcase sale in the atrium, another queue for the toilets, and queues in front of every single restaurant, necessitating a half-hour wait for a table. All around me people were speaking Mandarin, not Cantonese. If I'd been suddenly airdropped into the mall, I'd have guessed I was in mainland China, from the sheer cutthroat nature of the shopping and the volume of the eddying crowds.

I was there to meet a small, neat man with a monk's tonsure named Horace Chin Wan-kan, better known as Chin Wan, who has been nicknamed the "godfather of localism." Chin had recently published a book titled *Hong Kong as a City-State*, which advocated Hong Kong's autonomy within a federation with China as necessary to protect its values. We met just after a group of unnamed localists had placed a full-page newspaper ad calling mainlanders "locusts" and decrying their "unlimited infiltration" into Hong Kong. Chin Wan embraced this controversial view enthusiastically, telling me, "Locusts come in groups. When they come as individuals, it doesn't matter. When they come in thousands and thousands, it looks like a swarm of locusts."

There was no doubt that Hong Kong's economy was being lifted by the influx of mainland money, but Chin Wan feared this was benefiting property developers and conglomerates at the expense of ordinary people, who could not afford the sky-high property prices. He saw the economic ties as increasing Hong Kong's financial dependency, and he issued a stark warning about Beijing's designs on Hong Kong: "I would call it an imperialist approach. They think they will subsume Hong Kong people and make them more obedient. But that will destroy Hong Kong."

That day I was struck by how exhausting and unfamiliar this Hong Kong felt. Every time I went back, I revisited my familiar places, retracing old routes of love and childhood nostalgia. I also liked walking the rocky arteries and wild ridges of the mountains. But standing in that shopping mall in Sha Tin, I realized with a shock how mainlandized certain parts of my hometown had become.

I was also realizing that the more I wrote about Hong Kong's identity crisis, the less of a Hong Konger I felt myself to be. Localists like Chin Wan defined Hong Kongers as those who were born in Hong Kong and spoke a cosmopolitan style of Cantonese. Where was the place for someone like me, who was not a local and who still, despite my efforts, spoke horrible Cantonese? I'd always instinctively felt Hong Kong was my home, but I suddenly realized how little I fit in. The truth was that I was a postcolonial relic writing about an imaginary place, a dinosaur whose borrowed time had been handed back. People like me—the half-castes and mixed-bloods—had never really fit anywhere, but Hong Kong's own hybrid status had made it feel like a place where we could thrive. Now the forces that were changing Hong Kong were leaving me behind. It was around this time I stopped calling myself a Hong Konger. But I didn't really know what else I was.

It wasn't until the second time I met Chin Wan that I discovered that like me, he was an ardent admirer of the King of Kowloon. Chin Wan told me how he'd been drawn to the form of the King's work, which to him recalled Taoist talismans and Qing dynasty land certificates. He thought the King's claims struck a deep chord in Hong Kong because they invoked a historical yearning that extended back to the lost boy emperors of the Song dynasty who were an integral part of southern Chinese consciousness. "We remember him," he told me. "It is a sign of identity. He is a lost emperor. An emperor that we have lost."

To Chin Wan, the Cantonese mindset is characterized by a subversive and revolutionary yearning for lost dynasties. "The Cantonese always think that among us there will be some hidden princes, forced to live as commoners," he told me. "It's a whole mentality." Chin Wan believed that this insurgent streak was fed by an antipathy toward overlords from the north, no matter their political persuasion. "Deep in our minds, we do not respect Republicans as well as Communists, as we think we have royal roots older than them."

Whether it was driven by regional rivalries, a clash of values, or fear of economic dependence, the schism between Hong Kongers and their Beijing-backed rulers continued to deepen. A few months after my first meeting with Chin Wan, Hong Kong was rocked by an outbreak of opposition to government policy that mobilized tens of thousands of schoolchildren. In July 2012, a new chief executive had been sworn in: Leung Chun-ying, a millionaire property developer rumored to be an underground Communist. He had been chosen with just 689 votes from the 1,200-member Selection Committee, leaving him with a legitimacy crisis from the very start. Almost straightaway, he hit his first crisis when he tried to push through a new curriculum mandating Communist-style Moral and National Education in local schools. This was seen as political indoctrination, threatening the freedoms that Hong Kongers hold dear. Within days, Hong Kong's teenagers, mobilized by Joshua Wong, who was fifteen years old at this point, had begun protesting.

The students occupied government headquarters for ten days, staging a hunger strike that culminated in a sit-in attended by 120,000 black-clad citizens. Eventually the government made a U-turn and withdrew its plan for patriotic education. These early lessons in dissent set patterns in place. Twice, in the cases of Article 23 and patriotic education, the government had withdrawn unpopular proposals after massive displays of people power. The legislature might be toothless, but street politics was not, so long as the numbers were large enough. The King of Kowloon might be dead, but his descendants increasingly wanted a government that saw with the eyes of the people and heard with their ears. A rallying cry from Joshua Wong summed up their mood: "We've had enough of this government. Hong Kongers will prevail!"

PART 3

DEFIANCE

CHAPTER 7

THE FIRST GENERATION

I was standing on the hump of a flyover, looking down at the rainbow beads of tent encampments threading down the road far off into the distance, bathed in yellow streetlights. Two years had passed since mass protests had forced the government to withdraw the proposals for patriotic education. Now Hong Kongers' pent-up demands had burst out into the Umbrella Movement, which was an explosion of discontent, desire, and, above all, hope. An A4-sized poster tacked up on a wall said it all: "This is NOT a revolution." Hong Kongers wanted to hold their rulers to the promise that Hong Kongers would rule Hong Kong. It was, at heart, an expression of pure political idealism. The nonrevolution was as polite and reasonable as an occupation could be, with the occupiers building a study hall for students, organizing trash recycling, and even planting small vegetable patches in the ornamental flower beds.

At the heart of the occupation were the fears that S. Y. Chung had expressed over the vagueness of Hong Kong's electoral arrangement and the lack of a timeline for democracy in the Basic Law. Hong Kongers wanted to choose their own leader, and they laid all their trust in the talismanic date of 2017 that had been raised by the NPC Standing Committee. But on August 31, 2014, their hopes were dashed when the same body issued a decision that, although Hong Kongers could vote for a leader, their choices would be limited to two or three candidates nominated by a 1,200-person Selection Committee. It added that all candidates must love China and love Hong Kong. The aim was still universal suffrage, it said, but a steady and prudent path should be charted. When I tried to explain the import to my kids, I ended up using food metaphors: It's like the difference between an all-you-can-eat buffet offering endless quantities of lobster, sashimi, and chocolate cake, and an all-you-can-eat buffet offering only white bread and rice. Hong Kongers had been promised their all-you-can-eat buffet for so long that they couldn't countenance a spread of bread and rice. That night, at a rally near the main government complex, an assistant law professor named Benny Tai Yiu-ting announced that Hong Kong was entering a new era of resistance.

The first expression of that new era was the occupation of three important roads. The movement that ensued was named after the umbrellas that the young activists used to protect themselves from the clouds of tear gas fired by police in Admiralty, near the government headquarters and Legco. This was the first time that police had deployed tear gas against Hong Kongers since the 1997 return to Chinese sovereignty, and it was seen as a betrayal so great that thousands more rushed out to occupy the three sites, including streets in Causeway Bay and Mongkok. By the end of the occupation, seventy-nine days later, it was estimated that 1.2 million people—a sixth of the population—had taken part.

From the flyover, I was watching the last night of the occupation. Everyone knew the bailiffs would arrive at nine the next morning. So thick was the sense of impending loss that I could almost taste it. "People have come for the last dance," a forty-something professional told me, as she gave out yellow bookmarks. "It's like utopia. It's everyone's dreamland." We didn't know it at the time, but she was wrong. The last dance would turn out to be only a dress rehearsal for the carnival of discontent that would explode onto Hong Kong's streets five years later. But just then, the night felt weighted with significance.

I was standing beside a clump of tents known as Tung Village, whose inhabitants were swearing raucously as they downed beer and feasted on a last supper of hotpot and pizza. Ten weeks before, the Tung Villagers hadn't known each other. But they'd become a community of protest. By day they went to university or worked at their office jobs, and by night slept in tents on the flyover. The encampment had quickly become a settlement; the rows of tents had addresses, and it was even rumored that postal workers had delivered mail there. As the clock ticked toward midnight, the fluorescent lights of the study hall showed its young inhabitants, still in their school uniforms, spines curved over their textbooks. Others, in black robes and mortarboards, posed by the tents for graduation photos. It was a symbolic choice; the occupation was the site of their real education. The mood was one of nervy anticipation shot with bitter disappointment.

"We didn't gain anything at all," a chatty twenty-something man told me. "It's like we're back to square one. We won't trust the government anymore. We are all disillusioned. If the protestors do things like civil disobedience and the government still refuses to listen, what can people do to make the government listen?"

"I think this is the triggering point, the starting point of a whole-of-society movement," a security analyst chipped in.

"It's like a sinking ship, like the *Titanic*. We're all going to crash!" declared his garrulous companion. "We have to do something. We try to come out, speak out, actually not for something that is a luxury. It's just the thing we deserve, to select our leaders."

On the flyover, every person I spoke to was furiously articulate about Hong Kong's plight. A highly educated population could clearly see just how rigged the system was, and how powerless they were. As my new friend put it, "They don't actually need the votes of Hong Kong people. So why would they respond to us? That's the reason we want change. It's a vicious cycle."

Until the Umbrella Movement, Hong Kong's protest repertoire had been polite and predictable, consisting of orderly marches for which police permission had been granted in the form of a Letter of No Objection, as required under the archaic Public Order Ordinance. The political system allowed so few avenues for effecting change that street protests had become utterly routine, with more than three marches per day. No issue seemed too petty. One day at the Legislative Council I saw a spirited bunch of protestors waving a large caricature of the chairman of the Hong Kong Stock Exchange, Ronald Arculli, dressed in Nazi regalia. They turned out to be stockbrokers protesting that their two-hour lunch break was being cut to ninety minutes. The act of protest had become so ritualized that it was almost meaningless. But all that was about to change.

Benny Tai had been laying the groundwork for the new era of resistance for almost two years. He'd given hundreds of seminars on the principles of civil disobedience alongside a mild-mannered sociology professor named Chan Kin-man and a veteran democracy activist named Reverend Chu Yiu-ming. Their vision was a peaceful ten-thousand-person sit-in which they called Occupy Central with Love and Peace, which would be held on China's National Day, October 1, and would continue until all its participants had been arrested. In the run-up, they'd organized a public referendum asking Hong Kongers how they would like to elect their chief executive. Almost eight hundred thousand people— roughly a fifth of the electorate—had taken part, and all had voted for options that included civil nomination, or ordinary people putting forward candidates. This was a consultation exercise on a massive scale, in direct contrast to Beijing's plans for a Selection Committee of just 1,200 people.

But events on the ground did not follow Tai's vision of a single, orderly sit-in. Instead the action escalated very quickly, driven by two more radical-leaning student groups: the Hong Kong Federation of Students (HKFS) and Scholarism. The latter was a group of secondary students led by Joshua Wong, now seventeen, who organized a weeklong school boycott culminating in a massive sit-in at the legislature. He and fellow activist Nathan Law, along with some other students, had then tried to occupy the forecourt of the building, known as Civic Square. These were the events that led the police to deploy tear gas, which then launched the eleven-week occupation. Tai summed it up elegantly: "With twenty months of work, we planted the seeds in the community. But the tear gas caused the seeds to sprout."

Everyone was taken aback by the scale of the response. Nathan Law admitted to me, "We only planned for the class boycott, not for this massive occupation movement. No one has ever imagined that it would happen and it has that much momentum." The duration of the movement inevitably resulted in discord between the different factions, in particular about whether violent tactics were appropriate. In Mongkok, a grittier area on the Kowloon side, the occupation was marked by clashes. In one incident, unidentified men tore down the encampments and attacked occupiers while police stood to one side and watched. Afterward, nineteen people were arrested, including eight members of triads, or local crime syndicates, raising fears that Hong Kong's police were outsourcing their dirty work to mobsters. But the government's main strategy was to wait it out, refusing all concessions.

Each site had a different vibe, but one common feature was the colorful displays of political art that turned each site into an open-air gallery of political expression. The very first Lennon Wall was at Admiralty, where pastel Post-it Notes transformed a stark concrete stairwell into a multicolored explosion of ideals. One of my favorites was the single word "IMAGINE" on a white Post-it Note, echoing a yellow banner suspended from a footbridge that read, "You may say I'm a dreamer, but I'm not the only one." At Admiralty I saw giant insects made out of recycled trash, a two-meter-high statue of an umbrella-wielding man pieced together from woodblocks, and long curtains of tiny yellow origami umbrellas threaded together. Yellow posters declaring "I want genuine universal suffrage" were everywhere, including one carefully placed on top of a sleeping occupier, allowing him to continue protesting even as he napped. The very first banner hung by the guerrilla sign painters from Lion Rock, a gigantic sunshine-yellow call for universal suffrage topped with a picture of an umbrella, materialized during this period.

That final night, I spotted Kacey Wong, who'd designed the King of Kowloon's first exhibition catalog, sitting behind a folding table sketching protestors. Now an artist focusing on protest actions, he saw this moment as a turning point. "It's like taking the red pill," he said, alluding to the moment in *The Matrix* when the protagonist understands his world is a simulacrum. As we talked, his pen scratched and flicked across the page, sketching one protestor after another. "We have woken up and we realized we are not only Chinese, but we are Hong Kongese. We can stand tall and be proud of our identity for the first time. And that's what this movement is about." The unspoken threat, he warned, presaged a wider struggle: "This is a war on culture. If you lose, you have to change your language. That's why everybody came out: to support our culture, our way of life."

That particular episode turned out to be a skirmish ahead of a bigger battle. That first defeat, when it happened, arrived not by force but through the courts. A number of private transport companies—taxi, minibus, and tour coach—filed injunctions blaming the road obstructions for disrupting their business, and the High Court found in their favor, ordering the clearance of all the sites. As well as aiding their own commercial imperatives, the transport unions were using the veil of legality provided by Hong Kong's independent courts to serve the interests of both the Hong Kong and the Beijing governments. This was what people called "lawfare," the weaponization of the common law for repressive ends.

As the final night of the occupation wore on, messages of defiance began appearing. When the study hall finally closed at daylight, the sign on the entrance read, "We will be back." Another warning on the Lennon Wall read, "The clearing of the site is not the end, but the start of Round Two. Government are you ready?" Scrawled in black Sharpie on a highway divider were the words "Sand does not fear the wind. One day it will inevitably pile up." The biggest sign of all—a big orange banner erected for the bailiffs on a bamboo lattice over jerry-built barricades—simply read: "It's just the beginning."

To me, the signs seemed like bravado. The occupation was ending without even a symbolic victory. The disruption to everyday life had eroded public support, with 80 percent of Hong Kongers supporting an end to the action by this point. When the bailiffs marched in that morning, they were accompanied by five thousand policemen who helped dismantle the site, breaking only for lunch. By the end of the occupation, a total of 955 people had been arrested, including some of Hong Kong's best-known lawmakers, who sat cross-legged in the road, waiting to be carried away by police, as the Occupy planners had originally envisaged. But now the politicians' actions only earned them the contempt of the students, who accused them of grandstanding without having bothered to suffer through the occupation.

Two days later, I went to visit Occupy cofounder Benny Tai at his office at the law faculty of the University of Hong Kong, walking past a glass showcase containing a life-size model of a bewigged, lace-ruffed judge on the way. His personal email account had just been hacked, his voice was flat with exhaustion, and he looked dazed. To my surprise, he did not seem defeated at all. He still seemed stunned by the events of the past three months. "It was just an idea that came from my head, and it started to grow and grow and grow and develop into a situation now that is totally beyond my imagination. Ideas are very dangerous." In assessing Occupy's legacy, he commented on the change in protest tactics. "Now it's a much more active mode of struggle. You have people confronting the police. Though they still appear to use nonviolent principles, they are much more aggressive in their way of struggling. This is totally not within our plans."

Although he had been arrested, he was confident about his own fate. He'd researched the precedents and felt sure that he would be let off with a fine. "We have independent courts in Hong Kong, so it's very unlikely that we will be subject to imprisonment," he told me. "Even for all the organizers, they cannot lock us up in jail, as that is not the Hong Kong law—unless they want to give up the whole of One Country, Two Systems. Hong Kong laws provide the protection for us to have this kind of movement. I can continue to talk about all these things freely in Hong Kong. No one can stop us. I still have three columns in the newspaper and so I can continue to advocate. I cannot see that I will be stopped."

TWO YEARS PASSED before I saw Benny Tai again. By then, his faith in the legal system to which he had devoted his entire career was wavering. "We find that the law is not a very secure protection to our rights now," he said. "Because the law can be interpreted in any way, if the authorities think that is the way they want to interpret it." It was chastening to hear the shift in his views. The aftermath of the Umbrella Movement had seen Hong Kong's rights and freedoms salami-sliced away with accelerating speed, with the changes piling up one on top of the other. Day by day, One Country, Two Systems was tilting to favor One Country over Two

Systems. But calling it out also meant acknowledging the failure of the formula on which the future depended.

One incident that shook Hong Kongers to their very core was the disappearance of five men who became known as the Causeway Bay Booksellers. One of them, Gui Minhai, co-owned a publishing company called Mighty Current, which printed gossipy muckraking books about Chinese politics that had once crowded airport bookstores but were now becoming hard to buy. The other four worked at a small, independent bookstore called Causeway Bay Books, which mailed such books to customers in China. The five booksellers disappeared one by one between October and December 2015, mysteriously reappearing in custody in mainland China. The most frightening case was that of Gui Minhai, who disappeared from the city of Pattaya, near Bangkok, and surfaced in China, though there was no record of him leaving Thailand. He then appeared on Chinese television, confessing to having unintentionally killed someone in a drunk driving accident thirteen years earlier. The blatancy of the illegal rendition made it even more chilling.

One of the men, Lam Wing-kee, managed to escape China through a combination of chance, error, and guts. When we met on a street corner in Taipei in 2019, I immediately recognized his tall, rake-thin figure, even though his hat was pulled down low over his forehead. His eyes were sweeping the street the whole time. He took me to the noisiest coffee shop I've ever visited, full of clattering pots, chattering clients, and shouting staff, where he spoke in the quietest voice I've ever heard. As he described his ordeal, I noticed that he often used "you" rather than "I"—a dissociative practice typical of post-traumatic stress disorder.

He described the experience of being detained in Shenzhen in October 2015, as he tried to cross the border. When he asked what he'd done to warrant detention, he was simply told, "Whatever law you've broken, we won't tell you. You can guess." After a full day of questioning, his papers were confiscated and he was coerced into signing an agreement not to inform family members or to retain a lawyer. He was then blind-folded and taken on a train to Ningbo, where he was kept under twenty-four-hour surveillance for three months. At first he was interrogated several times a day, but gradually the sessions became less frequent. Even-tually Lam was told that he'd been accused of the "illegal sales of books," though he still couldn't really understand why the mighty Communist Party was focusing its efforts on a tiny bookshop. He felt that he had no choice but to confess, and to allow himself to be filmed delivering a state-ment of remorse scripted by his captors.

Utterly alone and desperate, he thought about killing himself, but the room's padded walls made that impossible. He considered hanging himself using his trousers, but both the ceiling and the showerhead were too high to reach. As he realized that the room had been designed to prevent suicide, he began wondering about the identity of its previous occupant, in particular how they had tried to kill themselves. Then Lam began to lose his grip on himself. He was never beaten, he says, because it simply wasn't necessary. As he described his plight, his hand trembled as he stirred his coffee. "I had mental problems because I was in an extraor-dinarily abnormal situation. They wanted to smother you. They said they could shut you up forever and no one outside would ever know about it. They didn't need to beat me."

Over time he learned that his colleagues were also being held. The focus of the interrogations seemed to be a book published by Gui Minhai that included details of President Xi Jinping's former relationships. By the end of February 2016, Lam had signed statements of guilt and filmed a confession, reading word for word from a script given to him by his cap-tors. In March, he was moved to Shaoguan, released "on bail," given a job at a library and a phone that functioned as a GPS tracker, and required to report daily to the police station. It was an odd type of unfreedom. One day, he was taken for a sumptuous dinner with two of the other booksellers, Cheung Chi-ping and Lee Bo, who'd not only been released on bail but had even been allowed to return to Hong Kong. The surreality of the meal was heightened by Lee Bo's relaxed and smiling demeanor, and his repeated assertions that he'd come back from Hong Kong voluntarily. Lee Bo even gave the others $1,500 (10,000 yuan) each, to express condolence for their difficulties. But all of them knew they were being watched. As I listened to Lam's account, I kept thinking of a metaphor that a friend of mine, the writer Zhang Lijia, had once used. China's like a birdcage, she said. Sometimes the bars are so far away that they can't even be seen, but they're always there.

Back in Hong Kong, Lam's ex-wife had lodged a missing persons report with the police, and that provided him with an unexpected opportunity. His handlers decided to send him to Hong Kong for a day to cancel the police report, and to bring back a computer so that its hard drive could be used as evidence. They also shared their longer-term plans, telling him that the bookshop had been sold to a new owner, and that after Lam's trial was over, he could return to his old job there so long as he kept informing on his customers. Thinking it over, he didn't see any other options.

Once he was in Hong Kong, however, everything changed. Lam managed to get online, where to his utter surprise he discovered that his disappearance had made international headlines. Six thousand Hong Kongers had marched to raise awareness of the booksellers' plight, and it had even been mentioned in the European Parliament. Lam stayed up all night thinking about what to do. Then he made a critical move that changed his fate. By mistake, he took the wrong computer from the bookshop. When he telephoned his handlers to tell them, they told him to stay another night to swap out the computer. That evening, he went to Temple Street night market, where he hadn't been for twenty years. People were sitting on portable stools on the pavement, slurping their food and shouting. As he watched them, he realized how much he loved watching Hong Kongers. He loved seeing them helping their fellow passersby, and he loved watching them jaywalk. He loved their efficiency. He even loved being pushed by crowds of Hong Kongers, because he could feel they were pushing him of their own free will. They had freedom and dignity. It was an absolutely banal scene—people sitting around at night, drinking beer and eating spicy clams—yet the contrast to that strained, surveilled, sumptuous meal he'd shared with his former colleagues could not have been greater.

It made him realize that without agency of his own, he was no longer a Hong Konger. He felt angry that his identity had been stripped from him. "I have become one of them today, and tomorrow I will cause more people to become one of us," he wrote in an account. He thought about how he would be expected to betray his fellow Hong Kongers, and that made him think of the six thousand Hong Kongers who'd protested for him. They should be his role models, and he should not let them down.

He spent the second night awake, thinking. Then he started his journey back toward the border. He was about to cross back into China when he stopped to smoke one last cigarette. As he took a drag on it, he thought of a famous poem by the Hong Kong writer Shu Xiangcheng that he'd learned in school.

> *I have never seen*
> *A desk kneeling*
> *But I have seen*
> *Scholars kneeling.*

If he returned to the mainland, what would have been the point of learning that poem or of reading all the books he had read? He would not kneel. As he tossed away his cigarette, he decided not to return. He knew this could lead to punishment for his girlfriend and his coworkers still in China on bail, but he also knew that he was the only one who could speak out, since the others all had relatives in China who could be used as leverage. He didn't. "They couldn't do this, but I could," he told me. Instead of returning to China, he called a very public press conference in Legco. It was an act of courage from someone who describes himself as not at all brave.

For a while, Lam Wing-kee lived in a safe house, protected by Hong Kong police from the mainland authorities. He was a living embodiment of the impossible contradictions of One Country, Two Systems. His colleagues remained unfree as well, a reminder that mainland security services were now operating with impunity in Hong Kong. In 2017, this kind of rendition happened again. Xiao Jianhua, a Chinese tycoon who'd been a student leader in 1989, was snatched from a luxury hotel in Hong Kong, from which he was escorted in a wheelchair, with a blanket over his head. The city, which had for so long offered a refuge for dissidents and dangerous ideas, was no longer a safe haven.

Hong Kong was in an accelerating slide into becoming a different city altogether. The freedoms that had distinguished it from China were being stripped away. In the post-Umbrella years, activists had at first retained enough confidence in Hong Kong's institutions that they tried to work within the system. There had been a blossoming of localist political parties focused on preserving Hong Kong's identity and autonomy; some of the more radical ones even openly advocated independence. Their radicalism reflected the shift into identity politics, as well as a repudiation of the moderate stance and methods of traditional political parties.

What they didn't foresee was just how the system itself would be changed to purposely exclude them. When the activists tried to start their own political parties, some were forbidden from opening bank accounts or registering the parties. When they tried to stand for election, a new rule was introduced requiring candidates to attest that they saw Hong Kong as an inalienable part of China. Six of those who signed the pledge were barred from running anyway. Another six localist candidates who ended up being elected were unceremoniously expelled from the legislature for breaking rules that hadn't even existed at the time they broke them. Politics was becoming ludicrously Kafkaesque.

The expulsion of the legislators—two in November 2016, another four eight months later—came to be known as Oathgate. Their crime was the way they'd taken their oaths of office. The first two had sworn allegiance to the "Hong Kong Nation" with flags reading "Hong Kong is not part of China" draped over their shoulders. One, thirty-year-old Leung Chung-hang, called Baggio after his favorite footballer, had been a Plan B candidate anyway, replacing Edward Leung Tin-kei, an unrelated localist politician who had been barred from standing because of his previous support for Hong Kong independence. "It's a mess," Baggio Leung told me despairingly when we met in a café below his lawyer's office. He was stick-thin, his black jeans bagging around his twiggy knees. He was now facing bankruptcy. His oath-taking behavior was being roundly panned by critics, even in the pro-democracy camp, who blamed him for baiting Beijing with childish antics. "How can you say this is childish?" he asked plaintively, pointing out that before the ceremony he had consulted earlier rulings on oath taking and judged there was sufficient precedent for his gesture. "This is part of our political agenda. You cannot judge our behavior because of the results." In fact, the infighting and accusations were distracting from the slippages that were beginning to unmake the system.

The next batch of those disqualified included Nathan Law, the student activist who at twenty-three had been the youngest lawmaker ever elected. His offenses included saying the words "People's Republic of China" in a questioning tone, and reading out a quote from Mahatma Gandhi after taking his oath. The quotation he'd chosen was, "You can chain me, you can torture me, you can even destroy my body, but you will never imprison my mind." "I consulted legal opinion beforehand," he told me. "It was actually a tradition of Hong Kong legislators to speak up before they took the oath, so I think the Beijing government has been abusing the power of reinterpretation, destroying our tradition in the council."

Another legislator kicked out was a diminutive forty-something sociology lecturer, Lau Siu-lai. When I visited her in the office she was soon to vacate, I noticed it was decorated with four large black-and-white photos of intellectuals and post-structuralists including Jürgen Habermas and Michel Foucault. They had inspired the act that got Lau ejected. She hadn't added anything to her oath or used any props. She'd been disqualified for speaking too slowly. She had paused six seconds between each word of her oath. "There's postmodern cultural theory behind it," she told me, explaining her actions, "how you inspire reflection on oath taking, how you inspire reflection by ritual."

The authorities were also inspiring reflection with their method of disqualification. The Hong Kong government had filed a legal action in the local courts, but before the judge could make his ruling, the NPC Standing Committee stepped in to issue its own reinterpretation of the Basic Law, making it retroactive to 1997. As China's top legal body, it had the legal power to do this. This was the fifth time the Beijing body had reinterpreted the Basic Law since the handover, and in doing so it managed to undermine Hong Kong's autonomy, its courts, and its political institutions in one fell swoop. The pattern was clear: if Beijing didn't like Hong Kong's laws, it would simply reinterpret them.

Eight days after Beijing's reinterpretation, it was the turn of the Hong Kong judge, Thomas Au Hing-cheung, to give his own ruling. I went along to the High Court out of curiosity. It was all reassuringly familiar, exactly as it had been twenty years before, when I worked for a Hong Kong paper: the jungle of photographers vying for space outside the court, the young journalists jeering when someone stole someone else's position. There was a flurry of excitement when the press officer came out with copies of the judgment and the credentialed reporters grabbed the reports and sprinted away to their respective newsrooms. Then suddenly it was all over. The main attraction was not the actual verdict, but the running of the young hacks; everyone had always known the judge would find in favor of Beijing's position.

Suddenly I felt as if I was colluding in an elaborate charade. This was not true news, since the broad contents of the ruling had never been in any doubt. Yet here we were, playing our assigned roles. The press pack was pretending to report news, while the judge was writing his own lines in a play ultimately directed by Beijing. It was a world where lawmakers pretended to be lawmakers even though everyone knew they had no real lawmaking powers, the public pretended they were taking part in elections even though the results were largely predictable, and the chief executive pretended to have autonomy though everyone knew he had almost none. Hong Kong's institutions were being hollowed out, but no one knew how to stop playing along. My own role in this pantomime nauseated me, but it was hard to know what else to do.

The recalibration of Hong Kong's identity was also leading to a reexamination of the territory's history. Around this time, it emerged that large swaths of policy files were missing. Around five thousand files had been relocated to the National Archives in the UK, with no duplicates publicly available in Hong Kong. Some had been publicly released in the UK, but even these had sections redacted. Around one thousand files had been sealed, some until 2049. These included around half of the files from the 1980s, especially those dealing with the period when the Joint Declaration was negotiated. From a bureaucratic and administrative point of view, the missing files were troublesome, since policymakers had no history of policy decisions or intentions, while court cases were sometimes complicated due to missing documents. But more than that, it was another reminder of Hong Kongers' powerlessness. In not being able to determine their own fate, they'd lost control of their future, and in losing their records, they'd lost control of their past.

On this front, some of the most interesting work was archival research done by young volunteers. I met a trio of endearingly serious young men, who described themselves as "nerdy, very nerdy." When we met, they described the missing files as posing an existential problem, with one spelling out the ramifications to me: "Records give a place and its people an identity. When the records are lost or removed, it's easy to change identity. When we talk about colonialism, it's understandable to want to make our own history obscure to its people to make our identity more easily changed and managed by the authorities. This colonial status hasn't really changed after the handover because we don't have the history. We don't even know about our own history. So it's very difficult to form a very solid identity about who we are."

The trio sometimes took part in archival marathons piecing together the past. Hong Kong students in London requested and copied documents from the National Archives in Kew, where I'd read the letters between Elliot and Qishan. Then they'd share them with volunteers in Hong Kong, who would work on them. The trio lit up with enthusiasm as they described one session when a roomful of volunteers had charted eight thousand pages—"the entire PREM19 series," as one put it in hushed tones—chronicling the sequence of events from the start of talks until the day the Joint Declaration was signed. The volunteers created a timeline, cross-referencing it to other material such as biographies and autobiographies to record different interpretations of events. It was the archivists' equivalent of a rock concert.

I honestly found it hard to believe that volunteers would sign up to wade through government archives. "Oh, there are many people interested!" one said. The three were growing increasingly animated, talking over one another. "Forty of them!" said another. "Mostly young people!" the third chipped in. "They want to know more about Hong Kong history but they cannot find other places or books that can tell them the whole picture of Hong Kong history, and they think records will help." The timing coincided with the rise of localism, as young Hong Kongers constructed their own narrative of Hong Kong history. Nerdy or not, what the young archivists were doing was surprisingly perilous, since they were fundamentally challenging Beijing's narrative. "When you try to touch on history issues and local identity, the Chinese Communist Party will always try to attack you," one of the three said.

The education sector was also being targeted, since students—and in particular university student unions—had been instrumental in the Umbrella Movement. Pro-Beijing chancellors were being installed at the territory's most politically active universities, teachers were warned that mentioning independence could cost them their qualifications, and Benny Tai was in trouble. He'd been found guilty of not following university guidelines in receiving Occupy-related donations and had been banned from receiving donations or supervising researchers for three years. Despite all this, Tai seemed surprisingly sanguine when we met again. "Personally, I do not feel direct threats at this stage," he told me cheerfully. "I just got three-year funding from the university supporting my work so I don't think I'm being penalized. In a way, I'm well supported."

He foresaw another round of mass protest. As we spoke, he laid out the failings of the Umbrella Movement: it went on too long, it was geographically concentrated in just three spots, internal communication was poor, and there was no mechanism to bring it to an end. As he mused on tactics, his words were uncannily prescient. "Actually, to block a road, you don't need ten thousand people. One thousand people will be able to block one road junction, and if you have ten thousand people you can block ten road junctions all over Hong Kong."

I hardly registered what he was saying. To me it seemed clear that the fallout of the Umbrella Movement had divided Hong Kong; older residents had been angered by the length of the occupation and the disruption it had caused, while those who took part were left depressed and demoralized. I could see no appetite for another round of action, and I thought Tai was misjudging the mood. But he was sure that an even greater confrontation was on the way, driven in part by the lack of concessions from the authorities. He told me he'd even written a warning letter to Beijing, and he described what it had said: "We are a group of very rational and moderate Democrats. We are committed to using nonviolent actions. What we were asking is very moderate in the sense that it's totally within the framework of the Basic Law. We warned that in case these very moderate things we ask for could not be satisfied, then people will resort to more radical moves and actions."

Two days later, I interviewed his fellow organizer Chan Kin-man in his Chinese University office high above the Sha Tin hillside. When I arrived, I found him peering into the back of his computer, along with a university IT worker. His computer had been hacked again, but for the first time he'd received a warning that the hacking might be state sponsored. No one seemed to know what to do. As we sat down to chat, I noticed a photo of Nelson Mandela on his bookshelf.

As a sociologist, Chan Kin-man was fascinated by the identity shift that was taking place, driven by the localism movement. The Hong Kong identity now was perceived as being in conflict with Chinese identity, rather than overlapping with it. The divergence that had begun when Hong Kongers started complaining about mainland locusts was picking up speed, and many young people felt entirely disengaged from China. They refused to attend the annual June 4 vigil remembering those who had died in 1989 because they felt China had nothing to do with them.

Chan Kin-man also warned of the possibility of a second, more serious round of social unrest. "This is a vicious cycle. I expect there's going to be very serious riots coming. Once they feel they are completely rejected by the institutions, of course they will resort to more noninstitutional or even violent means, because they're young, they're angry. It's quite dangerous."

I was so deaf to these warnings that I didn't even bother to report them at the time. I'd been having conversations with Umbrella activists who were so despondent that I couldn't imagine them going down the same path again. They'd expended so much energy and hope on the occupation that they seemed to have run out of both. My chatty friend from the Umbrella Movement was typical. When we met at a coffee shop, he was eloquent and dejected as he sipped mocha with cream. He had protest fatigue, and everything seemed hopeless. He'd stopped going to any demonstrations at all, including the June 4 Tiananmen vigils; they all seemed pointless. All his friends were trying to figure out how to leave Hong Kong. When we reminisced about the last day of the Umbrella Movement, he said, "We thought we were at the bottom then. But we have been slumping ever since. Now we are just waiting to be crushed by China."

I knew what he meant. Sometimes it felt like we were in a video game, falling into a bottomless pit. Our fall was sometimes slowed by a platform, but no sooner had we steadied ourselves than the platform would be whisked away to reveal a never-ending hole beneath. It seemed like there was no end to the fall.

But there were always new and depressing way stations on the descent. One was a court decision in 2017 that sentenced three student activists—Joshua Wong, Alex Chow, and Nathan Law—to prison terms of between six and eight months for the occupation of Civic Square. Originally they'd been given sentences of 120 hours of community service, but these were overturned on appeal after the government argued they were too lenient. The three activists were Hong Kong's first post-Umbrella political prisoners.

One day I visited a young graphic designer named Kit Man, whom people kept mentioning as a kind of latter-day King of Kowloon. Indeed, he had designed a chunky, stylized font called Hong Kong Kickass that was popular with some homegrown brands but was also often used for political messages. He was a slim young man with spiky hair and a quicksilver smile, but to my disappointment, he immediately dissociated himself from the King. He told me he thought that it was an unfortunate comparison. "It just keeps popping up," he said, with irritation. "But there's no solution to that because he is so famous in Hong Kong."

Kit Man had quit his job to throw himself into the Umbrella Movement, and had even taken out a bank loan to finance his participation without telling his long-suffering wife. Now he felt like Hong Kong was changing in front of his eyes. "Bit by bit, it is being diluted every day," he told me. He worried that the waiters in his favorite teahouse no longer spoke Cantonese, and the university campuses were full of students from mainland China. He couldn't seem to find a way to channel his political energies. He'd tried drawing political cartoons, but he couldn't find anywhere to publish them. I asked an innocuous question about calligraphy, and he suddenly fell silent. He passed his hand over his face, and his shoulders shook. A long minute passed as he wept painfully. Then he said, "This government is not composed of Hong Kongers. They're outsiders. They don't work for Hong Kong." When he thought about those young activists who were serving jail time, the tears began pouring down his face. He said, "Every time, I cannot hold the tears. We're still in the battle. It's just much harder to fight."

My path kept crossing with Occupy cofounder Chan Kin-man at various academic conferences. In March 2018, we met again when he was invited to speak at my university in Melbourne. He looked pale and sleepless. Benny Tai's confidence had been sadly misplaced; both of them were now under pressure at work, as well as being targeted by shady hate campaigns. Chan had received piles of hate mail, including envelopes containing razor blades. He received anonymous phone calls threatening to rape his wife and daughter, and he was trailed when he took his child to her weekend drama class. Benny Tai's belief in the power of precedents notwithstanding, all three Occupy cofounders, including the frail septuagenarian Reverend Chu Yiu-ming, were facing colonial-era public order charges: inciting public nuisance, conspiracy to incite public nuisance, and the extraordinary charge of incitement to incite public nuisance. Six other activists were also on trial, earning them the nickname of the Umbrella Nine.

Almost a year passed until Chan and I met again, this time in Hong Kong, when Graeme Smith and I interviewed him and Nathan Law for our *Little Red Podcast*. By then Law, at twenty-five, had been a student activist, started a political party, been elected as a legislator, been disqualified from the legislature, jailed, then released after the Court of Final Appeal overturned his sentence. So turbulent was Law's life that he described his six months in jail sharing a cell with triad members as peaceful.

It seemed like another lurch toward the bottom, hearing the young ex-prisoner giving advice to another political-prisoner-in-waiting. There was little doubt that Chan Kin-man would also serve jail time, and he said he was preparing to "travel light" into jail. He'd just taken early retirement from his beloved job with an erudite three-hour-long farewell speech attended by seven hundred students, during which he outlined his inspirations from the Chinese democracy activist Wei Jingsheng through Alexis de Tocqueville. Many more students had wanted to attend, but the university hadn't managed, or didn't want, to find an auditorium large enough.

To my surprise, Chan was not bitter, but cheerful and joking. Over my years interviewing dissidents in China, I was used to spending time with people for whom anger had become a driving force. But Chan's attitude seemed more like a weary resignation underpinned by a tenor of equanimity and a grim sense of humor. He seemed to view jail as an inevitability. "I guess I have read a lot of letters and books written in prison, even when I was a young man," he said, laughing. "So it seemed that I've been prepared for this for quite a while. I guess it is a must for society to go through this when fighting for democracy."

He attributed his attitude to the fact that Hong Kong activists had suffered less than their mainland counterparts, but to me, it was related to agency. Mainland dissidents are stuck in a bleak and Kafkaesque no-man's-land from which they are sometimes even forbidden from fleeing into exile. Chan, on the other hand, had received offers of political asylum from other countries, which he had rejected. He'd decided that he would stand trial, and that he'd also take the witness stand during that trial, even though lawyers warned him not to, saying the possibility of self-incrimination was extremely high.

Chan was the only one out of the nine Umbrella leaders who would do so, but he'd given the decision much thought. He explained it, saying, "I choose to give testimony in the witness box because if we don't do it, then we only have one version of the story. That is the government version, saying that we were creating a public nuisance. So I believe that it is our responsibility to retell the story, to restore history." I'd heard this very line before, but always from exiled Tiananmen activists explaining why they'd decided to write their life stories. Now Hong Kongers were also struggling to preserve their stories from the Communist Party's fearsome narrative control.

One reason Chan was so sure he would be imprisoned was the extraordinary and unprecedented charge of "incitement to incite." It was an *Alice in Wonderland*–style charge so broad it seemed meaningless, except as a deterrent. Once again, common law was being used as a weapon to hobble activists.

At this moment, it felt like the fight for democracy in Hong Kong had been lost. The movement had been crushed, its leaders imprisoned and marginalized, and the shock waves slowly rippling through the educational system seemed designed to cripple its ability to impart critical thinking skills. Many young people were throwing their energy into finding ways to leave Hong Kong entirely, as they had done in the early eighties. But Chan did not agree. Hong Kongers, he said, were like the children of asylum seekers in Sweden who suffer a physical condition known as resignation syndrome. This happens in families whose asylum applications have been rejected after years of waiting. Suddenly the children become catatonic, and can only lie in bed, unable to speak, eat, stand, or even open their eyes. "It seems that many people here also have this kind of resignation syndrome," Chan said. "They had been hoping for democracy for so long and the reality is so hard to take." But it was not over. Hong Kongers had not lost their values, they were just tired. "I would not make too hasty a conclusion," he said.

Chan's was shaping up to be the most important political trial in a generation. One night I had a beer with Sampson Wong Yu-hin, a political artist in his midthirties who was trying to formulate an artistic response. Wong, who had a distinctive mane of long, curly hair, was focusing his attention on a 2.7-meter-high statue of Lady Justice, a blindfolded classical Greek figure in flowing robes atop the Court of Final Appeal building. His idea was to put words in her mouth, but the tenor of the times was forcing him to spend hours studying law statutes to decide how to achieve that. He'd already considered and rejected the idea of a drone, as they were illegal in that part of the city. A Thai-style wishing lantern was potentially hazardous. Helium balloons were possible, though floating a balloon within sixty meters of a building was illegal. It occurred to him that the legal definition of "floating" was ambiguous enough to exclude tethered balloons, but he needed to consider the ancillary question of whether the artwork itself could be seen as a protest. Numbers were key; more than thirty people could constitute a public procession, requiring police permission. But being beneath that threshold wasn't necessarily a safeguard if the event was political in nature; illegal assembly was increasingly being used against activists as a catchall charge.

"We are trying to decide if we will get arrested," Wong said, grinning, as he sipped his craft IPA. Sampson Wong and his collaborator Jason Lam Chi-fai were part of an artistic collective called Add Oil Team, which specialized in political installations. For several years, they had been skating close to the edge. During the Umbrella Movement, they projected messages on-site at Admiralty. The next year, they'd been the highest-profile victims of artistic censorship when arts administrators switched off their light installation on the territory's tallest building, the International Commerce Centre. They'd embedded a countdown clock into their projection, which ticked down the seconds until the One Country, Two Systems formula expires in 2047. The administrators gave complicated, bureaucratic reasons to justify their censorship, but the disappearance of the countdown clock was itself horribly, unintentionally symbolic. With the acceleration of encroachments threatening all that marked Hong Kong out from mainland China, 2047 seemed imminent.

Wong had been outraged and had immediately written an op-ed about the censorship. "What was not sensitive yesterday has become sensitive today," he wrote. "Every day everybody becomes increasingly anxious. More and more tiny things are deemed to be 'potentially troublesome.' . . . Once that atmosphere exists, those with power simply have no need to issue any orders. Everyone will prematurely submit: there will be no day when a new standard for 'sensitivity' is not reached; fear will wipe everything out." He started keeping a tally of the number of cases of artistic censorship, and toyed with starting a Museum of Censorship. When we met, he said he'd recorded about forty cases, which seemed to me a lot. He laughed at my surprise. "Actually I thought that number was quite low. That just shows how much things have changed round here."

To no one's surprise, the Umbrella Nine were found guilty at the beginning of April 2019. The court judged that civil disobedience was not a defense in law, and that the obstruction to roads resulting from Occupy Central was unreasonable and unwarranted. Chan Kin-man was found guilty of conspiracy to commit public nuisance and inciting others to commit public nuisance. He was cleared of incitement to incite public nuisance, though five others were found guilty of this charge. When the verdicts were announced, there was a five-minute standing ovation in court for the activists. Two weeks later, Chan and Tai were both sentenced to sixteen months in jail. All Umbrella Nine had been convicted, but some were exempted from jail due to age or infirmity. Benny Tai was wrong again; the laws that were supposed to protect the movement had instead been used to stop him. It was the ultimate insult to a law professor.

On the day of the sentencing, I met Wong and his team in Statue Square, opposite the Court of Appeal's neoclassical granite porticoes, which had been designed by the architects responsible for Buckingham Palace. They were all watching scenes from the courthouse on their mobile phones, and the mood was despondent defiance. Then a van drew up, disgorging from its depths gigantic bulbous white helium balloons. Everyone gawped and giggled at the how large they were. The team had prepared a white banner with a black cartoon speech bubble containing the words "Not Guilty" in Chinese and English. Their plan was to float this upward until the words were coming from Lady Justice's mouth.

All of a sudden, it was time. Watching for police, we ran over to the courthouse, our every action livestreamed to the Add Oil Team's Facebook page by two cameramen. The team released the balloons, letting out string to hoist the sign higher and higher until "Not Guilty," twisting in the wind, reached Lady Justice's lips. The two designated sign-carriers stood still, while we—the erstwhile spectators—were tweeting, livestreaming, Facebooking, Insta-ing, WeChatting, and WhatsApping for all our worth, disseminating the images into every corner of the social media sphere. The team already knew that their action wouldn't be covered by the legacy media, now almost all acquired by pro-Beijing owners. The entire action had been designed for the virtual generation, and its success would be measured by its online visibility.

It was at this moment that I realized my role as an unwitting publicist for this artwork. My value to the team was in my Twitter following of sixty thousand people. I'd thought I was attending as a journalist, but in tweeting the work I was participating as effectively as if I'd been carrying a sign or shouting a slogan.

After about twenty minutes, the team lowered their sign and retreated. Wong posted a short statement to the team's Facebook page. It read, "If Lady Justice could speak, she would tell the world that they are not guilty. We all know that all Hong Kong people who fight for democracy are not guilty at all. Time will tell that those who participated in the Umbrella Movement in 2014 stand on the right side of history."

As I tweeted his statement, I had a niggling worry about whether I'd unwittingly crossed a line into activism. Doing a quick mental rundown, I assured myself that at no point had I done anything that would undermine my journalistic neutrality. The fact that I agreed with the statement and the banner was irrelevant. But the niggle was still there. I could sense that a moment might come at which journalistic neutrality might become immoral, as evenhandedness could undermine the very values I cherished. If I had to choose between being a journalist and being a Hong Konger, which one would I pick? It felt like that day was approaching.

The artistic operation had been successful. No one had been arrested. But the artists weren't euphoric. They remained solemn and largely silent as they popped the helium balloons and cleared up. The action seemed so tiny, so futile, highlighting the limited ability of art to confront political power. Nothing would stop the Umbrella Nine from serving jail time. Late into the night, Wong was still posting on Facebook, weeping as he read the speeches the Umbrella Nine had made after their verdicts were announced. He wrote, "The more I think about it, the angrier I am. It's hard to sleep at night. Is it OK that those in power can just throw a whole pile of people in jail? Isn't this a threat to people to obediently live a 'normal' life and just happily live in peace. The world shouldn't be like this."

CHAPTER 8

COUNTRY

A sea of alabaster flooded the city, shimmering between skyscraper canyons. Bodies clad in white, the traditional color of mourning in China, inundated every pedestrian overpass, every subterranean walkway. Viewed from above, they seemed to cohere into a single sinuous being, jammed together so tightly that movement was almost imperceptible. It was June 9, 2019, and one million demonstrators had taken to the streets to protest against the government's plans to change its extradition law. This extraordinary show of strength, pitting the people against the government, represented both the coming-of-age of a Hong Kong nation and the beginning of its end.

The political firestorm had started with a murder. A Hong Kong man killed his pregnant girlfriend in Taiwan, then fled to Hong Kong, and the lack of an extradition treaty prevented him from being sent back to face trial. Hong Kong's chief executive, the humorless former civil servant Carrie Lam Cheng Yuet-ngor, decided to use this case as a pretext to change the extradition law. The proposed legislation would permit suspects from Hong Kong to be extradited to stand trial in jurisdictions including mainland China, where the justice system was rife with arbitrary detention, unfair trials, and even torture. If passed, the law would spell the end of Hong Kong's status as a refuge for mainland dissidents and activists. And for Hong Kongers, it would mark the end of One Country, Two Systems.

At ground level, Hong Kongers' astonishment and euphoria at the turnout was tempered by a shrewd, bookie's-eye view of the future. The mood was encapsulated by a video clip that was circulating on social media.

"Do you think this march will bring change?" an off-camera reporter asked a young man.

"No, absolutely not," he replied, without hesitation.

The reporter pressed on: "So why are you doing it?"

His answer, a model of brevity: "At least you tried."

Everyone had turned out to try: Chinese and expats, old and young. The sheer press of numbers meant that marching turned to shuffling, then standing. It took some people nine hours to complete a route that could normally be walked in less than an hour. I, too, was marching, alongside my children. My twelve-year-old, Ave, had made their own protest sign. It read, "Xi Dada = Big Brother," referencing a sarcastic nickname ("Daddy Xi") for Chinese president Xi Jinping. I'd decided not to cover the march as a journalist, but to attend as a protestor; it had seemed more important to feel the moment than to report it. As the day wore on, however, I regretted my decision more and more. Just marching felt unsatisfying to me. I itched to interview the people around me, and I couldn't help mentally drafting a dispatch as I marched. Being a reporter had become my default mode, and by the end of the day, I realized that reporting a moment had become my way of feeling it. I was both a Hong Konger and a journalist, not one or the other.

As we lurched forward, a few steps at a time, a sixty-something Chinese man with a face blotched by vitiligo kept turning around to look at me. Finally he spoke.

"Why are foreigners marching today?" he asked me.

My heart clenched a little, and I realized I'd been waiting for someone to question my credentials.

"I grew up in Hong Kong," I replied. "I'm a permanent resident. I'm half-Chinese, and my children are three-quarters Chinese. We came to show our support because we believe that as many people as possible should come out today."

"Thank you!" he said, smiling broadly. "Thank you!"

This was my first indication that the crisis would change how Hong Kongers saw themselves, expanding the narrow, exclusionary, localist categories spawned by the Umbrella Movement. The march embraced all who elevated principle over pragmatism, hope over experience. The moment was a triumph of idealism from a people long stereotyped by their colonial masters as motivated only by the pursuit of money. In the only place on Chinese soil where political protest was allowed, Hong Kongers were performing their identity as a city of protest in order to defend it. They were coming together to raise their voices as one.

If Hong Kong's rulers were taken aback by the depth of feeling on display, it was only because they had perfected the habit of ignoring their people. As a Special Administrative Region of China, the government's authority stemmed not from the people, but from Beijing. The administration had honed the art of holding public consultations that were almost mockeries of the process. Sometimes it announced its final decision before the consultation period had even finished, or it rigged the process or ensured that it generated so few responses they could be ignored. This time, despite the far-reaching ramifications of the proposed changes to the extradition law, the government had shrunk the consultation period to a measly twenty days.

Meanwhile, murmurs of discontent had been building for months. In April, 130,000 people marched against the proposals. In May, the legislature erupted into vicious fistfights over the bill, a first in Hong

Kong. One legislator was rushed to the hospital and three others claimed injury after pro-Beijing and pro-democracy lawmakers fought for control over rival committees that could approve the contentious legislation. In June, the legal sector, clad in black like vultures, held a rare silent march. Even the normally supine business community was up in arms, spooked by the prospect of extradition for bribery or tax offenses committed, perhaps unwittingly, on the mainland. When we spoke, Nathan Law had described a "dual city" that was obvious only to those pushing the political boundaries. Now the bars of the cage were contracting, bringing them suddenly, horrifyingly, into view to the rest of the population.

Although I was living in Hong Kong at the time, true to form, I had failed to register the significance of the extradition law. My two adolescent children and I were living in a four-hundred-square-foot apartment on an outlying island, getting up at 5:45 every morning in order to catch the ferry that would get the kids to school on time. Our days passed in a daze of exhaustion, against an interminable soundtrack of squabbling. Our flat was so small and the children growing so fast that we were covered in bruises from bumping into furniture and each other. We learned to shrink ourselves to live in such a densely populated place; no singing, no dancing, no talking in loud voices. Exuberance was no longer possible, enthusiasm had to be tempered. Most of the public spaces near us— tiled squares outside supermarkets and children's playgrounds—were privately managed, with all kinds of interdictions. We had to moderate our personalities until the weekends, when we could unleash ourselves on the mountain hillsides that by default had become our backyard. When the children complained about the lack of space, I'd remind them we had exactly the average for public rental housing: just over 140 square feet per person.

Space and time had become luxuries that seemed entirely out of our reach. When I watched Netflix, I no longer cared what the actors were wearing. Instead, my eyes feasted on the rooms they inhabited. I was hungry for excess, scanning for walk-in closets or bathrooms with twin sinks. I was becoming addicted to space porn. Our tiny two-bedroom apartment was less than half the size of what we'd called the "amah quarters" in the government-assigned accommodation of my childhood. My current Hong Kong lifestyle—though still very privileged—was a world away from my childhood existence of swimming pool parties and junk trips. Even though my salary as a university lecturer was far above average, at the end of every month I was always in debt. My budget was straining from the daily ferry fares and the exorbitant cost of groceries at the local supermarket, which charged around three dollars (HK$23) for six slices of bread. At night as I totted up the outgoings, I wondered how shop attendants and janitors managed to survive. I'd come to Hong Kong to write about politics, yet the very act of living was sapping all my energy.

All this was a by-product of Hong Kong's economic system, whereby a few fabulously wealthy family-owned conglomerates controlled large blocks of land as well as key services such as telecommunications companies, public transport services, and utilities. I paid my mobile phone bill to one property developer and my electricity bill to another. When I rode on the bus, shopped in a mall, sipped coffee at Starbucks, or even bought the overpriced bread from my local supermarket, the tycoons ended up profiting. The city was an oligopoly whose economy was sliced up into sectors controlled in an almost feudal manner. This system had begun under the British and continued after the return of sovereignty. Beijing depended on the tycoons, and sometimes leaned on them, summoning them at times of political tension to ensure they kept the ship steady.

The idea of Hong Kongers as purely economic actors had so thoroughly informed—and been reinforced by—their British and Chinese rulers that Hong Kongers themselves had come to believe it. But it had never been true. Although Hong Kongers liked money, they were also political animals to the bone. When their interests were threatened, they protested in great numbers, as they had during the Tiananmen Movement of 1989, the Article 23 crisis of 2003, and to oppose patriotic education in 2012. Further back, during British rule, there had also been long-forgotten political protests, including a coolie strike against the population tax in 1844, just two years after British occupation, the Six-Day War of 1899, and sporadic labor strikes against unjust laws.

The June 2019 protest, as the young marcher had so confidently predicted, brought no change. Three days later, the government announced its determination to press ahead with the second reading of the extradition bill. The outrage was so intense that a public strike was called, resulting in widespread actions ranging from bus service work-to-rule measures forbidding drivers from overtaking other vehicles to the shutdown of porn sites. Young protestors opted for direct action, encircling the Legislative Council building and camping out all night to block lawmakers from reaching the chamber.

The mood of nervy calm was heightened by choruses of "Sing Hallelujah to the Lord!" echoing around the complex, which encompasses the central government headquarters, the Legislative Council, and the chief executive's office. Some of the singers were in fact devout Christians, but others were exploiting a legal loophole that was rumored to permit such gatherings to be classified as religious meetings rather than public assemblies, sidestepping the need for police permission. Over the next few days, the endless repetition of that single verse became so implanted in my brain that, like a victim of musical Stockholm syndrome, I even heard it as the background track to my dreams.

Throughout the next day, June 12, crowds gathered around the Legco building, swelling in number as the day went on. My fourteen-year-old son, Daniel, wanted to see what was happening, so I met him at the subway station after school. We were walking along an elevated walkway toward Legco when a shout—"Riot police!"—went up in the distance.

Suddenly a crush of people swelled toward us, pushing us roughly back the way we'd come.

"You'd better go home," I said.

"Yes," my tall son replied, clutching my hands, reverting instantly to childhood. I put him on a train, then went back outside. The crowd was roaring. Clouds of a white substance were pluming into the air. I was standing on a balcony when two cameramen with hard hats and respirators pushed past me to climb up a ladder for a better shot.

"What's happening over there?"

"Tear gas," one said. "It's fucking way strong. Eyes are fucking burning."

I was stunned. The only time Hong Kong police had used tear gas against their own people since the handover had been during the Umbrella Movement. That breach of trust had been considered so profound that T-shirts had been produced to mark it, featuring a picture of a tear gas canister and the numerals "87" in memory of the total number of rounds fired. I even owned one myself.

At that moment, I got my first whiff. My ears were stinging, my eyes watering, and my mouth burning. Around me, everyone was coughing and rinsing their eyes with bottled water. Just then my phone pinged with a message from a friend, an imperious Indian novelist whom I was due to meet for a drink at the Pacific Place mall, near the legislature.

"Where are you now?" she wrote. "Just out of yoga."

I messaged back. "They're tear-gassing."

"OMG get out of there!"

By the time I reached her table in the gleaming marble and chrome atrium, my friend had ordered two glasses of pinot gris. I demurred that it was no time to drink.

"What else are you going to do?" she replied briskly. "It's not safe out there. Wine will make you feel better, then you can go back out again."

This struck me as journalistically unsound, but I sat down, dazed.

Gulping down my wine, I watched as masked protestors rushed into the mall, coughing and spluttering, and sat down in knots to administer first aid to one another. Nearby, a woman in a pussy-bow shirt and high-heeled pumps plowed on with her business meeting, raising the volume of her French-accented English to be heard over the booms of the tear gas canisters outside. In that instant, the dual city had become a single city.

Meanwhile, the police were deploying not only tear gas but rubber bullets, and the protests had been declared a riot. When I went back out, the front line had advanced to right outside the mall, and a furious crowd was facing off against police. A man was screaming, his voice cracking, his body shaking with rage. Another clambered over a barrier brandishing a homemade poster that read, "Policemen, aren't you Hong Kong people too?" The policemen charged an encampment of colorful umbrellas, sending people scattering. "Animals!" gasped someone beside me. "Crazy!" The world was tilting. Our fall was accelerating.

By the end of the day, 150 rounds of tear gas had been fired, almost twice the amount deployed during the entire Umbrella Movement. Three days later, Carrie Lam announced a "pause" to the extradition law, but she stopped short of withdrawing it. The gesture was too late in any case. By then, new demands had been added, including an investigation into police brutality, amnesty for those arrested, and a retraction of the "riot" label. These, along with a demand for genuine universal suffrage, became the five demands symbolized in the protest gesture of a single outstretched hand held high overhead. On a walkway near the government headquarters, protestors held up signs saying, "Do not shoot. We are Hong Kongers!"

Another march was called, a week after the first, this time with a black dress code that reflected the shift in mood, from a hopeful celebration of people power to a furious denunciation of police violence. This time I was attending as a reporter. It was too big a story to miss. Hong Kong's newspapers, apart from the *Apple Daily*, had been acquired by businessmen tied to China, and their coverage of the protests showed a clear bias, quoting mainly government sources and downplaying police violence. I doubted whether my own coverage would make any difference, but I wanted to feel that I had done my very best to reflect the voices of the multitudes on the ground. "At least you tried" was becoming my mantra, too.

This time, I wore a fluorescent press vest and carried my recording equipment as I walked alongside Ave, whose new sign read, "Teargas Me. I dare you." The spontaneous organization that had sprung up was impressive, with people along the route thrusting water bottles into our hands, fanning us, spritzing our faces, refilling our water bottles, then taking the empty bottles to recycle.

As we neared the government headquarters in Admiralty, we climbed up to a pedestrian bridge overlooking the road to get a sense of the size of the crowd. As I peered down, I felt a hot flush rising through my body, suffusing my chest and burning my cheeks. I was suddenly so giddy that I had to steady myself against the railing. Looking down on the mass of tiny heads was like watching an Aboriginal dot painting come to life. Just then, a cheer of "*Heung gong yan, gaa yau!* 香港人加油!" rolled through the crowd. This is a shout of encouragement that translates literally as "Add oil, Hong Kongers!" As the sound wave bounced below me, my throat felt thick, as if it were closing up. I was hot and breathless. It was, I realized with a jolt, the way that you feel when you first start dating someone that you really, really like. When you go to meet them in a bar and you spot each other across the room and you feel that sense of rightness in your gut. Like the bookseller Lam Wing-kee, I'd fallen in love with Hong Kong all over again.

Politics was redefining Hong Kongers' relationship with the city. That day an estimated 2 million people—out of 7 million—marched. It was a day of epiphanies when the city became more than simply the place we lived. Hong Kongers could see themselves as a nation, a political community with a distinctive identity and an appetite for autonomy. With their feet, Hong Kongers were stamping pilgrimage routes across the soil of their city to defend that identity and their values. Two slogans that I saw that day stood out: "You Can't Silence Us," on a banner hanging from a pedestrian walkway, and "We Stand For What We Stand On," emblazoned on T-shirts worn by members of Demosisto, a political party started by Joshua Wong. The foreknowledge of defeat added a painful poignancy to this extraordinary show of political imagination. The moral high ground would offer no refuge from police batons and tear gas.

"It's the only thing we can do. To walk. To sweat. But they do not listen," the eighty-seven-year-old Catholic prelate Cardinal Joseph Zen Ze-kiun told me. I had spotted his diminutive figure on a makeshift platform under a flyover, alongside the legislator-turned-political-prisoner Nathan Law. He was beaming and holding two thumbs aloft to encourage the crowds, sweat from the blistering summer heat plastering his snow-white hair across his forehead. The churches were providing sanctuary to young protestors, and many pastors offered vocal support from their pulpits. Their work in mainland China was at risk.

"It's a real fight between the good and the evil," Cardinal Zen told me when I visited him the next day at the Salesian Missionary House, where he lived. It was a quiet oasis of serenity, with high ceilings and statue-studded courtyards, though the atmosphere did not seem to have tempered the elderly cardinal. He came rushing into the room at speed. He was very busy, he said, and had no time to talk. But the moment we started talking, he could not stop. The unshakable force of his convictions gave him a touch of Yoda, though it issued in firebrand political pulpitry instead of gnomic utterances.

Cardinal Zen saw the church as having been a formidable force in hardwiring a stubborn sense of moral conviction into the Hong Kong psyche. One legacy of colonialization was Hong Kong's education system, which saw half the region's students—including many of the governing elite—educated in church schools. Continuing his depiction of a Manichean struggle, the cardinal's voice rose to a squeak. "The evil forces are strong. Other people are paid by the government to create disorder, to use violence. Maybe they are encouraging the policemen to be harsh on the young people. I always pity the police because they are put in a dangerous situation by the government. It's all secret! All in the dark! This is the work of sin!" He was now pounding the table, red-faced and sweating, and I was worrying about his blood pressure.

The cardinal did not spare Hong Kongers responsibility for enabling their own suppression. "We really are too patient," he fumed. "We support so many things. We are *pretending* that there is still rule of law so they can condemn so many people to prison and they can disqualify elected legislators with hundreds of thousands of votes. And we don't know what to do until the moment they provoke us to come out to walk." This was the first time I'd heard someone else voice that feeling I'd had outside the High Court, that we were living in a kind of simulacrum, a political make-believe where our imaginations had been colonized for so long that we were desperate to believe whatever our rulers told us, no matter how much evidence there was to the contrary.

Just before I left, I asked the cardinal what he thought of Carrie Lam. Lam was a devout Catholic who had voiced her belief that she would go to heaven for the good things she'd done. The cardinal had no words of charity. "A servant of the devil!" he hissed, with such vehemence that I felt an involuntary twinge of sympathy for her. In just five words, he had consigned her soul to eternal damnation. With God on his side, he was a formidable foe.

With the marches, Hong Kongers were reclaiming politics, moving it out of the gerrymandered legislature and onto the streets. One day I went to Legco to meet Alvin Yeung Ngok-kiu, an Oxford-educated barrister who headed the pan-Democratic Civic Party. He was disheveled and exhausted after two days and nights on the streets, literally standing between police and protestors to try to forestall any violence. "We are not asking for the moon!" he said. "We are not asking for something that we never deserved! We are simply asking for something that is clearly written in the Basic Law, that should be a promise." This simple message was proving difficult for the government to counter, so it did not try, refusing to negotiate. And so the tension continued to ratchet up.

"But isn't this a dangerous game to play?" I asked.

He met my gaze. "If this is the game, we try to see how far we can get."

Soon there were deaths to mourn. The first was a thirty-five-year-old man named Marco Leung Ling-kit who had been holding a five-hour sit-in on the roof of the same shopping mall where I'd sipped wine amid the tear gas. He wore a yellow raincoat and perched next to a handwritten sign that included the words "Make Love, No Shoot!" As an emergency services team closed in on him, he'd fallen. Then a twenty-one-year-old student at the Education University jumped from a building, leaving a suicide note scrawled on a wall in red Sharpie. Her Chinese characters got larger toward the end of her message, as if she were shouting into a void, ending in, "I'm sacrificing my insignificant life in the hope the wishes of two million Hong Kongers will be honored. Please continue the fight."

The July 1 anniversary of Hong Kong's return was approaching, and it felt like this year's protest march would be explosive. The day started with rival flag-raising ceremonies. The administration officials, under physical and psychological siege, conducted theirs surrounded by riot police and heavy plastic barriers filled with water, with invited guests watching on closed-circuit television. The protestors had already held a preemptive sunrise ceremony outside the Legislative Council, hoisting a flag depicting a blackened and decaying bauhinia flower. The movement was reclaiming the symbols of state as their own.

I went to the march early with my kids, fearing trouble might break out as the day wore on. Ave's latest sign referenced the pro-police or "blue" rallies, as well as the already familiar sight of police hoisting black signs to warn of imminent tear gas. It read:

China is red
Violence is blue
Tear gas is black
Bruises are too.

The marchers were carrying white paper flowers, which they piled outside Pacific Place in remembrance of Yellow Raincoat Man. The mood this time was bitter desolation, with some sobbing as they bowed at a makeshift shrine. It felt like they were mourning their own futures.

While marching, we heard that protestors were trying to break into the Legislative Council building, so I sent the kids home and headed over. At Legco, the atmosphere reminded me of a medieval battle. Protestors had ripped metal rods from the side of the building and were using them as battering rams to break through its reinforced glass windows, while others beat time using the same poles. They were arming themselves with makeshift shields made from cardboard and dive floats, as if they were children playing at war. To everyone's surprise, the police had withdrawn completely. Watching from a raised walkway, I was transfixed by this ballet of destruction, set to the staccato beat of a building being ripped apart. Yellow-helmeted protestors surged and billowed in waves. They'd developed a sign language for getting supplies to the front, and every so often a wave of snipping fingers would cascade in one direction high above people's heads, answered by a stream of pliers or zip ties passed hand to hand overhead in return.

At one point, protestors let off a smoke bomb, and everyone put on their gas masks. Just then my phone rang. It was Ave.

"Hi! Is it okay if I watch a film on Netflix?"

"Fine!" I hollered through my gas mask, hoping they couldn't hear the sound of thousands of people yelling as they stumbled back and forth in panic.

"Okay, bye! Don't get tear-gassed, Mum!"

To break the strange mix of tedium and tension, I chatted with a journalist.

"What beat do you normally cover?" I asked.

"Politics," he laughed wryly as he removed his goggles to swab the rivulets of sweat streaming down his face. "I'm on the Legco beat."

"What do you think will happen?"

"The protestors will end up paying," he replied without hesitation.

When the protestors finally breached the building, I followed them gingerly inside. I was met by a scene of breathtaking defilement. An alarm was shrieking, papers were scattered all over the floor, and the walls were covered with anti-government graffiti. One of the first things I saw was a pillar spray-painted in Chinese with, "It was you who taught us that nonviolent protest is not effective." If the Umbrella Movement, which had been characterized as *wolifei*—peaceful, rational, and nonviolent—had failed to win a single concession, this new movement was consciously diverging from that path. Its most visible face was the *yongmou*, the frontline "brave warriors" with their respirators, yellow helmets, and goggles. Those who did not support violence refused to criticize it publicly, and that solidarity helped forge a common identity.

On closer inspection, the storming of Legco was a finely calibrated act of provocation. The protestors had targeted the emblems of power, for example spray-painting over half of Hong Kong's emblem to delete the words "People's Republic of China," while leaving the words "Special Administrative Region of Hong Kong" untouched. They defaced photographs of unpopular politicians, but left libraries and porcelain artifacts unharmed. They'd even left money in the fridge to pay for the drinks they'd consumed. It was an assault targeting the structural violence of a system that had disenfranchised its people, and it marked a widening of the movement to target Hong Kong's lack of democracy.

Inside the chamber, a skinny young man in a black T-shirt and shorts jumped onto a bench, removing his mask to reveal his gaunt face as other protestors tried to pull him down with their hands. Revealing his identity was a risky move since rioting carried a sentence of up to ten years. When the young man spoke, his voice was shaking with urgency. "I took off my mask to let everyone know that we Hong Kongers cannot lose any more," he said, jabbing the air with his finger. "If we retreat, we will be the 'rioters' tomorrow, as TVB will call us. They will be filming the destruction and mess in the Legco building and condemning us as rioters. Our entire civil society would not recover from this for the next ten years. Our students will be arrested. Our leaders will be arrested." His words made clear how entwined the political struggle was with the struggle for narrative control. That was why Chan Kin-man had taken the stand, and that was why this young man was risking ten years in jail.

Who was this young man? I had a nagging sense that I'd seen him somewhere, a reportorial ache in my gut that continued long after the protestors left the chamber and riot police cleared the streets with tear gas. It turned out that I knew him, by sight at least. Around ten days before, I'd attended an academic conference and seen him co-present a brilliant paper on authoritarianism, countermobilization, and civil society. His name was Brian Leung Kai-ping, and he was a twenty-five-year-old PhD candidate at the University of Washington. As an undergraduate in 2014, he'd edited a hugely controversial book called *Hong Kong as a Nation*, which had advocated the consolidation of Hong Kong nationalism to avoid assimilation into China. Back then it had been an edgy proposition, criticized by then chief executive Leung Chun-ying. Now it was political dynamite.

The conference had been—and I don't use this word lightly—electrifying. Leung had been part of a panel on political clientelism, which is the practice of vote buying or awarding favors for electoral turnout. His research uncovered the delicate network of ties between Beijing-friendly organizations catering to new migrants from the mainland. These hometown associations and federations gained huge amounts of funding from district councils and the business community, which they used to do China's bidding in Hong Kong, whether by mobilizing members to march in support of government policy or getting them to vote for pro-government candidates at elections. The effect was to crowd out preexisting civil society groups, diverting government funding for political ends. Leung's paper had included a graphic that illustrated Beijing's new networks of power in Hong Kong in a rainbow wheel of looping, intersecting ribbons. When I checked my notes to see what I'd written about his presentation, I read, "Repression may backfire. Cooptation does not necessarily absorb dissenting voices." Brian Leung had ended up living out his research.

The day after the storming of Legco, my children and I left Hong Kong to move back to Melbourne, as it was time to return to my teaching job. Until Covid hit, I shuttled back and forth to chart the horrifying escalation that was playing out. The protests quickly spread to every corner of Hong Kong, as protestors adopted tactics inspired by the philosophy of hometown kung fu master Bruce Lee: "Be formless, shapeless, like water. . . . [W]ater can flow or it can crash." In practice, this translated to the flash gatherings and equally sudden dispersals described to me years earlier by Benny Tai, though he himself was still incarcerated for charges relating to the Umbrella Movement. The police began withholding permission for marches, citing public safety, and sometimes even declaring them illegal halfway through. This meant that vast numbers of hitherto law-abiding people became used to violating the law on a regular basis.

The days and nights were melding into a single livestream of tear gas, deployed with horrifying and mesmerizing beauty. A smoking dragon tail of sparks from tear gas grenades would arc through the air before exploding into wispy tendrils that snaked their way across the ground, then plumed upward and outward to cloak Hong Kong's dense skyscraper-lined streets. From this disco haze, a whole new society was emerging.

At night the streets occupied by protestors served as a catwalk for frontliners, who accessorized their respirators with long black nylon gloves, flowing black capes, and fuck-off boots. Medics with red crosses inked on their helmets patrolled, and I even saw a dog collar–wearing clergyman whose hard hat advertised emergency pastoral services. "Firefighting crews" wearing yellow plastic gloves—sometimes just ordinary plastic dishwashing gloves—had figured out ingenious ways of quenching the noxious canisters. They'd pluck them off the road and pop them into a thermos flask, shaking it until the canister was disarmed. Or they'd place a traffic cone on top of the canister, then pour water through the tip of the cone to extinguish the canister.

The police response was a combination of more tear gas and violence. Within weeks, police had thrown tear gas grenades down crowded alleys and inside shopping malls and subway stations. They fired eight hundred rounds in a single day, depleting their reserves so quickly they began deploying expired canisters with use-by dates four years past. By the end of 2019, the police had fired sixteen thousand rounds of tear gas, violating both their own guidelines and the Chemical Weapons Convention.

At the end of July, in an echo of what had happened in Mongkok in 2014, local triads in Yuen Long near the Chinese border ran amok inside a subway station, rampaging through train carriages armed with long sticks and metal poles. The triads, who were dressed in white T-shirts, were looking for black-clad protestors but ended up beating anyone in their path. The police did not arrive for thirty-five minutes, even though their phone lines were jammed with twenty-four thousand calls for help. Hong Kongers were facing a new reality: public security as guaranteed by the police was well and truly dead. At the end of August, the police themselves attacked passengers on a subway train at Prince Edward station who they believed to be demonstrators returning home after a march. A young couple were filmed on their knees, clinging to each other, weeping and pleading for mercy. This was the face of a population under assault from its own police force. The sense of abandonment was palpable, as if the ground had been cut away from underneath, leaving the population in a frightening limbo.

When I wasn't in Hong Kong, I spent my nights hooked to a website that played nine different livestreams on a single screen, showing a perpetual panopticon of police brutality. I could no longer sleep. When I did doze off, my dreams were studded with pure fear, as I was chased by storm trooper–like policemen along streets slicked with blood, unable to find any doors that would open to offer shelter. Reality seemed to merge with fiction in the most appalling ways, such as when police began impersonating protestors. At one protest, I saw a young man wearing a brown McDonald's bag over his head to hide his identity, his eyes wild through the torn-out eyeholes. The same night, I met a young frontliner whose black T-shirt read, "#Scaredbaby @嚇死寶寶了."

At another protest I interviewed a pair of fifteen-year-olds dressed in black with red and blue bandannas across their faces. Three months before, they'd spent their weekends playing football. Now they worked as backup for the frontliners, tearing up bricks, building barricades, and running from the cops.

"The first and second time I was really scared, but now I'm not," one told me.

"Of course I'm scared, but we have no choice. We have to stand out here and fight for Hong Kong," said the other.

I had sometimes suspected the young protestors were drawn in by the video game glamour of a movement that offered adrenaline, camaraderie, and a kind of political Tinder all rolled up in one, along with the highest stakes possible. Speaking to these two made me ashamed of those thoughts. When I asked about the prospect of spending ten years—two-thirds of their lives so far—in jail, one replied, "I know what I'm doing. And I know if I was arrested what I will face. But we are fighting for freedom, democracy, and justice." They were only a year older than my son, and as we spoke, I remembered his clammy hand in mine the day we'd fled the riot police.

Sometimes the protestors acted with frightening and incomprehensible violence. In August, they descended en masse on the international airport, turning on two mainland Chinese men they believed were government agents. They surrounded them, beating them and even zip-tying one man to a luggage trolley. This act of mob justice carried on until the man, who turned out to be a journalist for China's state-run media, seemed close to death. The next day, the protestors apologized. Standing in the arrivals hall, they held up a handwritten poster reading: "Our police shot us, government betrayed us, social institutions failed us. Please give us a second chance." But a spokesman in Beijing was already describing the protests as showing "characteristics of terrorism."

The spiral of escalation was feeding off itself, with each act of violence begetting a mirroring response. The frontliners began picking up tear gas canisters and lobbing them back, then graduated to throwing bricks at police and setting fires in the streets. Then came Molotov cocktails. This behavior was stoked by the violence with which police carried out arrests, slamming young people to the ground, twisting their hands behind their backs, grinding their bleeding faces into the street.

Friends were being arrested. One day I woke up to see pictures of Johnson Yeung Ching-yin being detained. A policeman was shining a torch directly into his eyes, and his face was sheet-white and dazed. He described how the police punched him in the face and kicked him as he was lying on the ground when they recognized him as a human rights activist. He was released a few days later. It was his fifth arrest. He tweeted, "If I get arrested again, my bail will probably be denied. However, I feel freer when I am fighting with my people."

The protests were changing Hong Kong irrevocably, leaving pro-government and pro-democracy camps with no middle ground. Families were riven painfully apart, often along generational lines. This was the case with my own extended family. Our closest relatives in Hong Kong were some elderly cousins who'd fled China during the Cultural Revolution and moved to North Point, a stronghold of pro-China sentiment. For decades, they'd celebrated all the festivals with us, arriving beaming on our doorstep with red lai see packets for Spring Festival, mooncakes for Mid-Autumn Festival, and piles of presents for Christmas.

After the protests started, we met for dinner at a Thai restaurant. Almost immediately, my cousin, whom I'd always known as a kind and patient music teacher, started talking about the protestors. "They're so infantile!" she said, and I was shocked by the harshness in her voice. "They're ignorant! So ignorant! These young people haven't been well taught. There's something wrong with the education system here. They have all these opportunities to make money. And then they do this." Such views were typical of older migrants, who'd been victims of the unforgiving tides of Chinese history and feared political chaos with a visceral dread.

Her view—reinforced by the Chinese state-run media—was of spoiled children running amok, risking Hong Kong's hard-won safety and order. Beijing's line was to emphasize the economic factors stoking discontent, neatly shifting the blame for high property prices to the tycoons. Facing this criticism, the tycoons pledged land for affordable housing in a move that everyone knew was irrelevant to the protests but served to underline how beholden they had become to Beijing.

The pro-government camp had mobilized to organize a series of pro-China, pro-police rallies, likely harnessing the groups that Brian Leung had been researching. When I went to one, I arrived half an hour before the official finish time and found that almost everyone had already left. A few stragglers were still posing for selfies, bearing banners with the names of their universities or cities in China. I began chatting with a scientist, who, like my cousin, found the protestors' behavior inexplicable. "They say they have no freedom, no democracy. This is not true!" he said, his voice rising with agitation. Every day he saw footage from the pro-Beijing media of masked protestors attacking the police with bricks and hammers. To him, it looked like terrorism, and the police needed public support to crush it. "If the police use violence to stop another violence, it's good, there's no problem." By the time we had finished talking, the site was deserted. The waste bins were overflowing with crumpled Chinese flags that the pro-Beijing protestors had discarded after their photo ops, leaving some of the five-star flags blackened by footprints, having been trampled underfoot in the rush for the exit.

Meanwhile, the protest movement was coalescing into a political Hong Kong nation, with its own anthem and battle cry. The rallying cry was ambiguous and hard to translate: 光復香港時代革命, or "Liberate Hong Kong, Revolution of Our Times!" Some heard the slogan as an appeal to restore Hong Kong's freedoms, while others saw it as a call for independence. The phrase had been coined by Edward Leung Tin-kei, a young localist serving six years in prison on charges of rioting and assaulting a police officer during a violent scuffle known as the Fishball Revolution in 2016. Leung had founded a pro-independence political party called Hong Kong Indigenous, and had been banned from running in the 2016 elections and was now in prison. The resurgence of this slogan turned him into the intellectual godfather of this new movement.

A rousing unofficial anthem had also materialized. "Glory to Hong Kong" had been styled as a marching song by a twenty-something musician who called himself Thomas dgx yhl. He'd posted a draft version online, seeking feedback. The responses asked him to add the slogan "Liberate Hong Kong, Revolution of Our Times!" to the lyrics, which he did. Such crowdsourcing was a feature of the movement, a repudiation of the government's top-down directives. Its aim was democracy, and it tried to use democratic methods at every level. Within days, "Glory to Hong Kong" was being sung at every march:

Though deep is the dread that lies ahead
Yet still, with our faith, on we tread.
Let blood rage afield! Our voice grows evermore
For Hong Kong may glory reign!

With each rendition of its new anthem, the Hong Kong nation was finding its voice. Song became an act of protest, as flash mob choirs gathered in shopping malls. Sometimes the pro-Beijing groups mobilized rival choirs, who would try to drown out "Glory to Hong Kong" with shouted renditions of the Chinese national anthem. The symbolism was lost on no one.

The movement was redefining what it meant to be a Hong Konger, reducing a constellation of possibilities into a singular pole of opposition to the Chinese identity imposed by Beijing. Surveys showed that the overlap between identifying as a Hong Konger and as Chinese had disappeared; at one point, just 0.3 percent of Hong Kongers aged between eighteen and twenty-nine identified as Chinese. This was not a matter of birthright; some of the movement's most famous faces, like Nathan Law and Edward Leung, had been born in China but educated in Hong Kong, showing that it was possible to become a Hong Konger by embracing Hong Kong values.

One day I was at a rally in Central's Statue Square when Brian Leung, the young man who had unmasked himself in Legco and subsequently fled to the US, appeared on the big screen. Immediately a hush of almost religious intensity fell over the crowd. On-screen, Leung said, "The essence of 'Hong Konger' exists nowhere else but in our minds. And we reconstitute and strengthen this identity through our every struggle and daily practices. We take them as close as our own hands and feet, even if we have never seen their true likenesses; we take them as our kin even if we are never related to them in blood. Every sacrifice they made—their blood, their freedom, or even lives—are here to nurture this community of suffering." To be a Hong Konger was no longer race based or even location based. It was an imagined political community united by suffering.

The movement was also pouring its imagination into innovating the act of protest. Boys and girls so young they were sometimes too shy to hold hands gripped either end of a pen—"pen-zoning," as it became known—to form human chains around their schools before class or during lunch break. A human chain almost sixty kilometers long snaked around the whole of Hong Kong, straggling up the craggy ridge of Lion Rock to illuminate the entire territory with points of light from mobile phone screens. The "Ten O'Clock Call" became a nightly event, with people shouting protest slogans from the anonymity of their apartments. The first time I heard it, I was standing on a Sheung Wan street flanked by low-rise buildings. Suddenly I heard a frail male voice breaking the silence with a quavered, "Hong Kong people!" From the other side of the road, a confident voice responded loudly, "Add oil!" Tears pricked my eyes.

In early September, Carrie Lam finally withdrew the legislative proposals, but it was far, far too late. The battle for Hong Kong's soul had already spilled over its borders, causing clashes between Hong Kong supporters and mainland Chinese on campuses around the world. The atmosphere was so febrile that when I agreed to moderate a panel in Melbourne with Hong Kong pop star Denise Ho Wan-see, exiled Chinese artist Badiucao, and author Clive Hamilton, we were rejected by one venue after another on security grounds. When a location was finally secured, the threats against us were so credible that we held the event under the protection of a dozen police cars and mounted police. Even overseas, the space for discussing Hong Kong was shrinking.

On the ground in Hong Kong, the atmosphere was becoming increasingly dangerous. The police had stopped wearing their warrant numbers and were using new water cannons that marked protestors with indelible blue chemicals. Their aim was often directed at the press. When I asked a reporter friend to describe the sensation of being "smurfed," as it was nicknamed, she described intense pain, saying, "I felt like dying." As the risks escalated, I'd upgraded my half-face mask to an expensive full-face respirator. In August, I'd been slightly embarrassed to wear it. By October I was offering silent prayers of gratitude for my purchase.

I got used to being tear-gassed, but being pepper-sprayed was a shock. The first time it happened, I was videoing the arrest of a man in Causeway Bay. It was just after two on a Sunday afternoon, so early in the day that I hadn't bothered to don my protective gear. Suddenly a police officer squirted something at me, with no warning. I saw liquid slithering down the lenses of my spectacles. Then I felt the burning on my face, my neck, my arms, even sliding down my T-shirt to sting my chest and back. I was being bitten by a thousand fire ants, over and over again. I doused myself with a bottle of water, then stumbled into a nearby restaurant, where I stripped in the bathroom and washed. But each time I was tear-gassed throughout that day, my naked arms stung and throbbed as if they'd been flayed. And of course this was nothing compared to the Indonesian journalist who lost an eye from a beanbag, and the many other journalists who were beaten, harassed, and detained. The repeated exposure to tear gas was sickening some frontline reporters; one friend became so ill he was forced to spend a month in bed.

For me, the most terrifying moment of 2019 came on China's National Day, October 1. The contrast between the respective parades could not have been greater: the serried ranks of Chinese soldiers goose-stepping through Beijing's empty streets and the furious, messy spontaneity of the black-clad protestors congregating for Hong Kong's unofficial march, some wearing *V for Vendetta* masks. This march was unauthorized, but it seemed so peaceful that I stopped in Central to get a bubble tea. When I emerged five minutes later, the streets were pungent with freshly fired tear gas, and dozens of police buses were blocking the main waterfront road. That day, clashes broke out in thirteen places, and police used live ammunition for the first time, shooting an eighteen-year-old student in the chest at point-blank range after he attacked a policeman with a pole. The man survived but was charged with assault and rioting while still in his hospital bed.

I was standing on a Wanchai street with a bunch of reporters, filming a wave of policemen clad like storm troopers in black armor, with guns slung over their chests, as they came toward us, sweeping through the streets. As they approached, one policeman grabbed a nearby bystander—a portly man wearing a face mask, black clothes, and beige backpack—to arrest him. As we swiveled to film, another policeman stuck his gun in the face of the reporter right next to me, a young woman wearing jeans, a fluorescent jacket, and a green shirt. Then he swung his gun around to point at each of us in turn. I couldn't breathe. A gasp stayed stuck in my throat, and I backed away as fast as I could, hands shaking. I was ashamed of my own lack of bravery, but journalistic impulses were no match for my instinct for self-preservation. I ducked down an alley, sidestepping the ashes of a small fire, only to encounter another phalanx of equally aggressive policemen. Around the corner, I could see yet another. News organizations began withdrawing reporters from the street after a radio journalist was wounded in the head. It was clear that the accepted laws of war did not apply in this conflict zone. It was time to head home.

As I walked, I saw a metal door open, and an elderly man poked his head out to scan in all directions. When he saw that the coast was clear, he ducked back in. A long line of young people in colorful clothes hurried out the same door, their faces pale and pinched with fear. I understood straightaway what I was seeing; the man had been sheltering the protestors from the police, who were arresting anyone wearing black clothes. These were almost certainly total strangers to him, but he'd taken them in to allow them to change out of their protest gear. His furtive, fearful face was like a scene from the French Occupation. Indeed, to Hong Kongers, the police had become the visible face of an occupying force.

The next morning I attended a hearing for ninety-seven people, including two fourteen-year-olds. It was the biggest mass trial in Hong Kong's post-handover history. All but one were appearing on charges of rioting, which carried a ten-year maximum sentence. Almost as soon as the hearing began, it had to be adjourned; some among the first batch of dazed protestors who appeared in the dock hadn't yet seen their lawyers that morning. In some cases, charges hadn't even been readied, making it impossible for lawyers to put together an argument for release. The legal system was overwhelmed and tottering; due process had all but been suspended. Hundreds of black-clad protestors were occupying the lower levels of the court building to show their support for the defendants. When I asked one whether he knew them personally, he replied, "Ninety-seven people are in court today. They are all my brothers and family." Under attack, the Hong Kong nation was drawing together.

But Hong Kongers were soon to find out, in the very worst way, that they still had the capacity for horror. After the death of another student, protestors started a week of direct action, blocking roads and disrupting transport services. A policeman shot a protestor in the stomach, then protestors set a man on fire, leaving him with horrendous burns. From there, things got worse.

In November, police and student protestors fought a twenty-four-hour battle over a footbridge at the Chinese University of Hong Kong. This was straight-up urban warfare, with police firing endless fusillades of tear gas at students, who responded with petrol bombs and bows and arrows. By the end of the week, the students had moved to the Polytechnic University, blocking the entrance to the vitally important Cross Harbor Tunnel. Police locked down the university, arresting volunteer first-aiders who were trying to leave. A delegation of high school principals entered, to escort more than a hundred minors from the site under an amnesty arrangement. I spoke to one later, a seventeen-year-old. He didn't believe the promise that there would be no repercussions. "I'm on the list to be arrested," he told me, without flinching. "I'm just waiting."

This time there was no doubt the action would be violent. The protestors even practiced throwing Molotov cocktails into the university's fifty-meter swimming pool. The police response was an unrelenting barrage of tear gas, rubber bullets, pepper spray, water cannon fire, and even sound waves from a long-range audio device. A place of learning had become a battleground. Students escaped by crawling through sewers or lowering themselves from pedestrian bridges with ropes. The clashes lasted for nearly two weeks, and when they ended, 1,100 people had been arrested. The violence was so intense and unrelenting that many of those inside the university, including reporters, developed symptoms of PTSD.

Even the act of witnessing was becoming unbearable. I saw police marshaling girls dressed in black, with their arms on one another's shoulders, into a police van in a grotesque conga line. Police making people kneel in rows on the street so they could arrest them. Police detaining a woman in the lobby of her own building, because she had gone downstairs to check her mailbox. A policeman throwing a tear gas canister vertically so it fell straight back down on the policeman himself. It was a sign of how normalized tear gas had become that this made us laugh. But we could not look away. Witnessing was necessary so that we should all know—and remember—what the government had done.

Carrie Lam called the protestors "enemies of the people," a chilling phrase straight from the Chinese Communist Party lexicon. But it was hard to know who were the enemies and who were the people. Then, out of the bleakness, came a moment of clarity. For months, government officials had talked about a silent majority who supported their actions. The district elections in November 2019 offered a way of testing this assertion. When the results came in, it turned out that—yet again—the government had been deaf to the people; the silent majority supported the protest movement, which won in a landslide. Seventeen of the eighteen district councils flipped from pro-Beijing control to pan-democratic forces. But this did not change a government that had never been answerable to the people.

One of the new wave of politicians was Clara Cheung, a self-possessed artist whose hair was cut in a sharp bob. Her district, Happy Valley, had been held by a pro-Beijing incumbent for sixteen years. She'd run against his son out of sheer desperation. "I thought we've actually lost a lot, probably everything," she told me as she showed me round her office, a tiny triangle tucked into the side of a building. She won with a vote swing of 15 percent.

It was hard for me to square the cognitive dissonance of continuing resistance with the inevitability that the movement would be suppressed. Over noodles, I broached this with Cheung. She answered by describing a recent work of performance art, in which she had performed a symbolic farewell to Hong Kong. She buried her entire body in the soil of Hong Kong at a spot facing the hypermodern skyscraper-dotted skyline of Shenzhen. Through that action, she said she had found the strength to fight for election. "I am already dead," she told me. "I've already done that, so I would be brave enough to do whatever. I know I'm not going to commit suicide because I did that already." I understood what she was trying to say; we had lost our old city forever, and our old selves along with that. We had no choice but to reinvent ourselves.

As Hong Kongers reimagined and reshaped their identity, familiar sights were disappearing. Chinese state-run banks and certain outlets perceived as being pro-China, including Starbucks, were vanishing behind white wooden or metal hoardings fronted with signs claiming they were undergoing "maintenance" or "enhancement." They were bunkering up against protestors vandalizing Chinese-owned businesses and companies sympathetic to Beijing. "They've gone underground," one friend commented, "like the Communist Party itself." Despite Hong Kong's return to China, the Communist Party is still officially nonexistent in Hong Kong.

The armor of the shops represented the outward trappings of intensifying economic warfare. The protest movement was weaponizing economics by boycotting "blue" or pro-police, pro-government businesses, while redirecting business toward "yellow" or pro-protest businesses. A new app, Wolipay, helped identify businesses according to their political affiliation. In response, the government issued a plethora of commentary criticizing the "yellow economic circle" as nonsensical and even immoral.

There were other physical changes to the city. The authorities had caged in the sides of overhead pedestrian walkways with chicken wire to prevent protestors from throwing projectiles. Using them now felt like walking through a giant chicken coop, or a prison. Turnstiles were being installed on university campuses, and more and more foreign academics and activists were being barred from entering Hong Kong. The city was being locked down, and critics of Beijing were being kept out.

There were other disappearances. The Lunar New Year fair was a Hong Kong ritual. In my childhood, we'd gone to Victoria Park to buy toys, peach blossom sprays, and waist-high kumquat trees, whose fruit my mother would later use to make marmalade. I'd carried on the tradition with my own children; on the most recent Year of the Pig, we'd taken home a bubble tea–guzzling toy pig and a cushion that looked like a can of Spam. But in 2020, the government banned dry goods and political stalls. A group who tested the new rules by sharing political information on their stall saw it promptly shut down. No more boba pigs or boba anything else, for that matter.

One day I went to a Lennon Wall–building event near the Legislative Council. From afar I could see only the yellow and orange fluorescent vests of the press pack, ringed at a distance by small squads of Black Panthers, the elite response team from the Correctional Services Department who had been reassigned from suppressing prison riots to quelling urban unrest. With their full-body armor, including black bulletproof vests, black knee and shoulder pads, and lethal weapons, they looked like cosplayers. They had plastic zip ties tucked into their vests, guns holstered on their legs, and truncheons strapped across their backs. Earlier in the day, the police had warned that a hundred people had been arrested at Lennon Walls for criminal behavior over the previous six months. The intimidation worked. When I arrived, the tiny handful of protestors were already leaving without posting anything, and the wall remained bare. A single Post-it Note on the hanging roots of a nearby banyan tree read, "F__K police. F__K government."

Another day I met a friend involved in garment manufacturing. He had been unable to import black T-shirts from China. Although they hadn't been officially banned, everyone working in fashion knew about the curbs. (Rumor had it that Post-it Notes and yellow helmets were also on the banned list.) "The government is so nonsensical," he said. "They can ban all black outfits—black T-shirts, black pants—and they really think they can solve the problem? It's so stupid." Words had been disappearing, and now colors were starting to disappear, too.

After the earliest marches in Hong Kong, I had marveled at the ability of this megalopolis to reset itself, to shake off the unrest and return to normal overnight. Some days I'd get the ferry home after midnight, leaving behind streets occupied by hundreds of thousands of people, with black-clad protestors setting up barricades and building elaborate bamboo structures. By seven the next morning, when I returned to go to work, the streets were entirely clear. It was as if the events of the night before had been a fantastical dream. But slowly the dream was impinging upon everyday life as the government increased its interdictions. The majority of the population was still going about their everyday lives, shopping at the wet markets and reading newspapers over breakfast noodles. But people had slowly stopped talking about certain topics. First tear-gassing had become so run-of-the-mill that it hardly rated a mention, then the outrage at mass arrests had become blunted. It was hard to function with a perpetual sense of anger, yet the muting of emotion that accompanied the normalization of the abnormal was alarming.

The protest strategies kept changing. The movement had become so efficient that one friend told me that it took only a couple days to muster up a rally fifty thousand strong. Big weekend marches were bolstered by smaller pop-up actions such as "eat with me" lunchtime protests for office workers, and "sing with me" morning protests for schoolchildren. Protest activity was being integrated into everyday life.

The mood among protestors was bleaker than ever, laced with desperate humor. One day I met a group so young that some were still in secondary school. "Really, really bad things happen to our generation," one told me. "SARS. The Umbrella Movement. And now this." It was true. Their cohort, born around the time of the 1997 handover, had been nicknamed the Cursed Generation. The class of 2003 kindergarten graduation had been canceled because of the outbreak of SARS; their primary school graduation in 2009 was called off because of swine flu; their last year of secondary school had been interrupted by the Umbrella Movement. Now some of their university graduations had been canceled.

"Are you hopeful?" I asked.

"No."

"Not at all?"

"Not at all."

They all felt the movement was doomed, but that didn't change their determination to continue.

"We all stood up, but we all have our backs against the wall," said one young man.

"There's no turning back," said another.

"There's basically only one course right now. You either fight back or you get caught by police," said a solid, jovial-looking young man. He was a frontliner, and he had no compunction about using violence. "It's not like a normal struggle. It's like a war. The government is using military-grade weapons like real guns against the protestors. We need to fight back and stand together against this government." He'd been tear-gassed probably a hundred times, and pepper-sprayed five times. When I asked what they thought the movement should now do, one flicked two stickers from her pocket. One read, "Fuck your mother," and the other said, "Keep on fighting till the bitter end." They all burst into laughter.

One day I visited MC Yan in his studio, where he was holding court, dressed in a white lab coat and gray open-toed slippers. The room felt emptier without his precious pug, Gudiii, who had died just a few months before, at the age of seventeen. MC Yan had conducted more than a month of funerary rituals to aid his beloved dog's rebirth as a higher life form.

His band, LMF, had intended to retire after an upcoming twentieth-anniversary show on January 1. Instead, he'd ended up penning a song called "2019," which had become another anthem of the movement. The band's recording studio was in Mongkok, a few hundred meters from a police station targeted by protestors. For nights on end, they'd watched pitched battles unfolding, smelled the tear gas filtering into the studio. They'd ended up recording a dark, angry song over a thudding beat that echoed the soundtrack of *Lee Rock*, a 1981 film about police corruption. The name "2019" consciously invoked George Orwell's *1984*. "Hong Kong is actually a time machine," MC Yan told me gleefully in his slow hippie drawl, leaning forward conspiratorially and widening his eyes. "We're reversing back from 1997 to 1984."

Some people thought MC Yan was crazy, partly because he couldn't stop talking about topics that other people avoided. I'd become used to his torrent of words, often delivered with rolling eyes. I was never sure if he was a genius or a crackpot, a feeling that intensified after I rashly let him open my third eye with polyphonic sound. I'm still not sure if I believe in third eyes, but I can say that the experience left me shaken. Over the years I'd learned that MC Yan's observations, no matter how left-field they sounded, usually contained a hard kernel of undeniable truth. "Everything is cinema," he said, dropping his voice dramatically and moving his chair closer. "We've got police disguised as protestors starting to burn things. Because they want to capture violent scenes and provide it to the Chinese television channels."

He channeled his anger straight into his lyrics:

You've got guns. You've got bullets. You've got gas.
We use flesh and blood to resist. Fuck the popo.
You want to burn, we're lining up to play with you.
Tear-gas. Disperse. Return
Holding high the Umbrella of Liberty.

These were strong words, but even so, MC Yan believed he'd failed to capture what was happening on the ground. As he spoke, his incessant stream of words slowed, and he seemed to be faltering. "For us the reality is way, way more serious. What people in Hong Kong can see and feel. It's not about music. They can *smell* it."

Erasure was his greatest fear, not just of the past but of the present, too. In this city, erasure had become its own art form, practiced ad infinitum by the King of Kowloon. In 2017, the King had popped briefly back into the news, when a government contractor covered over one of his last remaining works, on an electricity box, with white paint. Before the protests had broken out, I'd often gone out to see if I could find any more pieces of his work. I'd stumbled over a wall near a train station, protected behind a locked iron grille, where traces of his words remained, though each had a big black patch painted over it, leaving only the distinctive spiky extremities protruding. At another site, I'd discovered ghostly efflorescent patches of King writing on round concrete pillars, the writing bleached by the sun almost to the point of invisibility. Nature was erasing the few pieces of his work that remained.

Around the time of the protests, I received a message from the King's friend and final curator, Joel Chung Yin-chai, agreeing to meet. Joel Chung was something of a mystery. He'd been polite but curt when we'd met five years before, giving me copies of the three books he'd written about Tsang Tsou-choi but then ignoring all my subsequent messages. In the meantime, everyone I'd spoken to seemed to have an opinion about him, often negative. Some of the artists who took part in the tribute show he'd organized had fallen out with him so badly that I'd heard through the grapevine some had refused to speak to him again.

Tsang Tsou-choi's other main collector, Lau Kin-wai, disliked Joel Chung intensely. He accused Chung of deliberately destroying pieces of the King's work. As he spoke with me about this, Lau became so agitated that his face turned red and he began stammering. He told me Chung had burned some of the King's works on paper to create his own piece of performance art. Even more disturbing, he accused Chung of erasing a very large piece of the King's calligraphy by spray-painting another work—an angular depiction of skyscrapers accompanied by the all-caps words ART IS NOT EVERYTHING BUT WE NEED IT—on top of it. Given the scarcity of Tsang's work, this seemed like an act of wanton destruction. Lau had been so disgusted that he'd gone to the police station to lodge a formal complaint. When I asked what he thought was driving Chung's actions, he'd replied with just two words. "Ego. Stupid."

Chung was certainly eccentric. He was a slim, eye-catching figure who wore trademark thick black circular spectacles. His office was like a magical museum of childhood. Dangling from the ceiling were string bags full of red-and-white plastic balls, sheaves of green-and-red skipping ropes, and old-fashioned wooden kite spools. Boxes of merchandise were piled up high, obscuring his Museum of Stationery, which was a repository of vintage fountain pens, novelty erasers, and wooden rulers smeared with the black-inked names of generations of schoolchildren past. Another corner was devoted to big-eyed bald dolls, gurning and gawking in their pink romper suits as they crawled along the shelves. Chung called himself a "librarian of history," but he seemed more like a Peter Pan figure with his tens of thousands of toys. The truth was that he had grown up in a family so poverty-stricken that he did not own a toy until he bought himself one after graduating from university. Chung had channeled his energy into setting up an NGO that collected surplus stationery and redistributed it to those in need in Hong Kong and on the mainland.

Though the movement was still unfolding, Chung didn't want to talk about politics. He had no interest in that at all, he said politely. So after some chitchat, I carefully broached Lau Kin-wai's accusations, asking Chung if he'd destroyed some of the King's calligraphy in order to make a video. He cheerfully pulled up the video in question. I found it physically painful to watch. The words "Seen; Disappeared" materialized on the screen, transposed against a wall covered in the King's faded calligraphy. As tense, haunting music played, slow-motion tendrils of flame in the foreground licked at a piece of paper covered with the King's black characters. Feathery puffs of ash spiraled into the air as a second piece of calligraphy, the words written in red, went up in flames. The conflagration was in a square iron can traditionally used to burn offerings during Hungry Ghost Festival. According to Chinese tradition, the vengeful spirits of the hungry ghosts—restless spirits who were not buried properly or were treated badly by their families—need propitiating with such offerings. The first time I watched the video, I gasped. The second time my hands involuntarily flew up to my head in horror.

Chung seemed delighted by my reaction. He explained that he owned more than five hundred pieces of the King's work, and he'd decided he could sacrifice a couple of them to create awareness of the King's legacy. When I asked if he'd used the visual metaphor of the hungry ghost on purpose, he nodded. What, I asked, did he think the King's spirit wanted, if it was still roaming the earth. "To still have some people remember him, still recognize what he did," he replied.

His tactics seemed counterintuitive, and I was nervous about broaching the question of the gigantic mural. But to my great surprise, Chung gleefully owned up to the crime. But that was only half the story, he told me. In fact, he'd taken measures to protect the King's calligraphy by covering it with a layer of plastic wrap, and then painting on top of that. The "destruction" was a trompe l'oeil, he said with satisfaction. He'd spray-painted his new picture on top of the plastic wrap, using a stencil, and after taking photos of it, he'd pulled off the plastic wrap, leaving the King's calligraphy unharmed.

If this was the case, I said, I couldn't understand why Lau had filed a police complaint. Chung giggled as he replied that Lau simply hadn't realized that the "destruction" was a total fake.

Then he let me in on his secret. Those two acts, he said, were just a small part of an elaborate mission Chung was waging, inspired by the King. He confided to me that he had been the mastermind behind a mysterious guerrilla graffiti campaign that had surfaced around 2012, when stencils of the King's face with his gap-toothed smile had appeared on electricity boxes. They were variously captioned "Who's afraid of the King?" or "I'm simply the King 1921–2007." "I had different versions!"

Chung said proudly. He'd carried stencils and spray paint in his car, and when the mood took him, he'd spray a picture on an electricity box or a wall as an act of remembrance. But there was nothing impromptu about the placement. He said he spray-painted his stencils only on locations that had once been graced with the King's own calligraphy. I doubted whether anyone would make that connection, but Joel Chung didn't care. "I'm not going to say this is an art action or not," he said. "I just wanted to do something to let people not forget that we had kings before."

I was reeling. I'd come prepared to confront Chung over acts of vandalism, and he'd completely wrong-footed me. But the biggest surprise was still to come. As I took my leave, Chung walked me to the lift. It was an ancient cage-type elevator with horizontal double doors that joined in the middle, requiring a lift operator to pull them up and down simultaneously to meet in the middle. "Are you in a hurry?" Joel Chung asked, casually. "Have you got five minutes?" He jumped into the lift with me, and we descended. When we reached ground level, he strode very quickly through the loading dock of the building, picking up his pace as he rounded a corner and headed down a very large road. There was no explanation, and I was struggling to keep up as he cantered dangerously across a highway, dodging cars. When we reached the median strip, he clambered up a bank. In front of us, through some scrubby bushes, was the rounded pillar of a flyover. I could hardly believe my eyes.

The circular column was covered with the King's words. This was not the kind of efflorescent sun-damaged writing I'd found in my searches, but thick black characters in excellent condition. The patch of writing was about one square meter—much larger than any other example of the King's work in the wild, and in much better condition. Given the value and scarcity of his work, this piece should have been worth a considerable amount of money, so how on earth had it survived unnoticed? As I was pondering that, I noticed that the edges of the work were still covered by paint. It was impossible to tell how much more of the King's work was still underneath.

This, it turned out, was Joel Chung's biggest project. As I goggled in disbelief, hardly able to take in what he was saying, he explained what he was doing. Chung said that he'd been with the King when he originally painted the pillar, and he'd noted its location on a spreadsheet. When the original work was covered up by a government contractor sloshing gray paint on top, he'd marked that down, too. Now he was methodically chipping away at the gray paint to expose the calligraphy underneath. It was slow and tedious work, and he'd already spent more than a week on this pillar. Once the whole work was visible, he'd cover it in a transparent oil to preserve it. Then, he'd paint over it with a fresh coat of gray paint, leaving no one any the wiser. As he slowly revealed his secret enterprise, he grew more and more delighted, beaming with the sly joy of a small child who has stolen and hidden his Christmas gift.

I was confused, stammering, flabbergasted at the thought of this invisible, baffling sleight of hand. It was hard to understand why Chung was going to all that effort just to cover up the calligraphy again. "It's because I think this is not the right moment to discover all the work in the public space," he said. He feared the government's lack of commitment to preserving the King's work meant that any new pieces could end up being erased again. "They have a lot of excuses," he told me darkly. "They will say it's a 'communication mistake.'" That had been the official excuse after the Choi Hung piece was destroyed. In effect, Chung was practicing destruction for the sake of conservation.

Moreover, Chung revealed, what I was seeing was only the latest piece in his campaign. For a decade, working from his spreadsheet, he had been slowly, methodically uncovering the King's hidden works, chipping away their coating of paint, restoring them, then painting over them again. He said he'd already restored six works, generally picking one a year, around the anniversary of the King's death. He was creating a clandestine museum of the King's work, known only to himself. It was the most quixotic, most secretive, most extraordinary act of preservation that I'd ever seen.

I wasn't sure how to fact-check this, but before we parted, Chung shared the locations of two more pieces that he'd uncovered, one partially and one fully. I went to both places and the calligraphy was exactly where he said it would be. In the first site—at the Peak Tram terminus—he'd peeled off strips of the white topcoat, revealing glimpses of the King's calligraphy peeking out underneath, as if to tease passersby. This find had been reported in a newspaper, and Lau Kin-wai had even told me about it. When I told Chung that, he grinned in satisfaction. The other piece was a big one on a concrete wall opposite the Kwun Tong police headquarters. I'd been there before, more than five years earlier, and hadn't found anything at all. This time, the topcoat of paint had been removed from large squares of the wall, revealing a calligraphy screed sprawling over the wall's expanse, enormous characters jostling up against smaller ones and even Roman numerals. An old paint scraper was stuffed into one of the drainage pipes, evidence of Joel Chung's labor.

The same cycle of destruction and reclamation was now playing out on the city's walls almost every day. Hong Kong's walls and pillars were scarred with newly painted gray squares, often themselves covered with a patchwork of white, black, or dark gray rectangles. The advertising billboards at tram stops were shrouded in protective plastic sheeting, which in turn was covered with massive black paint scribbles as if a giant demented toddler had thrown an artistic tantrum across the street furniture. All this frenzied paintwork covered up new political graffiti that the authorities deemed should not be seen. Sometimes the government contractors painted over the characters so carefully that they ended up emphasizing each word in boldface. In this way the characters 光復香港

時代革命, "Liberate Hong Kong, Revolution of Our Times," could still be read on highway dividers, and 香港人, "Hong Kong People," loomed out from a tram stop. They reminded me of the words of artist Jean-Michel Basquiat: "I cross out words so you will see them more." This was a lesson that Hong Kong's rulers had failed to understand, from the reign of the King of Kowloon onward.

EPILOGUE

There was a wall in Central, an absolutely unremarkable yellow-gray stone wall, a meter high and twenty-five meters long, scuffed from generations of passing pedestrians. I passed it all the time without noticing anything out of the ordinary. Then someone told me about its remarkable feat of alchemy. In the muggy torpidity of Hong Kong's post-rainstorm afternoons, the wall conjured a secret message to its surface, spectral characters looming through the gloaming.

It was, of course, a missive from the dead King, who had covered the entire length with his territorial claims. The characters had been hastily painted over by government workers, as usual, but in this spot something unexpected had happened. The King was using ink specially blended for him by Joel Chung, who had added acrylic and oil, making it unusually sticky. Over the years, as the King's characters melted away, they took the paint with them, leaving dark, character-shaped holes against a flaking dove-gray backdrop. The effect was almost imperceptible except after rainfall, when the empty spaces left by the King's words glistened darkly from the wall, like a photographic negative.

The day that I discovered the wall, back in 2015, I took Tanya Chan to see it. A barrister and lawmaker who cofounded the Civic Party, Chan is known for her film-star looks and her assertive brand of retail politics, which included shaving her head in protest against the election rules imposed by China. In 2010, she had asked the legislature for an official survey of the King of Kowloon's extant pieces in public space and upbraided the government for its ineffective efforts at conserving his work. We'd been having coffee nearby when I told her about the wall. Her eyes lit up, and she demanded to see it straightaway.

It had just been raining, and the wall was still moist and warm to the touch, almost steaming in the dank afternoon humidity. Despite her stiletto heels and pristine white dress emblazoned with orange and pink flowers, Chan knelt on the pavement and leaned into the wall to pick out the remnants of the King's script. "This is a *big* word over there," she yelped in excitement. "*Tin!* Sky! Interesting!" A passel of somber-suited businessmen yapping into their phones slowed as they passed, bemused at the sight of this well-known politician crouching on the ground and shrieking as she examined an ostensibly bare wall.

Chan had passed the wall thousands of times—every day in the period when she shuttled between her office and the legislative chamber—without noticing a thing. It was testament to the King that he could hide his work in plain sight in the center of Central, the political and economic heart of Hong Kong. His legacy was so deeply woven into the city's psyche that, as with the protest slogans, the visibility of his work hardly mattered anymore. "This work is part of Hong Kong's history," Chan said, tracing the characters with her finger. "It's part of us."

In the years since we'd explored the wall together, a lot had happened to Chan. She was reelected to the legislature. Then she was found guilty of public nuisance charges related to Occupy Central. She became one of the Umbrella Nine, alongside Chan Kin-man and Benny Tai, though she'd avoided serving jail time because she needed to undergo surgery for a brain tumor that had grown larger than a Ping-Pong ball. She'd also written a book, *My Journeys for Food and Justice*. Then, overnight, Chan's book, a striking magenta paperback, was banned from library shelves.

It was an early victim of the draconian national security legislation that Beijing imposed on Hong Kong just before midnight on June 30, 2020, on the eve of the annual protest march marking the anniversary of Hong Kong's retrocession. The new law outlawed sedition, subversion, terrorism, and collusion with foreign forces, though it did not provide any clear guidelines for how these crimes were to be defined. It overrode the existing mini-constitution known as the Basic Law, and it also established a separate legal framework for national security crimes that theoretically allowed suspects to be tried on the mainland. This was Beijing's response to the year of protests, whose very catalyst had been the issue of extradition.

The very means by which the national security legislation was enacted underlined Beijing's continued disregard for Hong Kongers. It had already been made amply clear that Beijing wasn't respecting its pledge to leave Hong Kong unchanged for fifty years. Three years before, Beijing had airily disavowed the same Joint Declaration that had taken two long years of negotiation and over which the Unofficials had undergone such agonies. A Chinese Foreign Ministry spokesman had simply shrugged it off as a historical document without any real import. This time, however, no one in Hong Kong—not even Carrie Lam—had so much as seen the law before it was put into effect. The legislation was simply appended to an annex of the Basic Law, a move that allowed Beijing to bypass Hong Kong's institutions and the due process they required.

This was, people said, the second handover, the real one, when Hong Kongers' worst fears were finally realized. Beijing had waited seventeen years, since the massive Article 23 protests, for Hong Kong to promulgate its own national security legislation. Now it had lost patience. After the bill was enacted, China's feared internal security agencies moved into Hong Kong, requisitioning a hotel in the dead of night for their new Office for Safeguarding National Security. On the first day of the law's existence, it was used to arrest ten people at the annual July 1 protest, including a fifteen-year-old girl waving a Hong Kong independence flag and a motorcyclist who'd mounted a 光復香港時代革命, "Liberate Hong Kong, Revolution of Our Times!," flag on the back of his bike. He became the first person to be tried under the National Security Law. From that day on, it seemed the most popular protest slogans had suddenly been deemed illegal, and so the few remaining Lennon Walls were hastily dismantled. The image that stayed with me from that day was of eight people standing in the street, each holding up a blank sheet of paper. It was both a protest against censorship and the only way they could safely express the eight-character slogan. Language itself was beginning to vanish.

Within days, books were vanishing from library shelves, including Chan's. She didn't know the reason, but wondered aloud if it was related to the Chinese-language title, *Walking, Eating, and Resisting*. "Is the word 'resisting' problematic, or is it the name Tanya Chan, or that I as a person have become a problem after the national security law? I do not have an answer." The vagueness of the law made self-protection impossible, and the worries she voiced soon became ubiquitous. "You don't know when you will step into these traps or even when you will step on these red lines, because red lines are everywhere, and they move constantly." A Democracy Wall at one university was stripped of posters, then access to it was blocked by plastic barricades, presenting a horrible, unmistakable metaphor: democracy had literally become a no-go area. The lacunae were gaping ever wider, swallowing not just words and books but also ideas and whole ways of thinking.

Beijing's endgame was total dominance. Its actions sabotaged its own

One Country, Two Systems formula, exposing it for the sham it was. In imposing the legislation, Beijing had in one fell swoop undermined the high degree of autonomy it had promised to Hong Kong, sidelined its judiciary and canceled its rule of law. It was as if, in order to fix a leaky pipe, the builders had pulled down the entire house and plowed up the land under its foundations.

Next, the government used Covid safety as a pretext to ban gatherings of more than two people and to postpone Legislative Council elections initially for a year, hoping to avoid a repeat of the stinging pan-Democratic landslide in the 2019 district council polls. Arrests were picking up speed, with the law sometimes invoked retroactively. Shouting protest slogans suddenly could be seen as "uttering seditious words." Lobbying foreign countries to impose sanctions on Hong Kong and China had become "collusion with a foreign country." It sometimes seemed as if the authorities were waging a war on language itself. And the battlefield was global; Beijing insisted it would enforce the legislation worldwide, even laying charges against activists who weren't Hong Kong residents or even in Hong Kong.

The impact was intense and immediate. My phone, which had buzzed incessantly with notifications from the dozens of Telegram groups that Hong Kongers had used to communicate and plan protest actions, fell silent. People were so fearful of China's internet surveillance capabilities that they were shutting down their accounts and asking contacts to delete their chat records. They began worrying about what they were posting on Facebook and Twitter, so they deleted those, too. This was more than self-censorship. In the digital era, it was an act of mass self-cancelation.

Something else was happening that was even harder to process. Hong Kong's government officials had generally been respected and trusted as colorless but competent bureaucrats whose efficiency allowed the city to function smoothly. But now the most senior officials were regularly telling outlandish, barefaced, verifiable lies in their press conferences, right from the very top down.

Carrie Lam's public statements were a case in point, almost every time she spoke in public. In December 2019, she insisted that Hong Kong's freedoms had not been eroded even as police banned protest marches. In September 2020, she argued that Hong Kong's system of government provided for no separation of powers between the executive, legislative, and judicial branches. The refutation could be found in any Hong Kong secondary schoolers' textbooks, but Lam said the textbooks needed rewriting to correct what she called a historical misunderstanding. In March 2021, when Beijing rewrote Hong Kong's electoral system to reduce the number of directly elected seats and allow police to vet electoral candidates, Carrie Lam even framed it as a move toward greater democracy. It wasn't just history that was being revised; the present itself was being rewritten, even as it happened.

She knew what she was saying was patently untrue, and she knew that everyone knew she was lying. These acts of mass gaslighting served as a raw exercise of power, forcing the population to swallow statements that blatantly contradicted themselves. But it went deeper; these attempts to muddy the epistemological waters seeded doubts about the nature of reality and knowledge itself. It was a tried-and-tested move straight out of the authoritarian playbook, and an uncanny echo of the Chinese Communist Party's efforts to rewrite the history of the Tiananmen killings of June 4, 1989.

Back then it had mounted a massive campaign to change the narrative. It was a multistep process, with the Communist Party first flooding the population with propaganda presenting the events of that night as counterrevolutionary rioting rather than peaceful protests in an attempt to rewrite memories of a moment many had witnessed. Over time, the propaganda leaflets disappeared from library shelves, the television stations stopped running scenes of fugitives being arrested, and silence took over, first eroding, then excising those implanted memories.

The party-state has been so successful in this effort that many young Chinese had no idea anything had happened on June 4, 1989. While writing my book, I'd also uncovered a second bloody crackdown on the same day in the city of Chengdu that had been wiped from the record, sponged out rather like the Six-Day War of 1899. I knew that type of historical erasure happened in Communist China, where the state controlled information so tightly, but I'd never imagined I would see the same process beginning to unfold in Hong Kong, with its highly educated, highly networked global population.

When the movement started, I'd initially resisted drawing parallels with the Tiananmen crackdown, but the similarities kept mounting. Right at the very beginning, Carrie Lam's description of largely peaceful protests as "riots" recalled a famous *People's Daily* editorial in 1989 that labeled the student protests as "turmoil." These moments were, in Confucian terms, acts that "rectified the names," ensuring that the proper name was attached to an event to signal the correct political stance. When Hong Kong officials blamed the protests on "black hands" backed by hostile foreign forces, I recognized this vocabulary as coming straight from the Tiananmen lexicon. Even the use of police to beat protestors, rather than having the army open fire on them, replayed the quelling of the Chengdu protests with horrible familiarity to me. Massive civil unrest in Chengdu had been crushed not with tanks but by riot police, known as Paramilitary Armed Police, using water cannons and the brute force of truncheons. In the streets of Hong Kong, the weaponry had been updated to include water cannons that shot blue liquid laced with chemicals, sonar devices, and huge quantities of tear gas. But the tactics were the same, including violent beatings given to protestors by the police.

A year after the protests began, I went to a June 4 candlelight vigil organized by the Hong Kong community in Melbourne. The organizers had rigged up screens and were projecting a highlights reel of state violence that flashed between scenes from Beijing in 1989 and Hong Kong in 2019. I watched a Hong Kong cop casually breaking the arm of a protestor who was lying facedown on the ground. Then a scene of mass arrest, with rows of young people kneeling on the pavement, their hands behind their backs. Then the fleshy thud of a police officer beating a protestor's head with his truncheon. In a moment of sickening clarity, I suddenly realized that all these were scenes I'd already written, as I set down on paper eyewitnesses' descriptions of what they'd seen in Chengdu. Now those very same scenes were being replayed in Hong Kong, night after night, for months on end.

In 2020, the June 4 candlelight vigil in Hong Kong—which had been the only such memorial on Chinese soil—was forbidden for the first time, on the grounds of Covid safety. Despite the ban, Hong Kongers turned out anyway. The instinct to remember en masse was so ingrained that they didn't know what else to do. Their feet carried them to Victoria Park, where they sat quietly in socially distanced clumps, or to local parks where small groups coalesced organically to mourn together. This represented an about-turn, since in recent years many young Hong Kongers had refused to attend the June 4 vigil, arguing that what happened so many years before in China had nothing to do with their lives. Now the events of three decades ago had become horribly, undeniably relevant. As Chan Kin-man told me, "Now we are also facing a similar crackdown. In Hong Kong we took almost nine months to experience the crackdown, but in 1989 it was just one evening. It's not just a piece of history. It's happening now."

It was at that vigil that I heard a new slogan for the first time: "Hong Kong independence! The only way!" The movement was demolishing all the old sacred cows. Almost no one thought that Hong Kong independence was a possibility; the power of the words lay in the solidarity they expressed, the defiance, the rejection of the Communist Party's China.

By 2021, the authorities were threatening five-year sentences for any-one attending the vigil. The most prominent of those who had been at Victoria Park the year before were already serving sentences of up to ten months for illegal assembly. My book, too, had been deemed sensitive and had been removed from public library shelves to be placed in the reference library, from where it could not be borrowed. Seven thousand police officers were deployed, many encircling the park to forestall any acts of collective memory. Once more, Hong Kongers refused to be cowed. Circling the perimeter of the park at 8:09 p.m., the moment can-dles are traditionally lit, they brought out candles, or simply raised their mobile phone screens aloft, torches on. There was new graffiti, in par-ticular "64" marking the date in Chinese scrawled on building struts. Someone had spray-painted a picture of a candle in black on a salmon-pink wall, below which they'd written, "People's hearts never die." The authorities hastily covered up the words with a black plastic bag; the flame of the graffiti candle was still visible, burning on.

I sometimes thought back to the day when I'd been having lunch with a lawyer friend, years before, when he'd used the term "dissident" to refer to a prominent Hong Konger. Then he stopped and corrected him-self. "Not a dissident," he said. "A popularly elected lawmaker." China's moves had turned so many Hong Kongers into dissidents. Now they were creating exiles, political refugees, and, most shocking of all, boat people. The first case involved twelve young people, the youngest just sixteen, who, facing protest-related charges, had tried to flee by speed-boat to Taiwan. They were stopped by the Chinese Coast Guard, held incommunicado in China for months, then charged with illegally cross-ing borders. Hong Kong—historically a place of refuge that had offered safe harbor to Vietnamese boat people and Tiananmen-era student leaders—had become a place that people were fleeing from.

The changes were coming so fast that we could hardly even write them down before they were superseded by even worse. The fate of the legislature was a case in point. Four moderate Democratic lawmakers were expelled "for endangering national security" after they'd called for the US to sanction Chinese officials for human rights abuses. In protest, the fifteen other Democratic lawmakers resigned en masse. Just like that, the opposition was gone, and the legislative chamber was transformed. When Carrie Lam gave her policy address, she spoke to a curiously quiet chamber. The remaining lawmakers—all from the progovernment camp—dozed in their seats or watched videos of those sleeping. One even used the time to order exorbitantly priced hairy crab for dinner. Politics was over. Hong Kong's feisty legislature had become a rubber stamp. Just to be sure, Beijing overhauled the electoral system to ensure only "patriots" could run for office, introducing national security police vetting for electoral candidates and reducing the number of directly elected seats. As one politician commented, Beijing now had "a 100 percent guarantee" it would get the results it wanted.

Freedom of the press ended just as abruptly, when Jimmy Lai Cheeying, the seventy-something founder of *Apple Daily*, appeared in court on national security charges, not only handcuffed but with chains around his waist. Among his charges was one of collusion with foreign elements to endanger national security, citing his tweets and interviews with foreign media. In June 2021, *Apple Daily* printed its last copy after its funds were frozen and a swath of senior executives, including editorial writers, were arrested on national security grounds. Its last mournful headline read: "Hong Kongers bid a painful farewell in the rain; 'We support Apple Daily.'" This was printed over a photo of the crowds who had flocked to the newspaper's headquarters to shine the points of light from their mobile phones toward the journalists working on the obituary issue. A million copies were printed for this city of 7.5 million. They sold out. The next day, the newspaper's entire archive vanished from the internet. As Beijing imposed its narrative control by force, it was simply too dangerous for other versions of the past to exist.

Internet freedom was also narrowing, with websites blocked on national security grounds. The cherished neutrality of the civil service was swept away when civil servants were ordered to pledge allegiance to the government. Schoolteachers were facing lifetime bans for teaching classes that "distorted" history or spread independence messages. Freedoms weren't being chipped away or eroded. They were being torn down and trampled over with indecent, gleeful haste. Capital was fleeing overseas as people tried to figure out their exit strategies en masse.

Hong Kong was being absorbed, by decree, into China's security state. Overnight, a mostly free society had become an authoritarian one.

Every day seemed to bring worse news. Friends and interviewees were being arrested at a startling rate. On a single day, more than fifty people were rounded up and detained for their involvement in primary polls held by the pan-Democratic camp to decide which candidates to field at election. Their marathon bail hearing, which stretched out into the early hours of morning, led to eight defendants being rushed to hospital on stretchers, due to lack of food. It was "an unthinkable travesty of justice" according to an expert of Chinese law, Jerome Cohen. Forty-seven people ended up being charged with conspiracy to commit subversion, which can carry a life sentence. It was a reminder that the Communist Party viewed Hong Kong's system and its attendant freedoms as a threat to its own security, and it was using the national security law to dismantle those freedoms.

Among the forty-seven were Umbrella cofounder Benny Tai and politician Alvin Yeung, who had stood between the police and protestors. When they appeared in court, some of the forty-seven still flashed protest signs. They had lost everything in this dangerous game except the one thing that could not be taken away, even by jail time: their freedom of thought. The words of Tai's Umbrella Movement court submission now applied to a new generation of political prisoners: "If we were to be guilty, we will be guilty of daring to share hope at a difficult time for

Hong Kong. I am not afraid or ashamed of going to prison. If this is the cup I must take, I will drink with no regret."

One politician was convicted of assault after police said his use of a loudspeaker assaulted their eardrums. A bus driver who honked at police during the protests was given one hundred hours of community service for dangerous driving. Five speech therapists were arrested on suspicion of inciting hatred toward the government for picture books they had published, including *The Guardian of Sheep Village*. The charges were sometimes so absurd they would have been laughable had it not been for the endless parade of familiar faces flickering through my social media timelines, dazed and pale, being escorted into police cars.

Universities and schools were being wrested under control, with national security education introduced, even into subjects like biology and geography. History books were being rewritten all the way back to 220 BCE to emphasize Hong Kong's role as part of Chinese soil since time immemorial. Teachers who dared to question the official line were being struck off. Pro-Beijing politicians, and even tycoons, were increasingly calling for all lessons to be taught in Mandarin, warning that otherwise Hong Kong could be left behind from China's economic development. When the organizer of the massive 2019 protests, the Civil Human Rights Front, announced it was disbanding, the police chief warned an investigation would probe whether the 2019 protests had violated the national security legislation, which had not been imposed until the following year. The legislation, it seemed, defied the space-time continuum. The war on Hong Kong's culture was underway. It was a shock-and-awe blitzkrieg rolled out on all fronts simultaneously.

Hong Kong was a dual city no more, as people left en masse. By August 2021, a new law allowed the government to impose exit bans. Even the freedom to leave was being denied. For Hong Kongers, every day was a litany of losses, both big and small. But the loss of the future was perhaps the most devastating of all. For so long, Hong Kong had been a city untrammeled, except by the limits of imagination. It was a place always in motion, its endless land reclamations creeping outward to displace the sea, its skyscrapers challenging the air itself. Politically, too, it was the living exercise of an impossible thought experiment that held together until it didn't. We'd grown up thinking we had the best of both worlds. Now we were stranded in a completely different universe. We'd imagined this improbable city into existence, and now its very future had become unthinkable. And there was no way to go home; home no longer existed.

Those days of marching had changed us. In the sauna heat of summer, with the midday sun refracted off the skyscrapers, we had felt the power of collective imagination made flesh, sweating onto one another's bodies as we crammed six-lane highways to capacity. We were daring to write our own story, even though the conclusion had already been written for us. Looking back, those days of protest felt like a fever dream, at once beautiful and harrowing.

One day, buried in a box, I found a memento I'd bought at one of the first marches. When I unfolded it, my heart caught. It was a cream flag bearing a picture of birds flying through turquoise clouds against the words "100% 自由" and "100% Free" written in black graffiti-style characters. In one corner were the English words "Let us stand up as Hong Kongers." I felt as though the flag was speaking to me as a journalist. To stand up is not to kneel, or to crouch, or to hide behind the convenient shield of reportorial neutrality. In circumstances where morality demands a stance, evenhandedness is an act of cowardice. A fisherman at sea cannot be neutral about an approaching typhoon; his very existence depends upon not being swallowed by the towering walls of water pummeling his tiny boat. But the closer he is to the storm, the better he can describe its keening winds, its stinging rain, the sickening pitch and swell of the unsettled seas, the sheer destructive force that shreds everything in its path.

When I worked at the BBC, we used to talk about the value of "stand-back pieces," where the correspondent is removed from the situation like a kind of journalistic demigod. But distance is a privilege that Hong Kongers—no matter where—cannot enjoy. There is no escape from the horror of watching your home be destroyed. From a journalistic point of view, standing back would be a dereliction of my duty as a Hong Konger, although standing up feels like the repudiation of a career of carefully weighed distance and neutrality. It is, however, the most honest approach that I can muster.

By this point, I'd long since abandoned my original journalistic mission. The questions that had been so central to me when I set out in search of the King of Kowloon no longer mattered. I still didn't know if the King was mentally competent or not. I'd utterly failed to confirm or deny the truth of his territorial claim. To me, the King's dominion was both moral and symbolic. What mattered was not the substance of his claim but how that fictional claim was made real. Our old, mad King had an imagination so immense that it overflowed onto things we'd never noticed—postboxes and lampposts, curbs and walls—giving voice to sentiments we didn't know we felt until he voiced them for us.

His imagination became our own, for we turned him into the monarch that he imagined himself to be. We did that with our eulogies and obituaries, our poems and songs, our wallpaper designs and whiskey brands. Even as a commodity, he still whispered to us, his subversive message susurrating through the hipster sneakers daubed with his words or the faux-King calligraphy on the wall of a Starbucks.

Under the spell of his mental sovereignty, we'd been forced to theorize our own. Now our dreams had been outlawed, our anthems and slogans banned, our very thought bubbles choked off before they could form. Now we all were Kings of Kowloon, dispossessed of our very idea of ourselves, left only our loss to own.

The King's work was, however, still ambiguous. So much so that when Hong Kong finally opened its multimillion-dollar M+ art museum in November 2021, the very first piece in the exhibition was a pair of large wooden doors daubed with the King's graffiti. They had been chosen, curator Tina Pang said, because they represent Hong Kong's visual culture. The notes given to reporters spun the King's work in a pro-China light as "an act of resistance to British colonial rule," yet such a reading strips the King of the throne he spent his lifetime claiming.

One day, years before the protests, I had been to visit a well-known Hong Kong artist who counted himself among the King's court. He told me he considered the King his hero. I asked him what he'd learned from him.

"Just determination," he replied simply. "As a person, not as an artist. Someone taking action for what he believes in, for years after years. I don't see anyone that can compare with him."

Another of the King's courtiers gave me a different answer; when I asked what he'd learned from the King, he replied, "To be a Hong Kong person, I tell my story to others. I tell the Hong Kong story to others."

When I thought back to that afternoon when I'd taken up a brush to join in painting a protest banner on a sweltering rooftop, I decided that I hadn't transgressed after all. I was simply another descendant of the King. I'd taken on his mantle the moment I'd started my doomed pursuit of the old trash collector. Even as he held his own hidden history close, he'd inspired me to write my own saga of defiance and dispossession, my own idiosyncratic story of Hong Kong.

I thought about the courtier's words after I returned to Australia. I was part of a study group there, of fellow Hong Kong PhD students whose research revolved around Hong Kong identity. Throughout the long Melbourne Covid lockdown, we met once a week on Zoom to read relevant academic papers. We were on one such call when the national security legislation was announced. After that, we stopped meeting, stopped reading papers, stopped discussing Hong Kong identity at all. The day after the law went into effect, I put the flat in Hong Kong that I'd always hoped to live in again on the market. It wasn't only the risk of arbitrary detention, which would soon make other countries warn against travel to the region; it was that I instinctively understood that this was no longer a place to raise my children.

We'd all unexpectedly become exiles, even those of us still in Hong Kong. For my study group, suddenly our research seemed irrelevant. After all, how can you research something whose very expression could be a criminal act? It was hard even to focus under the circumstances, and one by one, my friends applied for a leave of absence. Their parents were ringing them up, warning them not to come home. One friend, after watching *Unorthodox* on Netflix, asked the group, "Are we Hong Kongers going to be like the Jews after the Holocaust? Has it now become my duty to have children overseas in order to keep us alive?"

Months passed, and as Melbourne finally emerged from lockdown, my study group started to meet again. We blinked blearily in the unfamiliar sunshine as we ate sweet, sticky slices of mango in the park. When the restaurants reopened, we shared plates of plump steaming dumplings. At Christmas, we listened to Cantopop as we dunked lotus root and fishballs in the rolling boil of a hotpot. Halfway through the meal, someone arrived with warm egg waffles and we passed them round the table like a sacrament, each of us carefully breaking off a few doughy bubbles so we could savor the taste of home together. Slowly, painfully, we were imagining our own small Hong Kong into being.

In Hong Kong, the spaces for imagining Hong Kong identity have narrowed almost to extinction. The Lennon Walls are gone, the internet is increasingly monitored, and the protest stickers that were once everywhere have become samizdat circulated behind locked doors. *Apple Daily* is no more. For a while, it had offered a window of defiance and Hong Kongers had shown their support for it by buying stock in Jimmy Lai's company and placing personal ads in the newspaper to boost its revenues. Those notices were sometimes organized in pastel checkerboard squares, like newsprint Lennon Walls. "We really fucking love

Hong Kong" appeared over and over, one of the few acceptable assertions of Hong Kong identity that remained.

One day, an antique jewelry shop took out a full-page ad, front and back. The first page was mostly blank, apart from a picture of an old-fashioned photographic slide that bore the image of a gray brick wall, marked by four swirling, blackish smudges where Chinese characters had been sponged out. Above were the words: "No matter how black the dark is, it cannot block out the light." The back of the page was blank, except for four black graffiti-style Chinese characters written in mirror image. This allowed the paper to perform a magic trick that was uncannily similar to the King's hidden message on that gray wall. When lifted up to the sun, the gray smudges faded and thick black words began to take shape, shining straight through the paper. They read: "Hong Kong will see light again," 香港重光.

ACKNOWLEDGMENTS

This book could not have been written without all the Hong Kongers who gave me their time and their stories. The risks of doing so have escalated dramatically over the years, and I hope I can do justice to the trust they have placed in me. There are so many who cannot be named, but I will not forget their kindness and support.

For so many years, the King of Kowloon has held me in his thrall, and I am indebted to all who humored me and encouraged me on my merry dance with him. In particular, I could not have written this book without the King's three regents—Simon Go Man-ching, Lau Kin-wai, and Joel Chung Yin-chai—and I thank them for sharing their stories, collections, and secrets over the years.

I am especially indebted to Steve Tsang, whose interviews for the Hong Kong Project form the backbone of chapter 4. I spent many hours in the Weston Library exploring this treasure trove of information, with a growing sense of wonder at the richness and detail of this extraordinary archive. "Such a record might be of interest to eventual historians," former Hong Kong governor Baron MacLehose of Beoch wrote in a declassified Foreign

Office letter from 1988. In it, he also predicted that Hong Kong government records would not be all that illuminating. He was right on both counts. I am most grateful to the librarians of the Bodleian Library's Special Collections for their patience with my queries and their scanning assistance, especially Lucy McCann, Sam Sales, and Angie Goodgame.

I spent five interminable years doing a PhD researching how Hong Kong newspaper coverage elevated the King of Kowloon to icon status. I was sustained during those years by the academic generosity and patience of Gloria Davies, whose wisdom imbricates every page of this book. I would not have made it to the finish line without the formidable tag-team of Johan Lidberg and Mia Lindgren, who carried me through my crises with unwavering support and sage guidance. By the end, my dislike of the PhD process was counterbalanced by the pure pleasure of the advisory process, which is in itself a testament to their success.

This work owes its current form to the steady hand of Becky Saletan at Riverhead Books, who gave me the confidence to write a book that terrified me. I'm also thankful to Catalina Trigo, L. Huang, Helen Yentus, Glory Plata, Lavina Lee, Anna Jardine, Raven Ross, Michael Brown, and Eric Wechter at Riverhead for all their work. I had enormous help from my agents, Peter and Amy Bernstein, who believed in the King and shaped the book proposal. Thank you to Jeff Wasserstrom for that introduction, as well as many years of friendship and shared interests.

So many others helped out at various stages, but my deepest thanks go to Victoria Tin-bor Hui, Michael C. Davis, Antony Dapiran, Edouard Perrin, and Mark Leong for their careful readings of various drafts of the book. Kelly Chan took on the mammoth task of fact-checking with aplomb, and Patrick Cummins dug out his amazing photographs for my use.

In Hong Kong, I am hugely indebted to Keith Richburg for inviting me to be a writer in residence at the Journalism and Media Studies Centre at the University of Hong Kong, and to the whole JMSC team who made me so welcome. My heartfelt thanks to all those in Hong Kong who housed me and my children over the years, in particular Yuen Chan, Mishi Saran, Scott Keller, Gerry Mullany, Georgia Davidson, and Tara Duffy.

I salute Ilaria Maria Sala, who has acted as a sounding board and companion in making sense of developments as we wrote through them, both in our own work and in jointly authored opinion pieces. I am ever grateful to my podcasting partner in crime, Graeme Smith, for his friendship, his fundraising abilities, and his willingness to fly to Hong Kong at the drop of a hat. Over the years, we have been lucky enough to interview an extraordinary cast of Hong Kongers. Thanks, too, to Julia Bergin, Andy Hazel, Xu Cheng Chong, Wing Kuang, Gavin Nebauer, and Sarah Logan for their services to *The Little Red Podcast*.

In Melbourne, I could not have had a better support crew than Lucy Smy, Natasha Mitchell, Jo Chandler, Vanessa O'Neill, and Licho Licho López, who were there when I needed it most. Thanks also to Kathleen McLaughlin, Denis Muller, Govin Ruben, Niccolò Pianciola, Alex Dukalskis, Austin Ramzy, and Adam Vise for their whiskey-fueled conversations and support. I owe a special debt of thanks to my reading group, who provided inspiration, PDFs, Hong Kong snacks, and solidarity in some exceedingly bleak times, in particular Hugh Davies, Kelly Chan, Katy Chan, Joyce Cheng, Christa Tom, and Nikki Lam. I have been lucky to work for Andrew Dodd, who made it possible for me to have time off from teaching to work on the project, and Rachel Fensham, Peter Otto, and Jennifer Milam, who approved that request. I am grateful to my colleagues including Jeff Sparrow, Liam Cochrane, Sami Shah, Rachel Fountain, Tim Stoney, and Paul Connolly for all their help and support.

Some parts of the book grew out of earlier writing, published in different form. I am grateful to all those editors who commissioned me to write about Hong Kong, including Jyoti Thottam and Yaya Bayoumy at *The New York Times*; Robert Yates, Paul Webster, Yohann Koshy, Jonathan Shainin, David Wolf, Bonnie Malkin, and Emma Graham-Harrison at *The Guardian*; Mili Mitra at *The Washington Post*; Lorien Kite at the *Financial Times*; India Bourke at *New Statesman*; and James Palmer at *Foreign Policy*. I was also honored to contribute a memoir piece to the PEN anthology *Hong Kong 20/20; Reflections on a Borrowed Place*, edited by Tammy Ho Lai-Ming, Jason Y. Ng, Mishi Saran, Sarah Schafer, and Nicholas Wong.

ACKNOWLEDGMENTS

I have benefited immensely from residencies at Varuna, the National Writers' House, in the beautiful Blue Mountains, despite my record of aborted stays. My thanks to Veechi Stuart for her aid in evacuating me speedily twice over, as well as to Carol Major for her astonishing writer-whispering skills and to Amy Sambrooke and the whole varuna team. Parts of the book were written in Old Melbourne Gaol as part of Writers' Victoria's Cells for Writers program. Even though my cell was haunted, I miss it daily.

The seeds of this book were planted long before I even began thinking about it by my mother, Patricia Lim, as she dragged her reluctant brood around the study halls and walled villages of the New Territories. I have learned from her boundless curiosity and her perseverance. From my father, Poh Chye Lim, I have received the gift of steadfast support, offered in the face of his obvious skepticism about the sanity of this project. Big love to the world's best sisters, Emma and Jo Lim, for their unending encouragement and for taking on child-minding duties, and to their partners, Rick Fielding and Kingsley Evans. Finally, this book would not have been possible without my children, Ave and Daniel, who reluctantly moved to Hong Kong and then fell in love with the city themselves. One day we will return.

NOTES

EPIGRAPHS

vii **"Your furious characters"**: Jennifer Wong, "King of Kowloon," in *Letters Home* (London: Nine Arches Press, 2020).

PROLOGUE

4 **90 percent of the population:** Sheridan Prasso, "Millions in Hong Kong Have Been Exposed to Tear Gas since June," *Bloomberg*, November 5, 2019.

4 **post-traumatic stress disorder:** *The Lancet*, "The Lancet: Study Suggests Mental Health Impact of Ongoing Social Unrest in Hong Kong," news release, January 9, 2020.

8 **an estimated 55,845 works:** *Memories of King Kowloon* exhibition catalog, Island East, Hong Kong Creates, 2011.

8 **"everyone is missing him":** Lin Zhaorong, "Exhibition of Optimism: Mourning the King of Kowloon," *Ming Pao*, July 29, 2007; Deng Jinghao, "Farewell to the King of Kowloon Tsang Tsou-choi," *Ming Pao*, August 4, 2007.

8 **"his people are crying and wailing":** Li Chunen, "The Idiot Is the Way," *Apple Daily*, August 2, 2007, A21.

8 **"his ink treasures were poetic masterpieces":** Jinghao, "Farewell to the King of Kowloon Tsang Tsou-choi."

8 **"the writer is sad"**: "The King of Kowloon's Ink Treasures," *Singtao Daily*, July 27, 2007, A32.

8 **"who will succeed him"**: "Finding a Successor for the King," *Hong Kong Economic Times*, August 1, 2007.

10 **by writer Fung Man-yee:** Fung Man-yee, "King of Kowloon: In Memory of the Last Free Man in Hong Kong 「九龍皇帝」街頭御筆捍衛記," *City Magazine*, May 2009.

10 **an outspoken university lecturer:** Chin Wan, "Remembering Tsang Tsou-Choi's Significance 紀念曾杜財的意義," in *Post No Bills* 禁止標貼, ed. S. Y. Chung (Hong Kong: CUP Magazine Publishing, 2009).

10 **legislator Tanya Chan:** Chris Lau and Sum Lok-kei, "Four of Nine Occupy Leaders Jailed for up to 16 Months over Roles in Hong Kong's 2014 Umbrella Movement," *South China Morning Post*, April 24, 2019.

CHAPTER 1: 字 WORDS

17 **Chinese script preceded the spoken language:** Simon Leys, "One More Art," *New York Review of Books*, April 18, 1996.

18 **a Mao-style signature:** Qian Gang, "Keeping to the Script," January 6, 2019, https://chinamediaproject.org/2019/01/06/keeping-to-the-script.

18 **"an imaginative communion":** Leys, "One More Art."

18 **he was born in Guangdong province:** David Spalding, ed., *King of Kowloon: The Art of Tsang Tsou-choi* (Bologna, Italy: Damiani, 2013), 236.

19 **"have always been calligraphers":** "Emperors in China Have Always Been Calligraphers," *Colors*, October 2005.

20 **"The country is prosperous":** Spalding, *King of Kowloon*, 208; "'Kowloon King' Is an Emperor without Male Offspring. He Constantly Bears in Mind the Prosperity of His Country and the Peace of His People," *Ming Pao Evening News*, July 7, 1970.

20 **Simon Go Man-ching, a photojournalist:** Spalding, *King of Kowloon*, 210.

20 **told a film crew:** Joanne Shen and Martin Egan, *King of Kowloon* television documentary, 1998.

21 **When his daughters moved overseas:** Joel Chung, "The Art of Treason," *CUP Press, Hong Kong* (2007).

22 **"They should just give me back my throne":** "Emperors in China Have Always Been Calligraphers."

25 **"Calligraphy with much strength":** Dawn Delbanco, "Chinese Calligraphy," *Heilbrunn Timeline of Art History*, April 2008.

31 **The first contained maps:** *Memories of King Kowloon* exhibition catalog, Island East, Hong Kong Creates, 2011.

33 **"a culture of disappearance":** M. A. Abbas, *Hong Kong: Culture and the Politics of Disappearance* (Minneapolis: University of Minnesota Press, 1997), 7.

34 **leaking personal information about police officers:** Kris Cheng, "Dozens of Police in Riot Gear Remove Flyers with Officers' Personal Information from Tai Po Lennon Wall," *Hong Kong Free Press*, July 10, 2019.

34 **a Lennon Wall on a footbridge:** "Lennon Wall Message Wall in Fanling Set on Fire by Arsonist," *Dimsum Daily*, July 14, 2019.

34 **a not-so-subtle death threat:** Kris Cheng, "Busloads of Pro-Government Activists Vandalise Tai Po Lennon Wall Message Board at 2am, Pasting Ads for Saturday Rally," *Hong Kong Free Press*, July 19, 2019.

34 **fights began to break out at Lennon Walls:** Elizabeth Cheung, "Fight over Lennon Wall Leaves Two Men Injured as Tensions Escalate between Anti-Government Protestors and Opponents," *South China Morning Post*, September 29, 2019.

34 **a mainlander attacked three people:** Victor Ting, "Three Hong Kongers Stabbed after Revealing Political Views," *Inkstone News*, August 20, 2019.

CHAPTER 2: 祖 ANCESTORS

37 **a late sixteenth-century map:** Hal Empson, *Mapping Hong Kong: A Historical Atlas* (Hong Kong: Government Information Services, 1992).

37 **earliest known mention of Hong Kong:** Liu Shuyong, *An Outline History of Hong Kong* (Beijing: Foreign Languages Press, 1997), 6.

37 **a recognizable coastline:** Empson, *Mapping Hong Kong*, 85, 86.

37 **Hung Kong (Red River):** Empson, *Mapping Hong Kong*, 96.

37 **Red Incense Burner Hill:** Empson, *Mapping Hong Kong*, 18, 87.

37 **Incense Harbor or Fragrant Harbor:** Empson, *Mapping Hong Kong*, 21.

37 **"Fan-chin-chow or He-ong Kong":** Empson, *Mapping Hong Kong*, 94.

37 **eventually stretching to encompass Hong Kong:** Cecile Kung, "Guanfu Salt Farm and Hong Kong in the Song Dynasty (960–1279)," *Social Transformations in Chinese Societies*, May 17, 2020.

38 **a verbal collection of maps:** Dung Kai-cheung, *Atlas: The Archaeology of an Imaginary City*, ed. Anders Hansson and Bonnie S. McDougall (New York: Columbia University Press, 2012), xii.

38 **"enough fictitious Hong Kongs":** Dung, *Atlas*, xi.

39 **the textbook my son studied:** *Chinese Language Yr 7*, ed. Jinan University Chinese Department (Jinan, China: Jinan University Press, 2007).

39 **In the story, "Visiting Hong Kong":** *Chinese Language Yr 7*, 7.

40 **"Britain's persistent aggression":** Liu, *An Outline History of Hong Kong*.

40 **the definitive, state-approved version:** Liu, *An Outline History of Hong Kong*.

40 **details of the settlement:** Liu, *An Outline History of Hong Kong*, 15.

41 **Hong Kong's administrative place:** Liu, *An Outline History of Hong Kong*, 6–7.

41 **Liu Shuyong's official history cites:** Liu, *An Outline History of Hong Kong*, 13.

41 **Some said they lived in thatched huts:** Information from wall plaque at Hong Kong Museum of Art.

41 **textual references to the Lo Ting:** Kai-wing Chow, *A General History of Hong Kong: Ancient Times* 香港通史: 遠古至清代 (Hong Kong: Joint Publishing Co., 2017).

42 **television show *HK Enigmata*:** Oscar Ho Hing-kay, "Lo Ting: Hong Kong's Lantau Mythology 盧亭: 大嶼山的香港神話."

43 **"History is like glasses":** Lam Tung-pang website: www.lamtungpang.com.

45 **the burial place of an official:** Patrick H. Hase, "Beside the Yamen: Nga Tsin Wai Village," *Journal of the Hong Kong Branch of the Royal Asiatic Society* 39 (1999).

45 **a salt monopoly:** Hase, "Beside the Yamen," 1.

45 **that of Emperor Wu:** Christopher DeWolf, "Hong Kong's Salty History: Rebellion, Smuggling and Shrimp Paste," *Zolima CityMag*, September 7, 2017.

45 **a paper published in 1999:** Hase, "Beside the Yamen."

45 **he believed it likely:** Hase, "Beside the Yamen."

45 **Chinese historians, too:** Liu, *An Outline History of Hong Kong*, 11.

45 **Hase even speculates that:** Patrick H. Hase, *Forgotten Heroes: San On County and Its Magistrates in the Late Ming and Early Qing* (Hong Kong: City University of Hong Kong Press, 2017).

46 **"strong proof":** Liu, *An Outline History of Hong Kong*, 6.

47 **dating back to 1464:** Mick Atha and Kennis Yip, *Piecing Together Sha Po: Archaeological Investigations and Landscape Reconstruction* (Hong Kong: Hong Kong University Press, 2016), 6.

47 **Pak Lo Mountain or Pok Liu:** Atha and Yip, *Piecing Together Sha Po*.

48 **eight sites of similar age:** Liu, *An Outline History of Hong Kong*, 2.

48 **fisher-hunter-foragers:** Atha and Yip, *Piecing Together Sha Po*, 39.

48 **two or three extended families:** Atha and Yip, *Piecing Together Sha Po*, 47.

48 **the site had been in continuous use:** Atha and Yip, *Piecing Together Sha Po*, 40.

48 **fifty-nine different salt production sites:** Kung, "Guanfu Salt Farm."

49 **Guanfu Salt Farm:** Kung, "Guanfu Salt Farm."

50 **"After rebels on the island":** Liu, *An Outline History of Hong Kong*, 11.

50 **"without leaving any survivor":** Kung, "Guanfu Salt Farm."

51 **circular disks of quartz:** Daniel Finn, *Archaeological Finds in Lamma Near Hong Kong* (Hong Kong: University of Hong Kong, 1958), 147.

51 **jewelry of some kind:** Finn, *Archaeological Finds in Lamma Near Hong Kong,* 143.

52 **It took another sixteen years:** Allan Pang, "Manipulating the Past: History Education in Late-Colonial Hong Kong," University of Hong Kong, 2018.

52 **found by a survey:** Gary Cheung, "New Hong Kong Story Museum Exhibits Include Controversial Events from the 1967 Riots to the July 1 March to Occupy," *South China Morning Post,* November 24, 2018.

54 **once the museum reopens again:** Cheung, "New Hong Kong Story Museum."

55 **In 2015, it was earmarked:** "All Going to Plan in FT's latest Zone," *China Daily,* December 7, 2015.

56 **"They want to have more extreme buildings":** Louisa Lim, "Beijing's Building Revolution," BBC, March 9, 2004.

56 **Rem Koolhaas's OMA and Norman Foster:** Christele Harrouk, "Construction Begins on OMA's CMG Qianhai Global Trade Center in Shenzhen, China," *ArchDaily,* May 11, 2020.

57 **high-speed railway:** Eric Cheung, "Launch of HK-China High-Speed Rail Link Goes Smoothly, but Fears Remain," CNN, September 23, 2018.

57 **the value of that plot of real estate:** Denise Tsang and Alvin Lum, "Mainland China Will Only Be Charged HK$1,000 Per Year for Hong Kong High-Speed Rail Terminus," *South China Morning Post,* August 31, 2018.

58 **visited by half the enclave's tourists:** Muhammad Cohen, "How the Venetian Made Macau Great Again," *South China Morning Post,* August 28, 2017.

59 **39 million visitors:** Devin O'Connor, "Macau Visitor Volume Sets Record, 39m People Traveled to Enclave in 2019," Casino.org, January 2, 2020.

59 **The Greater Bay Area strategy:** Niall Fraser, "Macau Poised to Become Richest Place on the Planet by 2020," *South China Morning Post,* August 8, 2018.

59 **civil disobedience statutes:** Raquel Carvalho, "Macau's Youngest Lawmaker Sulu Sou, Suspended from Office and Found Guilty over 2016 Protest, Hopes to Retake His Seat," *South China Morning Post,* June 2, 2018.

59 **free government-sponsored exhibitions:** Hong Kong Government, "'Understand: Greater Bay Area' Exhibition," news release, September 27, 2019, www.info.gov.hk/gia/general/201909/27/P2019092700692.htm.

59 **museum exhibits that use historic artifacts:** Stuart Heaver, "When Hong Kong Was a Way Station on the Maritime Silk Road—New Exhibition Showcases Recent Discoveries About City's Trading Past," *South China Morning Post,* Spetember 4, 2018.

61 **"Our ancestors were from the sea":** Anja Ziegler, "Hong Kong Incarnated" (master's thesis), 7.

64 **"The best weapon against myth":** Roland Barthes, *Mythologies,* trans. Annette Lavers (New York: Noonday Press, 1972).

CHAPTER 3: 九龍 KOWLOON

67 **"Eurasians were too different":** Vicky Lee, "The Code of Silence across the Hong Kong Eurasian Community(ies)," in *Meeting Place: Encounters across Cultures in Hong Kong, 1841–1984*, ed. Elizabeth Sinn and Christopher Munn (Hong Kong: Hong Kong University Press, 2018), 40. Much of the information about Eurasian communities is from this source.

69 **"Macaulay's Minute":** Thomas Macaulay, "Minute by the Hon'ble T. B. Macaulay, dated the 2nd February 1835."

69 **Hong Kong history was not taught:** Allan Pang, "Manipulating the Past: History Education in Late-Colonial Hong Kong," University of Hong Kong, 2018.

70 **"There were . . . certain historical reserves":** Transcript of interviews with Lord MacLehose by Steve Tsang, 1989–1991, MSS.Ind.Ocn. s.377, 285, Weston Library, University of Oxford, UK.

70 **Hong Kong as an entity:** Dung Kai-cheung, *Atlas: The Archaeology of an Imaginary City*, ed. Anders Hansson and Bonnie S. McDougall (New York: Columbia University Press, 2012), xi.

71 **three separate tranches:** *Encyclopaedia Britannica*, "Convention of 1898."

71 **"A war more unjust in its origins":** Julian Gewirtz, "'Imperial Twilight' Review: An Explosive Mix of Trade and Politics," *Wall Street Journal*, May 17, 2018.

72 **a famously corrupt official:** Frank Welsh, *A History of Hong Kong* (New York: HarperCollins, 1993), 27.

72 **an opium addict himself:** Peter Perdue, "The First Opium War: The Anglo-Chinese War of 1839–1842," in Visualizing Cultures, Massachusetts Institute of Technology, 2010.

72 **effectively blockading the foreign traders:** Stephen R. Platt, *Autumn in the Heavenly Kingdom: China, the West, and the Epic Story of the Taiping Civil War* (New York: Vintage Books, 2012), 352.

72 **More than twenty thousand chests:** Julia Lovell, *The Opium War: Drugs, Dreams, and the Making of China* (Sydney: Picador, 2011), 66.

72 **naval captain named Charles Elliot:** Platt, *Autumn in the Heavenly Kingdom*.

72 **the British government would compensate them:** Steve Tsang, *A Modern History of Hong Kong: 1841–1997* (London: I. B. Tauris & Company, 2007), 10.

72 **a draft treaty:** Welsh, *A History of Hong Kong*, 106.

73 **The battle for Chusan:** Lovell, *The Opium War*, 133.

73 **six fruitless months:** Ernest John Eitel, *Europe in China: The History of Hong Kong from the Beginning to the Year 1882* (Oxford: Oxford University Press, 1983), 121.

73 **Accounts by British soldiers:** Lovell, *The Opium War*, 132.

73 **"bespattered with brains":** Platt, *Autumn in the Heavenly Kingdom*, 404.

73 **The first envelope:** Letter from C. Elliot to Ch'i Shan, January 11, 1841, FO682/ 1974/12, UK National Archives, Kew.

74 **Qishan's reply:** Letter from Ch'i Shan to C. Elliot, January 15, 1841, FO682/1974/ 20, UK National Archives, Kew.

74 **Qishan points out:** Liu Shuyong, *An Outline History of Hong Kong* (Beijing: Foreign Languages Press, 1997), 30.

74 **In his reply:** Letter from C. Elliot to Ch'i Shan, January 16, 1841, FO682/1974/21, UK National Archives, Kew.

74 **according to Chinese historians:** Liu, *An Outline History of Hong Kong*, 30.

74 **"a surprise to all concerned":** Eitel, *Europe in China*, 124.

74 **known as the Convention of Chuenpi:** Tsang, *A Modern History of Hong Kong*, 11.

75 **"the bona fide first possessors":** K. J. P. Lowe, "Hong Kong, 26 January 1841: Hoisting the Flag Revisited," *Journal of the Hong Kong Branch of the Royal Asiatic Society* 29 (1989).

75 **He and his crew drank:** Eitel, *Europe in China*, 124.

75 **"diplomatic blackmail":** Liu, *An Outline History of Hong Kong*, 31.

75 **differences between the English and Chinese versions:** George H. C. Wong, "The Ch'i-Shan–Elliot Negotiations Concerning an Off-Shore Entrepôt and a Re-Evaluation of the Abortive Chuenpi Convention," *Monumenta Serica* 14, no. 1 (1949).

75 **George H. C. Wong:** Wong, "The Ch'i-Shan–Elliot Negotiations."

75 **"A barren rock with nary a house":** Hong Kong Government, "Speech by FS at Asian Financial Forum Cocktail Reception," news release, 2010, www.info.gov.hk/gia /general/201001/20/P201001200262.htm.

76 **"Even this cession as it is called":** Wong, "The Ch'i-Shan–Elliot Negotiations," 570.

76 **The Qing government was equally outraged:** Christopher Munn, *Anglo-China: Chinese People and British Rule in Hong Kong* (Richmond, Surrey, UK: Curzon, 2000), 25.

76 **His assets were confiscated:** Lovell, *The Opium War.*

76 **1841 census figures:** Fan Shuh-ching, *The Population of Hong Kong* (Committee for International Coordination of National Research in Demography, 1974).

76 **It did not officially become a Crown Colony:** R. L. Jarman, *Hong Kong: Annual Administration Reports 1841–1941* (Cambridge: University of Cambridge, 1996).

76 **no proper authority to do so:** Many of the details of the first land sales derive from Roger Nissim, *Land Administration and Practice in Hong Kong*, 4th ed. (Hong Kong: Hong Kong University Press, 2016).

76 **all unoccupied land lots were Crown land:** Many of the details about the British misunderstanding of traditional landowning practices come from Munn, *Anglo-China.*

76 **traditional Chinese land-owning practices:** Patrick H. Hase, *The Six-Day War of 1899: Hong Kong in the Age of Imperialism* (Hong Kong: Hong Kong University Press, 2008), 58.

77 **ninety-six pounds each:** Again, details about the first land sales are from Nissim, *Land Administration and Practice in Hong Kong.*

77 **a performing orangutan:** Lovell, *The Opium War*, 245.

78 **an enormous jail:** "The History of Tai Kwun" (2019).

78 **the first city plan:** Hal Empson, *Mapping Hong Kong: A Historical Atlas [Hsiang-Kang Ti T'u Hui Chih Shih]* (Hong Kong: Government Information Services, 1992).

78 **more than 8 percent of the population:** Munn, *Anglo-China*, 111.

78 **a hawkish major general:** Tsang, *A Modern History of Hong Kong.*

78 **the settlement was too advanced:** Details regarding Pottinger are from George Pottinger, *Sir Henry Pottinger: First Governor of Hong Kong* (New York: St. Martin's Press, 1997).

78 **He later admitted:** Pottinger, *Sir Henry Pottinger*, 196.

78 **an 1847 report:** Perdue, "The First Opium War."

78 **"future Great Emporium of Commerce and Wealth":** Munn, *Anglo-China*, 37.

79 **a curfew banning all Chinese:** Munn, *Anglo-China*, 131.

79 **"warping to the mind":** Jan Morris, *Hong Kong: Epilogue to an Empire*, final ed. (London: Penguin, 1997), 88.

79 **"dishonest, potentially dangerous, malevolent":** Peter Wesley-Smith, "Anti-Chinese Legislation in Hong Kong," in *Precarious Balance: Hong Kong between China and Britain, 1842–1992*, ed. Ming K. Chan and John D. Young (Armonk, NY: M. E. Sharpe, 1994).

79 **The graveyard on a hillside:** Details of the expropriation of Wong Nai Chung village are from Patricia Lim, *Forgotten Souls: A Social History of the Hong Kong Cemetery* (Hong Kong: Hong Kong University Press, 2011), 7–8.

80 **two cultural heritage guidebooks:** Patricia Lim, *Discovering Hong Kong's Cultural Heritage: Hong Kong and Kowloon: With 19 Guided Walks* (Oxford: Oxford University Press, 2002); Patricia Lim, *Discovering Hong Kong's Cultural Heritage: The New Territories* (Hong Kong: Oxford University Press, 2002).

80 **the social history of the graveyard:** Lim, *Forgotten Souls.*

80 **"All Hong Kong history is here":** Louisa Lim, "Deaths Tell the Story of Life in Early Hong Kong," NPR, August 21, 2012.

81 **Lieutenant Benjamin Fox:** Lim, *Forgotten Souls.*

81 **three-quarters of the Indian opium crop:** Joseph Ting Sung-pao, "1860–1898: The Establishment of Entrepot Trade" in *History of the Port of Hong Kong and the Marine Department*, ed. Chin-pang Lau (Hong Kong: Marine Department, 2017).

81 **"He fell lifeless from his chair"**: Lim, *Forgotten Souls*, 175.

81 **a trading station free from Chinese jurisdiction**: Law Wing-sang, *Collaborative Colonial Power: The Making of the Hong Kong Chinese* (Hong Kong: Hong Kong University Press, 2009).

82 **He poisoned some four hundred Europeans**: Lim, *Forgotten Souls*.

82 **In Bowring's sobering assessment**: Munn, *Anglo-China*, 1.

83 **"a lot to pay for a dog"**: Lim, *Forgotten Souls*, 167.

84 **a book he wrote about his time in Japan and China**: Edward Barrington de Fonblanque, *Niphon and Pe-Che-Li: Or, Two Years in Japan and Northern China* (London: Saunders, Otley, 1862).

84 **"so warped in their judgment"**: De Fonblanque, *Niphon and Pe-Che-Li*.

85 **"half maddened with fear"**: De Fonblanque, *Niphon and Pe-Che-Li*, 128.

85 **"golden josses or ingots"**: De Fonblanque, *Niphon and Pe-Che-Li*, 196.

86 **Kowloon's military and strategic value**: Tsang, *A Modern History of Hong Kong*.

86 **"a seat of anarchy and a source of embarrassment"**: Eitel, *Europe in China*, 358.

86 **"In the afternoon to Lau"**: Welsh, *A History of Hong Kong*, 226.

86 **"In spite of the pretensions of our diplomatists"**: De Fonblanque, *Niphon and Pe-Che-Li*, 262–63.

87 **the slapdash attitude of MacDonald**: Tsang, *A Modern History of Hong Kong*.

87 **an up-to-date map of the land**: Wesley-Smith, "Anti-Chinese Legislation in Hong Kong."

88 **a permanent cession in disguise**: Tsang, *A Modern History of Hong Kong*.

88 **the British saw them as triads**: Information about the events of 1899 is mainly from Hase, *The Six-Day War of 1899*. And Peter Wesley-Smith, "Unequal Treaty, 1898–1997: China, Great Britain, and Hong Kong's New Territories" (Revision of thesis [PhD], University of Hong Kong, 1976, 1980).

88 **"like a rock, crushing"**: Hase, *The Six-Day War of 1899*, 56.

89 **"Everything is being systematically changed!"**: Hase, *The Six-Day War of 1899*, 47.

89 **Tang genealogy**: Hase, *The Six-Day War of 1899*.

90 **"pass a sponge over the events"**: Hase, *The Six-Day War of 1899*, 128.

90 **"a glorious page in Hong Kong's history"**: Wesley-Smith, "Unequal Treaty, 1898–1997," 83.

90 **the villagers seen as patriots**: Liu, *An Outline History of Hong Kong*.

90 **the target of an assassination attempt**: "1912 Attempt to Assassinate Governor," from the *International Herald Tribune* 100, 75, 50 Years Ago, *New York Times*, July 4, 2012.

90 **the most racist governor of them all**: Wesley-Smith, "Anti-Chinese Legislation in Hong Kong."

90 **"he is white right through":** Esther Morris, *Helena May: The Person, the Place and 90 Years of History in Hong Kong* (Hong Kong: Helena May Institute, 2016), 9.

90 **"little short of a calamity":** David M. Pomfret, "Raising Eurasia: Race, Class, and Age in French and British Colonies," *Comparative Studies in Society and History* 51, no. 2 (2009): 324.

91 **"The English barbarians are about to enter":** Hase, *The Six-Day War of 1899*, 46–47.

91 **One clue signals:** Hase, *The Six-Day War of 1899*, picture plate 17.

92 **a modern iteration of the photograph:** Lam Yik-fei, *Woh Yuhng: Photographs from the 2019 Hong Kong Protests* (Hong Kong: Brownie Publishing, 2020), picture plate 35.

92 **"Like a valiant mantis":** Hase, *The Six-Day War of 1899*, 187.

CHAPTER 4: 新界 NEW TERRITORIES

95 **Thatcher had gone in hoping:** Margaret Thatcher, *The Downing Street Years* (London: HarperCollins, 1993), 259.

96 **described him as cruel:** Percy Cradock, *Experiences of China*, new ed. (London: John Murray, 1999), 179.

96 **could do so that very day:** Thatcher, *The Downing Street Years*, 261–62.

96 **"We will not be Li Hongzhang":** China: No 10 Record of Conversation, September 24, 1982, Thatcher MSS (Churchill Archive Centre): THCR 1/10/39-2 f52, Margaret Thatcher Foundation, www.margaretthatcher.org/document/122696.

96 **Thatcher features Hong Kong:** Thatcher, *The Downing Street Years*, 87, 91–92, 93, 94, 95, 259–62, 466.

97 **five of his 774 pages:** John Major, *John Major: The Autobiography* (New York: HarperCollins, 1999), 118–19, 495, 506, 507.

97 **Hong Kong's most important figures:** Hong Kong Archive, Weston Library, University of Oxford, UK.

97 **extraordinarily difficult negotiations:** Robert Cottrell, *The End of Hong Kong: The Secret Diplomacy of Imperial Retreat* (London: John Murray, 1993).

98 **no governor had acted against its advice:** Chim Lo Yui, "The Last Stand of Colonialism? The Unofficial Members of the Executive and Legislative Councils and the Sino-British Negotiations over Hong Kong, 1982–1984," *Journal of Imperial and Commonwealth History* 48, no. 2 (2020): 371.

99 **"the Chinese in the colony most knowledgeable":** Sze-yuen Chung, *Hong Kong's Journey to Reunification: Memoirs of Sze-Yuen Chung* (Hong Kong: Chinese University Press, 2001), 25.

99 **born with silver spoons:** Transcript of interviews with Sir Sze-yuen Chung by Steve Tsang, 1989–1990, MSS.Ind.Ocn. s.328, p. 60, Weston Library, University of Oxford, UK.

99 **A hard worker who spent every Sunday:** Mark Roberti, *The Fall of Hong Kong: China's Triumph and Britain's Betrayal*, revised and updated ed. (New York: John Wiley & Sons, 1996).

99 **"not to be seen by anybody":** Transcript of interviews with Sir Sze-yuen Chung, 282.

99 **"These are the facts":** Transcript of interviews with Sir Sze-yuen Chung, 167.

99 **"This is confidential":** Transcript of interviews with Sir Sze-yuen Chung, 158.

99 **"twenty-five years from now":** Transcript of interviews with Sir Sze-yuen Chung, 166.

99 **"this disclosure could lead me into trouble":** Transcript of interviews with Sir Sze-yuen Chung, 167.

99 **"Thank you for the interview":** Transcript of interviews with Sir Sze-yuen Chung, 419.

100 **an estimated 213,000 Vietnamese:** Carina Hoang, "Vietnamese Boat People Crisis in Hong Kong" presentation at Curtin University, Lecture at Curtin University, July 2018, https://businesslaw.curtin.edu.au/wp-content/uploads/sites/5/2018/07/Vietnamese-boat-people-crisis-in-HKG-Carina-Hoang.pdf.

100 **"I don't think we faced any pressure":** Transcript of interviews with Li Fook-Wo by Steve Tsang, 1990, MSS.Ind.Ocn. s.334, p. 25, Weston Library, University of Oxford, UK.

100 **"They didn't really have a policy":** Transcript of interviews with Lord MacLehose by Steve Tsang, 1989–1991, MSS.Ind.Ocn. s.377, p. 508, Weston Library, University of Oxford, UK.

100 **"Secretary of State's hair":** FCO papers 1988-FCO 40-2581 334 p10.

101 **"government in a hurry":** Transcript of interviews with Lord MacLehose, 118.

101 **refused to call his outings "walkabouts":** Transcript of interviews with Lord MacLehose, 361.

101 **"an effective and more immediate substitute":** Transcript of interviews with Lord MacLehose, 298.

101 **"Pandora's box of drastic constitutional reform":** Transcript of interviews with Lord MacLehose, 350.

101 **Hong Kong's system could outperform electoral politics:** Transcript of interviews with Lord MacLehose, 371.

102 **mentioning 1997 was seen as a "crime":** Transcript of interviews with Li Fook-wo, 55.

102 **"Nobody ever dared to touch the question":** Transcript of interview with Ann Tse-kai by Steve Tsang, MSS.Ind.Ocn. s.332, p. 15, Weston Library, University of Oxford, UK.

102 **"an inescapable source of crisis":** Transcript of interviews with Lord MacLehose, 492.

102 **grossly irresponsible:** Transcript of interviews with Lord MacLehose, 494.

102 **indeed indefensible:** Transcript of interviews with Lord MacLehose, 494.

102 **Beijing would not hesitate to intervene:** Transcript of interviews with Lord MacLehose, 389–90.

102 **Hong Kong's survival depended:** Transcript of interviews with Lord MacLehose, 580.

102 **"a conspiracy of silence":** Transcript of interviews with Lord MacLehose, 616.

102 **the first official Chinese acknowledgment:** Steve Tsang, *A Modern History of Hong Kong: 1841–1997* (London: I. B. Tauris & Company, 2007), 212.

102 **a carefully thought-out plan:** Transcript of interviews with Lord MacLehose, 616.

103 **agreement whereby Britain could continue:** Cottrell, *The End of Hong Kong*.

103 **a trial balloon to investigate Beijing's intentions:** Tsang, *A Modern History of Hong Kong*. Cradock, *Experiences of China*, 166.

103 **he would be meeting Deng Xiaoping:** Ezra F. Vogel, *Deng Xiaoping and the Transformation of China* (Cambridge, MA: Belknap Press of Harvard University Press, 2011).

103 **tried to dissuade him from the plan:** Roberti, *The Fall of Hong Kong*.

103 **MacLehose was determined to push ahead:** Tsang, *A Modern History of Hong Kong*.

103 **Beijing would respect Hong Kong's special status:** Tsang, *A Modern History of Hong Kong*.

103 **It was not clear whether Deng had understood:** Cottrell, *The End of Hong Kong*.

103 **"put their hearts at ease":** Cradock, *Experiences of China*, 166.

104 **"It is rather attractive":** Transcript of interviews with Lord MacLehose, 518.

104 **MacLehose and his team decided:** Transcript of interviews with Lord MacLehose, 517.

104 **dressed down by Chinese foreign minister Huang Hua:** Cottrell, *The End of Hong Kong*.

104 **"the result would have been the same":** Cottrell, *The End of Hong Kong*, 495.

104 **One factor was polling:** Chung, *Hong Kong's Journey to Reunification*, 25.

105 **MacLehose was concerned:** Roberti, *The Fall of Hong Kong*.

105 **"catastrophic" effect on markets:** Transcript of interviews with Lord MacLehose, 504.

105 **"it was perfectly legal":** Transcript of interviews with Lord MacLehose, 506.

105 **"it would put a strain on them":** Transcript of interviews with Lord MacLehose, 504.

105 **the letter was never answered:** Transcript of interviews with Sir Sze-yuen Chung, 151.

106 **He firmly opposed:** Transcript of interviews with Sir Sze-yuen Chung, 264.

106 **a key role in watering down British proposals:** Roberti, *The Fall of Hong Kong*.

106 **"Y. K. Kan knew something I did not":** Transcript of interviews with Sir Sze-yuen Chung, 153.

106 **"History will never know":** Transcript of interviews with Sir Sze-yuen Chung, 150.

106 **"Nobody would ask the Governor":** Transcript of interviews with Roger Lobo by Steve Tsang, 1990, MSS.Ind.Ocn. s.405, p. 84, Weston Library, University of Oxford, UK.

107 **an "external war":** Transcript of interviews with Sir Sze-yuen Chung, 280.

107 **This disagreement scarred the relationship:** Mark Chi-kwan, "Decolonising Britishness? The 1981 British Nationality Act and the Identity Crisis of Hong Kong Elites," *Journal of Imperial and Commonwealth History* 48, no. 3 (2020).

107 **a second-class citizenship:** Cottrell, *The End of Hong Kong.*

107 **no copies of the paper:** Roberti, *The Fall of Hong Kong.*

107 **Unofficials wanted to go to London:** Mark, "Decolonising Britishness?"

107 **nationality was a dead issue:** Transcript of interviews with Roger Lobo, 103.

107 **the vote had already been decided:** Transcript of interviews with Roger Lobo, 93–94.

107 **"We don't mind having you people in":** Transcript of interviews with Li Fook-wo, 58.

107 **defeated by just three votes:** Mark, "Decolonising Britishness?"

108 **"I was in the boat and they were not":** Transcript of interviews with Lord MacLehose, 554.

108 **He suggested two possibilities:** Transcript of interviews with Roger Lobo, 175–76.

109 **They were assured:** No 10 Record of Conversation (MT, Youde, Cradock, Donald, Haddon-Cave, SY Chung) ["Record of a meeting between the Prime Minister and unofficial members of the Executive Council"], September 27, 1982, PREM19-0790 f108, Margaret Thatcher Foundation, https://839d6adc517f14a0ad6a-b9527bc5dce0df4456f4c5548db2e5c2.ssl.cf1.rackcdn.com/820927%20no.10%20cnv%20PREM19-0790%20f108.pdf.

109 **he sent an official memo:** Youde Minute to No 10 (meeting with Umelco), September 26, 1982, PREM19-788 f95, Margaret Thatcher Foundation, accessed February 16, 2021, https://839d6adc517f14a0ad6a-b9527bc5dce0df4456f4c5548db2e5c2.ssl.cf1.rackcdn.com/820926%20youde%20min%20PREM19-0788%20f95.pdf.

109 **"inside a drum":** Chung, *Hong Kong's Journey to Reunification*, 58.

109 **under orders from Thatcher:** Chung, *Hong Kong's Journey to Reunification*, 60–62.

109 **Chung gave him an ultimatum:** Chung, *Hong Kong's Journey to Reunification*, 61.

109 **he made a threat:** No 10 Record of conversation between the Prime Minister and SY Chung CBE, December 10, 1982, PREM 19/1059 f199, Margaret Thatcher Foundation, accessed February 16, 2021, https://839d6adc517f14a0ad6a-b9527bc5dce0df4456f4c5548db2e5c2.ssl.cf1.rackcdn.com/821220%20no.10%20cnv%20PREM19-1053%20f199.pdf, Accessed February 16, 2021.

109 **The British would not even permit:** Transcript of interviews with Sir Sze-yuen Chung, 205.

109 **To Beijing, they were nonexistent:** Transcript of interviews with Sir Sze-yuen Chung.

110 **Cradock described them:** Cradock, *Experiences of China*, 111.

110 **Beijing would act unilaterally:** Cradock, *Experiences of China*, 184.

110 **starting with a weak hand:** Cradock, *Experiences of China*, 185.

110 **"*prepared* to recommend":** Ngok Ma, "The Sino-British Dispute over Hong Kong: A Game Theory Interpretation," *Asian Survey* 37, no. 8 (1997): 741.

110 **not all the cards were on the Chinese side:** No 10 Record of Conversation (MT, Youde, Cradock, Donald, Haddon-Cave, SY Chung) ["Record of a meeting between the Prime Minister and unofficial members of the Executive Council], September 27, 1982, PREM19-0790, f108, p. 7, Margaret Thatcher Foundation, https://839d6adc517f14a0ad6a-b9527bc5dce0df4456f4c5548db2e5c2.ssl.cf1.rackcdn.com/820927%20no.10%20cnv%20PREM19-0790%20f108.pdf.

110 **"'We have no cards to play'":** Transcript of interviews with Roger Lobo, 145.

111 **they weren't being given access:** Transcript of interviews with Roger Lobo, 42.

111 **"Oh, this will be very messy":** Transcript of interviews with Roger Lobo, 141.

111 **a twelve-point plan for Hong Kong's future:** Cottrell, *The End of Hong Kong*.

111 **"moments during the period of negotiations":** Transcript of interviews with Roger Lobo, 143.

112 **"They are making opening bids":** Transcript of interviews with Sir Sze-yuen Chung, 224.

112 **set down in an official memo:** UKE Beijing telegram to FCO ("Future of Hong Kong: Calls on Chinese Leaders"), December 9, 1983, PREM19-1059 f168, p. 3, Margaret Thatcher Foundation.

112 **sobbing from two councillors:** Chung, *Hong Kong's Journey to Reunification*, 75.

112 **an untenable position:** Cradock, *Experiences of China*, 191.

113 **"a little scared of the Chinese":** Transcript of interviews with Li Fook-wo, 108.

113 **"I could not even tell my wife":** Transcript of interviews with Roger Lobo, 195.

113 **"the desperate position":** Transcript of interviews with Roger Lobo, 196.

113 **"the cards that we possessed":** No 10 Record of Conversation (MT, Howe, Luce, Acland, Cradock, Evans, Youde, SY Chung/Exco), January 16, 1984, PREM19-1262 f119, p. 5, Margaret Thatcher Foundation, https://ee9da88eff6f462f2d6b-873dc3788ab15d5cbb1e3fe45dbec9b4.ssl.cf1.rackcdn.com/840116%20no.10%20cnv%20PREM19-1262%20f119.pdf.

113 **the last nail in the coffin:** Youde Telegram to FCO ("Future of Hong Kong: Consultation with Exco"), March 29, 1984, PREM19-1263, f16, Margaret Thatcher Foundation, www.margaretthatcher.org/document/139893.

114 **one diplomatic memo from their meeting noted:** No 10 Record of Conversation (MT, Howe, Michael Havers, Luce, Acland, Cradock, Youde, SY Chung) ["Meeting with the Unofficial Members of Exco"], April 6, 1984, PREM19-1264 f197, p. 6, https://ee9da88eff6f462f2d6b-873dc3788ab15d5cbb1e3fe45dbec9b4.ssl.cf1.rackcdn.com/840406%20no.10%20cnv%20PREM19-1264%20f197.pdf.

114 **"It seems the Unofficials were right":** UKE Beijing telegram to FCO ("Future of Hong Kong: call on Zhou Nan on 13 April") [Howe in China; MT: "seems as if the

Unofficials were right in their judgement"], April 13, 1984, PREM19-1264 f146, www.margaretthatcher.org/document/139737.

115 **Youde tried to lean on Chung:** Chung, *Hong Kong's Journey to Reunification*, 85–86.

115 **a whispering campaign:** Chung, *Hong Kong's Journey to Reunification*, 86.

115 **Even Howe chided them:** Chung, *Hong Kong's Journey to Reunification*, 88.

116 **"I will never forgive them":** Transcript of interviews with Sir Sze-yuen Chung, 228.

116 **"unforgivably stupid":** Transcript of interviews with Lord MacLehose, 558.

116 **It was a crisis point:** Chung, *Hong Kong's Journey to Reunification*, 88.

116 **more than eight thousand letters and telegrams:** Chim Lo, "The Last Stand of Colonialism?" 385.

117 **"Kindly ask Lord MacLehose":** Roberti, *The Fall of Hong Kong*, 90.

117 **"the true views of the Hong Kong people":** Chung, *Hong Kong's Journey to Reunification*, 90.

117 **the highlight of all his trips to London:** Roberti, *The Fall of Hong Kong*.

117 **"'let's close the deal'":** Transcript of interviews with Sir Sze-yuen Chung, 227.

117 **Since May 1983:** Chung, *Hong Kong's Journey to Reunification*, 95.

118 **the concerns of Hong Kongers:** Transcript of interviews with Sir Sze-yuen Chung, 2.

118 **"three main worries":** Chung, *Hong Kong's Journey to Reunification*, 101.

118 **"It is you who have no faith":** Chung, *Hong Kong's Journey to Reunification*.

118 **All-caps headlines greeted them:** Roberti, *The Fall of Hong Kong*, 98.

118 **target of an assassination threat:** Transcript of interviews with Sir Sze-yuen Chung, 164, autobiography, 118.

119 **"the die was cast":** Transcript of interviews with Sir Sze-yuen Chung, 168.

119 **S. Y. Chung pushed for a referendum:** Joyce Ng, "'Godfather of HK Politics' Chung Sze-yuen Once Described by Top British Advisor as 'Not Reliable,'" *South China Morning Post*, January 14, 2019.

119 **determined to finish on Deng's schedule:** Transcript of interviews with Sir Sze-yuen Chung, 223.

119 **"they refused to talk about the details":** Transcript of interviews with Sir Sze-yuen Chung, 350.

119 **September 26, 1984:** Roberti, *The Fall of Hong Kong*.

120 **This document stipulated:** The Joint Declaration can be seen here: www.cmab.gov.hk/en/issues/jd2.htm.

120 **The document was greeted enthusiastically:** Roberti, *The Fall of Hong Kong*, 116.

120 **"No one was happy":** Transcript of interviews with Sir Sze-yuen Chung, 283.

120 **"no agreement at all":** Cottrell, *The End of Hong Kong*, 173.

120 **the singularly unenviable position:** Chung, *Hong Kong's Journey to Reunification*, 77.

121 **"It was not easy for us":** Transcript of interviews with Sir Sze-yuen Chung, 162.

122 **at times risking his life:** Transcript of interviews with Sir Sze-yuen Chung, 287.

CHAPTER 5: 香港政府 HONG KONG GOVERNMENT

124 **"in the light of the actual situation":** Basic Law is available at: www.basiclaw.gov.hk /en/basiclawtext/index.html.

125 **"The Chinese cannot resolve it":** Transcript of interviews with Sir Sze-yuen Chung by Steve Tsang, 1989–1990, MSS.Ind.Ocn. s.328, p. 255, Weston Library, University of Oxford, UK.

126 **"the worst abuses of British eighteenth-century parliamentary history":** Chris Patten, *East and West* (London: Macmillan, 1998), 58.

126 **"embarrassingly moderate":** Jonathan Dimbleby, *The Last Governor: Chris Patten and the Handover of Hong Kong* (London: Little, Brown & Co., 1997).

127 **"ride on a through train":** Christine Loh, *Underground Front: The Chinese Communist Party in Hong Kong* (Hong Kong: Hong Kong University Press, 2010), 180.

127 **"an absolutely tight grip":** Dimbleby, *The Last Governor*, 161.

128 **"we need China more than they need us":** Dimbleby, *The Last Governor*.

130 **a solo exhibition:** Lu Pan, "Writing at the End of History: Reflections on Two Cases of Graffiti in Hong Kong," *Public Art Dialogue* 4, no. 1 (2014).

130 **"I don't see any artistic value":** Keith Richburg, "Words of Calligrapher Perplexing Hong Kong," *Washington Post*, May 12, 1997.

131 **"new blossoms on a decayed branch":** David Spalding, ed., *King of Kowloon: The Art of Tsang Tsou-choi* (Bologna, Italy: Damiani, 2013), 215.

131 **the kind of scene that Lau had hoped for:** Oscar Ho Hing-kay, "The Betrayal of the King," *Artlink* 34, no. 1 (2014).

133 **he did not think he could get the land back:** Richburg, "Words of Calligrapher Perplexing Hong Kong."

139 **"simpering and shimmering":** *Sze-yuen* Chung, *Hong Kong's Journey to Reunification: Memoirs of Sze-Yuen Chung* (Hong Kong: Chinese University Press, 2001), 273. Chung writes that the new chief executive, Tung Chee-hwa, had not realized the seating arrangement until it was mentioned to him by the Singaporean prime minister, Goh Chok-Tong.

140 **"We shall not forget you":** Agence France Presse, "Words of a Prince and a President: Continuity, Change and Assurances," *New York Times*, July 1, 1997.

140 **Hong Kong's flagpole was lower:** Regional flag and Regional emblem bill can be found here: www.legco.gov.hk/yr97-98/english/bills/bills03/bills03.htm.

140 **a written account for friends:** Agence France Presse, "Prince Charles Wins Diary Battle," *ABC Australia*, December 21, 2006.

141 **"The return of Hong Kong to the motherland":** Jiang Zemin's speech can be found here: www.fmprc.gov.cn/mfa_eng/wjdt_665385/zyjh_665391/t24924.shtml.

141 **"We are Chinese":** Martin Lee's speech can be found here: www.martinlee.org.hk /July1Declaration.html.

CHAPTER 6: 國皇 KING

148 **As Tung later described in a newspaper interview:** Cliff Buddle, "Hong Kong's First Chief Executive Tung Chee-Hwa Takes a Trip Down Memory Lane," *South China Morning Post*, July 2, 2017.

149 **"threatening piece of legislation":** Elson Tong, "Reviving Article 23 (Part I): The Rise and Fall of Hong Kong's 2003 National Security Bill," *Hong Kong Free Press*, February 17, 2018.

149 **"We are not introducing":** "HK Needs Laws to Protect National Security by Secretary for Security, Mrs Regina Ip," news release, January 28, 2003, www.basiclaw23 .gov.hk/english/focus/focus5.htm.

151 **"There may be riots in the future":** "Huge Protest Fills HK Streets," CNN, July 2, 2003.

152 **"at several US institutions":** Louisa Lim and Julia Bergin, "Inside China's Audacious Global Propaganda Offensive," *The Guardian*, December 7, 2018.

153 **bailed out of bankruptcy:** Eric Guyot, "Tung Chee Hwa Admits China Aided His Shipping Firm in '80s," *Wall Street Journal*, October 24, 1996.

153 **godfather deal that couldn't be refused:** S. C. Yeung, "Cosco Takeover of Orient Overseas Fits a Pattern," *EJ Insight*, July 11, 2017.

153 **an eight-hundred-person Selection Committee:** Keith Bradsher, "Beijing Asserts New Control over Election Laws in Hong Kong," *New York Times*, April 6, 2004.

156 **there's still no consensus:** Victor Mair, February 25, 2017, https://languagelog.ldc .upenn.edu/nll/?p=31255.

156 **not an official language:** Johnny Tam and Stuart Lau, "Education Bureau Rapped over Cantonese 'Not an Official Language' Gaffe," *South China Morning Post*, February 2, 2014.

156 **"its own language":** Rey Chow, "Between Colonizers; Hong Kong's Postcolonial Self-Writing in the 1990s," *Diaspora, a Journal of Transnational Studies*, vol. 2, no. 2 (Toronto: University of Toronto Press, Fall 1992), 155.

160 **"dare to speak out":** Louisa Lim, *The People's Republic of Amnesia: Tiananmen Revisited* (New York: Oxford University Press, 2014), 84.

160 **"oppressed collective unconsciousness":** Hou Hanru, "How to Remember Tsang Tsou-choi?" in *King of Kowloon: The Art of Tsang Tsou-choi*, ed. David Spalding (Bologna, Italy: Damiani, 2013), 124.

160 **"a poet whose page"**: Hans Ulrich Obrist, "Foreword: A Protest against Forgetting," in *King of Kowloon*, ed. David Spalding, 4.

165 **He wanted to figure out:** *King of Kowloon*, 236.

167 **Zone of Urgency:** Details of the Venice Biennale's Zone of Urgency are here: http://universes-in-universe.de/car/venezia/bien50/zou/english.htm.

167 **a relapse of his leg injury:** Spalding, *King of Kowloon*.

168 **His writing jumped:** Joel Chung, *Post No Bills* (Hong Kong: CUP Magazine Publishing, 2009).

169 **a newspaper article taking the media to task:** Lau Kin-wai, "The Media Is Out of Control," *Apple Daily*, August 7, 2007.

169 **"His writing remains"**: Chip Tsao, "Chip Tsao Writes: Tsang Tsou-choi's First Family Under Heaven," *Apple Daily*, July 28, 2007.

169 **"Everyone is writing about him"**: Li Bafang, "Walls Have Ears: Emperors Show with No Family," *Apple Daily*, July 31, 2007.

169 **"a political figure seeking justice"**: Chip Tsao, "Another King," *Apple Daily*, July 29, 2007.

169 **"his relics remain"**: Li Bafang, "Walls Have Ears: Searching for the Emperor's Ink Relics," *Apple Daily*, July 28, 2007.

169 **"'ink treasures'"**: Chip Tsao, "Grandpa Tsang Tsou," *Apple Daily*, July 27, 2007, E05.

169 **"Hong Kong people's collective memories"**: "Respecting Wishes, Government Agrees to Leave the King's Ink Treasures," *Singtao Daily*, July 27, 2007, A08.

169 **his approval rating dropped**: Details of chief executive popularity polls are here: www.hkupop.hku.hk/english/popexpress/ceall/cerq/poll/poll_chart.html?cat=poll&str=2&end=249.

170 **should have been given an OBE:** "Save the Queen: Calling for People Power; 3 Days Movement to Stop Destruction," *Apple Daily*, July 27, 2007, A08.

170 **"the most honourable emperor in history"**: Xiao Hua, "Seeking: King of Kowloon, he always kept his head down," *Apple Daily*, July 27, 2007, A26.

170 **"for half a century"**: Chan Ye, "The Emperor's Legacy," *Apple Daily*, July 30, 2007, E8.

170 **an embodiment of Lion Rock Spirit:** "Real person's story becomes 'Hooligan Emperor,'" *Apple Daily*, July 26, 2007, A04.

170 **"not living above others"**: Xiao Hua, "Seeking: King of Kowloon, he always kept his head down," *Apple Daily*, July 27, 2007, A26.

170 **"a moral teacher"**: Chip Tsao, "Living in Catalogues, King of Kowloon Edition/Tsang the Survivor," *Ming Pao*, July 29, 2007.

170 **"No matter if he's a true or fake"**: "MC Yan: The First Person to Use HK Streets as a Canvas," *Ming Pao*, July 26, 2007.

171 **it was a decoy:** He Jiamin, Peng Bice, Chen Pei, "The Emperor Sleeps Quietly at Wo Hop Shek," *Ming Pao*, August 7, 2007.

171 **"Empty City Strategem":** William Tang, "Brocade Journal," *Hong Kong Economic Journal*, August 7, 2007.

172 **Thirteen protestors:** Minnie Wong, Howard Tang, and Vivienne Tsang, "From Local Identity to the Pursuit of Independence: The Changing Face of Hong Kong Localism," *Hong Kong Free Press*, November 11, 2016.

173 **"Hong Kong people remember the King of Kowloon":** Lee Yee, "Commentary: The Emperor Has Gone, Can the Queen Remain?" *Apple Daily*, July, 28, 2007, A8.

173 **"The rise of the new Hong Konger had begun":** Joshua Wong and Jason Y. Ng, *Unfree Speech: The Threat to Global Democracy and Why We Must Act, Now* (New York: Penguin Books, 2020).

175 **"Locusts come in groups":** Louisa Lim, "For Hong Kong and Mainland, Distrust Only Grows," NPR, March 23, 2012.

177 **"Hong Kongers will prevail":** Wong and Ng, *Unfree Speech*, 34.

CHAPTER 7: 一世祖 THE FIRST GENERATION

182 **the same body issued a decision:** Details of the decision can be found here: www .basiclaw.gov.hk/en/basiclawtext/images/basiclawtext_doc23.pdf.

184 **street protests had become utterly routine:** Antony Dapiran, *City of Protest: A Recent History of Dissent in Hong Kong* (Australia: Penguin Random House, 2017).

185 **nineteen people were arrested:** Chris Buckley, Austin Ramzy, and Edward Wong, "Violence Erupts in Hong Kong as Protesters Are Assaulted," *New York Times*, October 3, 2014.

185 **outsourcing their dirty work to mobsters:** Louisa Lim, "The Thugs of Mainland China," *New Yorker*, October 8, 2014.

187 **ordering the clearance of all the sites:** Johannes Chan, "A Storm of Unprecedented Ferocity: The Shrinking Space of the Right to Political Participation, Peaceful Demonstration, and Judicial Independence in Hong Kong," *International Journal of Constitutional Law* 16, no. 2 (2018).

187 **955 people had been arrested:** Lin Jing, "Hong Kong Police Clear Last Pro-Democracy Protests as Leaders Vow Movement Will Continue," Radio Free Asia, December 15, 2014.

189 **no record of him leaving Thailand:** Human Rights Watch, "China: Release Abducted Swedish Bookseller," news release, October 17, 2016, www.hrw.org/news /2016/10/17/china-release-abducted-swedish-bookseller.

192 **"Scholars kneeling":** Thanks to poet Tammy Ho Lai-ming for supplying this poem.

193 **snatched from a luxury hotel:** Michael Forsythe and Paul Mozur, "A Video, a Wheelchair, a Suitcase: Mystery of Vanished Tycoon Deepens," *New York Times*, 2017.

198 **teachers were warned:** Kris Cheng, "Teachers Warned They Could Lose Qualifications for Advocating Independence in Schools," *Hong Kong Free Press*, August 15, 2016.

198 **He'd been found guilty:** Joyce Ng and Shirley Zhao, "Occupy Central Founder Benny Tai Banned from Supervising Researchers for Three Years Following HKU Donation Scandal," *South China Morning Post*, August 26, 2015.

200 **a court decision in 2017:** Alan Wong, "Joshua Wong and 2 Others Jailed in Hong Kong over Pro-Democracy Protest," *New York Times*, August 17, 2017.

202 **colonial-era public order charges:** Chris Lau, "Nine Key Occupy Figures—Including Co-Founders Benny Tai, Chan Kin-Man and Chu Yiu-Ming—Chant Slogans with Hundreds of Supporters at Hong Kong Court Just before Public Nuisance Trial Begins," *South China Morning Post*, November 18, 2018.

204 **as resignation syndrome:** Graeme Smith and Louisa Lim, "Resignation Syndrome? Democracy and Jail in Post-Umbrella Hong Kong," *The Little Red Podcast*, April 8, 2019.

204–205 **illegal assembly was increasingly being used:** Alice Woodhouse, "Two Disqualified Hong Kong Legislators Arrested," *Financial Times*, April 26, 2017.

205 **an op-ed about the censorship:** Sampson Wong, "When Everything Becomes 'Sensitive' 當一切都變成「好敏感」," The Stand News, July 1, 2017.

CHAPTER 8: 國 COUNTRY

211 **public consultations that were almost mockeries:** Stephen Vines, "In Hong Kong, Public Consultations Are Effective—at Keeping the Public at Bay," *South China Morning Post*, October 24, 2018.

211 **before the consultation period had even finished:** Tony Cheung and Shirley Zhao, "Hong Kong's Artificial Islands Plan 'Not Ignoring Land Task Force and Public Consultation,' Minister Says, Defending HK$500 Billion 'Lantau Tomorrow Vision,'" *South China Morning Post*, October 12, 2018.

211 **it rigged the process:** Shirley Zhao, "Land Supply Consultation 'Rigged,' Ex-Hong Kong Planning Official Says of Public Exercise to Tackle City's Housing Crisis," *South China Morning Post*, September 22, 2018.

211 **a measly twenty days:** Holmes Chan, "'Jumping the Gun': Barristers, Scholars and Democrats Oppose Update to Hong Kong Extradition Law as Consultation Ends," *Hong Kong Free Press*, March 5, 2019.

211 **130,000 people marched:** Sum Lok-kei and Ng Kang-chung, "Estimated 130,000 Protestors Join March against Proposed Extradition Law that Will Allow the Transfer of Fugitives from Hong Kong to Mainland China," *South China Morning Post*, April 28, 2019.

211 **the legislature erupted into vicious fistfights:** Sum Lok-kei, Su Xinqi, and Alvin Lum, "Hong Kong Government Condemns 'Disorderly and Uncontrollable Con-

ditions' after Legco Chaos Halts Meeting of Committee Reviewing Extradition Bill," *South China Morning Post*, May 19, 2019.

212 **a rare silent march:** Alvin Lum and Sum Lok-kei, "'Record 3,000' Hong Kong Lawyers in Silent March against Controversial Extradition Bill," *South China Morning Post*, April 6, 2019.

212 **the average for public rental housing:** Statista, "Average Living Space of Public Rental Housing Tenants in Hong Kong from 2007 to 2020" (2020).

213 **Beijing depended on the tycoons:** Kelvin Chan, "Trouble in Hong Kong? Beijing Summons Tycoons," Associated Press, September 25, 2014.

214 **they protested in great numbers:** Leung Po-lung, "Hong Kong Political Strikes: A Brief History," *Lausan*, August 3, 2019.

215 **that T-shirts had been produced to mark it:** Ng Kang-chung and Christy Leung, "Eleven Arrests, Double the Tear Gas Fired During Occupy Movement and 81 Injured: Police Chief Paints Disturbing Picture of Hong Kong Extradition Bill Protests," *South China Morning Post*, June 13, 2019.

217 **see themselves as a nation:** This definition of "Hong Kong nation" draws on work by Brian C. H. Fong, "Stateless Nation within a Nationless State: The Political Past, Present, and Future of Hongkongers, 1949–2019," *Nations and Nationalism* 26, no. 4 (2020), using the definition of "nation" of Michael Keating, *Nations against the State: The New Politics of Nationalism in Quebec, Catalonia, and Scotland*, 2nd ed. (Basingstoke, Hampshire, UK: Palgrave, 2000).

218 **Hong Kong's education system:** Christopher DeWolf, "How Did Christianity Become So Influential in Hong Kong?" *Zolima CityMag*, August 21, 2019.

219 **Lam was a devout Catholic:** Carrie Gracie, "Hong Kong's Carrie Lam: 'I Am No Puppet of Beijing,'" BBC, June 21, 2017.

220 **a suicide note scrawled on a wall:** Picture of the note is here: https://twitter.com/RealHKNews/status/1145016582013431808.

223 **"we Hong Kongers cannot lose any more":** Video of Brian Leung's speech is here: https://twitter.com/dlachina_lau/status/1147491671543668736.

223 **a hugely controversial book:** Chapman Chen, "Washington Univ. Ph.D. Student-Occupier of HK Legco on Hong Kong Nationalism," *Hong Kong Bilingual News*, June 10, 2020.

224 **police began withholding permission:** Holmes Chan, "Hong Kong Police Restrict Sunday's Anti-Police Violence Demo, in Second Move to Limit Protests This Week," *Hong Kong Free Press*, July 26, 2019.

225 **eight hundred rounds in a single day:** Mary Hui, "In Hong Kong, Almost Everyone, Everywhere—Including Pets—Is Getting Tear Gassed," *Quartz*, August 8, 2019.

225 **sixteen thousand rounds of tear gas:** Antony Dapiran, *City on Fire: The Fight for Hong Kong* (Australia: Scribe, 2020), 5.

225 **the Chemical Weapons Convention:** Simon Parry, "The Truth About Tear Gas: How Hong Kong Police Violated All Guidelines for the 'Non-Lethal Weapon,'" *South China Morning Post*, August 16, 2019.

227 **police punched him in the face:** Human Rights Foundation, "Complaint Concerning Johnson (Ching-Yin) Yeung," New York, 2020.

229 **"Liberate Hong Kong, Revolution of Our Times!":** "Who Wrote 'Glory to Hong Kong'?" *South China Morning Post*, video, https://www.youtube.com/watch?v=bLooy sg9idY.

230 **just 0.3 percent of Hong Kongers:** Details of Hong Kongers' identity surveys are here: www.pori.hk/pop-poll/ethnic-identity/q001/chinese.

230 **"The essence of 'Hong Konger'":** Geremie Barme, "I Am Brian Leung: They Cannot Understand; They Cannot Comprehend; They Cannot See," *China Heritage*, August 20, 2019.

232 **expensive full-face respirator:** Suzanne Sataline, "Hong Kong's Worsening Press Climate," October 11, 2019.

233 **clashes broke out in thirteen places:** SCMP Reporters, "As It Happened: Hong Kong Protester Shot in Chest, Six Live Rounds Fired on National Day," *South China Morning Post*, October 1, 2019.

233 **shooting an eighteen-year-old student:** Helen Regan and James Griffiths, "Man Shot with Live Round in Major Escalation of Hong Kong Protests," CNN, October 2, 2019.

233 **The man survived:** Tripti Lahiri, "The Teen Protester Shot by Hong Kong Police Faces Charges of Assault and Rioting," *Quartz*, October 3, 2019.

234 **the biggest mass trial:** Jasmine Siu, Brian Wong, and Chris Lau, "97 Protesters Hauled to Court over Sunday's Clashes on Hong Kong Island, with Prosecutors Accused of Rushing Charges," *South China Morning Post*, October 2, 2019.

234 **charges hadn't even been readied:** Suzanne Sataline, "The Other China Emergency," *The Atlantic*, May 24, 2020.

235 **practiced throwing Molotov cocktails:** Rosie Perper, "Behind the Barricades: Hong Kong Protesters Share What Happened During the Violent Clashes with Police on University Campuses," *Insider*, December 24, 2019.

235 **"enemies of the people":** Sarah Clarke, "Hong Kong's Carrie Lam: Protesters Now People's Enemy," Al Jazeera, November 11, 2019.

236 **Seventeen of the eighteen district councils flipped:** Jeffie Lam, Sum Lok-kei, and Ng Kang-chung, "Hong Kong Elections: Pro-Democracy Camp Wins 17 out of 18 Districts While City Leader Says She Will Reflect on the Result," *South China Morning Post*, January 25, 2019.

236 **vote swing of 15 percent:** Election results breakdown is here: https://en.wikipedia .org/wiki/Happy_Valley_(constituency).

237 **a plethora of commentary:** Alex Lo, "Why the 'Yellow Economic Circle' Is Immoral," *South China Morning Post*, December 31, 2019.

237 **the government banned dry goods:** Kris Cheng, "Hong Kong Gov't Bans Dry Goods, Including Satirical Items, at Lunar New Year Fairs," *Hong Kong Free Press*, November 7, 2019.

237 **A group who tested the new rules:** Lilian Cheng, "Lunar New Year Market Stalls in Victoria Park Shut Down by Officials over Hong Kong Protest Displays," *South China Morning Post*, January 20, 2020.

238 **a hundred people had been arrested:** Police tweet is here: https://twitter.com /hkpoliceforce/status/1215840598663426048.

243 **"librarian of history":** Elisa Luk and Sharon Pun, "Collect the Past, Inspire the Future," *The Young Reporter*, April 2017.

248 **"I cross out words":** Sotheby's, "Sotheby's Evening Auction: Jean-Michel Basquiat, Tuxedo," 2012.

EPILOGUE

250 **upbraided the government:** Hong Kong Government, "Lcq12: Mr Tsang Tsou-Choi's Ink Writing," news release, January 13, 2010, www.info.gov.hk/gia/general /201001/13/P201001130222.htm.

251 **she needed to undergo surgery:** Chris Lau and Sum Lok-kei, "Four of Nine Occupy Leaders Jailed for Up to 16 Months over Roles in Hong Kong's 2014 Umbrella Movement," *South China Morning Post*, April 24, 2019.

251 **She'd also written a book:** Laura Westbrook, "National Security Law: Hong Kong Libraries Pull Books by Some Localist and Democracy Activists for Review," *South China Morning Post*, July 4, 2020.

251 **A Chinese Foreign Ministry spokesman:** Reuters staff, "China Says Sino-British Joint Declaration on Hong Kong No Longer Has Meaning," Reuters, June 30, 2017.

252 **On the first day of the law's existence:** "Hong Kong: First Arrests under 'Anti-Protest' Law as Handover Marked," BBC, July 1, 2020.

252 **"I do not have an answer":** Ted Jeffery, "China Strips Hong Kong Libraries of Pro-Democracy Books and Forces Nursery Pupils to Learn Law," *Daily Express*, July 6, 2020.

252 **"red lines are everywhere":** Haley Ott, "Hong Kong Politician Whose Book Was Yanked from Shelves Says, 'I Don't Know How I Can Protect Myself,'" CBS News, July 24, 2020.

252 **A Democracy Wall at one university:** Picture of the fate of the City University's Democracy Wall here: https://twitter.com/antd/status/1301083972546355200.

253 **"uttering seditious words":** Agence France Presse, "Hong Kong Activist Tam Tak-Chi Arrested for 'Uttering Seditious Words,'" *Hong Kong Free Press*, September 6, 2020.

253 **"collusion with a foreign country":** Reuters staff, "Hong Kong Media Tycoon Jimmy Lai Charged under National Security Law," December 11, 2020.

254 **Carrie Lam's public statements:** Kris Cheng, "Hong Kong's Freedom Has Not Been Eroded, Says Leader Carrie Lam as US Passes Law in Support of Protestors," *Hong Kong Free Press*, December 3, 2019.

254 **no separation of powers:** Tony Cheung and Chris Lau, "Hong Kong Leader Carrie Lam Sides with Education Chief on No 'Separation of Powers' in City, Defends Move to Delete Phrase from Textbooks," *South China Morning Post*, September 1, 2020.

254 **a historical misunderstanding:** Jennifer Creery, "No Separation of Powers in Hong Kong Says Chief Exec. Carrie Lam, Despite Previous Comments from Top Judges," *Hong Kong Free Press*, September 1, 2020.

254 **Lam even framed it:** Jeffie Lam, "Hong Kong Can Still Move Towards Greater Democracy after Changes to Electoral System, Carrie Lam says," *South China Morning Post*, March 8, 2021.

255 **Lam's description of largely peaceful protests:** Louisa Lim and Graeme Smith, "Hong Kong and the Tiananmen Playbook," in *China Dreams: China Story Yearbook 2019*, ed. Jane Golley et al. (Australia: ANU Press, 2020).

257 **authorities hastily covered up:** Louisa Lim, "This Is How Much China's Communist Party Fears the Power of Public Memory," *Washington Post*, June 4, 2021.

258 **"for endangering national security":** "Hong Kong Disqualifies Legislators for 'Endangering Security,'" Al Jazeera, November 11, 2020.

258 **fifteen other Democratic lawmakers resigned:** Lily Kuo and Helen Davidson, "Hong Kong Opposition Lawmakers All Quit after Four Members Ousted," *The Guardian*, November 12, 2020.

258 **"a 100 percent guarantee":** Austin Ramzy and Tiffany May, "How Beijing Will Control Hong Kong's Elections," *New York Times*, March 30, 2021.

258 **Jimmy Lai Chee-ying:** Emma Graham-Harrison, "Hong Kong Democracy Campaigner Jimmy Lai Denied Bail," *The Guardian*, December 12, 2020.

258 **Among his charges:** "Citing Tweets and Op-Eds, Hong Kong Police Charges Media Tycoon Jimmy Lai with Foreign Collusion," The Stand News, December 15, 2020.

258 **"we support Apple Daily":** "Hong Kongers Bid a Painful Farewell in the Rain; 'We Support Apple Daily,'" *Apple Daily*, June 24, 2021.

259 **websites blocked on national security grounds:** Zen Soo, "Hong Kong Internet Firm Blocked Website over Security Law," Associated Press, January 14, 2021.

259 **civil servants were ordered:** Candace Chau, "Video: Hong Kong Civil Servants Take Oaths Pledging Loyalty to Gov't," *Hong Kong Free Press*, December 16, 2020.

259 **lifetime bans for teaching classes:** Ho-him Chan, "Lifetime Ban for Hong Kong Teacher Who Taught Distorted Class on Sino-British Opium War 'Too Harsh,' Some Parents Say," *South China Morning Post*, November 30, 2020.

259 **"an unthinkable travesty of justice":** Timothy McLaughlin, "What the Hong Kong Protesters' Trial Reveals about Beijing," *The Atlantic*, March 23, 2021.

259 **conspiracy to commit subversion:** Helen Davidson, "Hong Kong: 47 Key Activists Charged with Subversion and Face Life if Convicted," *The Guardian*, March 1, 2021.

260 **"with no regret":** "Closing Submission of Benny Tai Yiu-ting," *Citizen News*, December 13, 2018.

260 **convicted of assault:** RTHK, "Ex-Lawmaker Au Nok-Hin Guilty of Loudhailer Assaults," April 6, 2020.

260 **dangerous driving:** Rhoda Kwan, "Horn-Honking Hong Kong Driver Guilty of Careless Driving during 2020 Protests," *Hong Kong Free Press*, June 8, 2021.

260 ***"The Guardian of Sheep Village":*** "Five Arrested for 'Inciting Young Children's Hatred,'" RTHK, June 22, 2021.

260 **lessons to be taught in Mandarin:** "All Schools Should Teach in Mandarin: Ronnie Chan," RTHK, June 10, 2021.

260 **imposed until the following year:** "CHRF Rallies May Have Violated NSL: Police Chief," RTHK, August 13, 2021.

BIBLIOGRAPHY

"1912 Attempt to Assassinate Governor." From the *International Herald Tribune* 100, 75, 50 Years Ago. *New York Times*, July 4, 2012.

Abbas, M. A. *Hong Kong: Culture and the Politics of Disappearance*. Minneapolis: University of Minnesota Press, 1997.

Agence France Presse. "Prince Charles Wins Diary Battle." *ABC Australia*, December 21, 2006.

Agence France Presse. "Words of a Prince and a President: Continuity, Change and Assurances." *New York Times*, July 1, 1997.

Atha, Mick, and Kennis Yip. *Piecing Together Sha Po: Archaeological Investigations and Landscape Reconstruction*. Hong Kong: Hong Kong University Press, 2016.

Barme, Geremie. "I Am Brian Leung: They Cannot Understand; They Cannot Comprehend; They Cannot See." *China Heritage*, August 20, 2019.

Bradsher, Keith. "Beijing Asserts New Control over Election Laws in Hong Kong." *New York Times*, April 6, 2004.

Buckley, Chris, Austin Ramzy, and Edward Wong. "Violence Erupts in Hong Kong as Protesters Are Assaulted." *New York Times*, October 3, 2014.

Buddle, Cliff. "Hong Kong's First Chief Executive Tung Chee-Hwa Takes a Trip Down Memory Lane." *South China Morning Post*, July 2, 2017.

Chan, Holmes. "Hong Kong Police Restrict Sunday's Anti-Police Violence Demo, in Second Move to Limit Protests This Week." *Hong Kong Free Press*, July 26, 2019.

Chan, Holmes. "'Jumping the Gun': Barristers, Scholars and Democrats Oppose Update to Hong Kong Extradition Law as Consultation Ends." *Hong Kong Free Press*, March 5, 2019.

Chan, Johannes. "A Storm of Unprecedented Ferocity: The Shrinking Space of the Right to Political Participation, Peaceful Demonstration, and Judicial Independence in Hong Kong." *International Journal of Constitutional Law* 16, no. 2 (2018): 373–88.

Chan, Kelvin. "Trouble in Hong Kong? Beijing Summons Tycoons." Associated Press, September 25, 2014.

Cheng, Kris. "Busloads of Pro-Government Activists Vandalise Tai Po Lennon Wall Message Board at 2am, Pasting Ads for Saturday Rally." *Hong Kong Free Press*, July 19, 2019.

Cheng, Kris. "Dozens of Police in Riot Gear Remove Flyers with Officers' Personal Information from Tai Po Lennon Wall." *Hong Kong Free Press*, July 10, 2019.

Cheng, Kris. "Hong Kong Gov't Bans Dry Goods, Including Satirical Items, at Lunar New Year Fairs." *Hong Kong Free Press*, November 7, 2019.

Cheng, Kris. "Teachers Warned They Could Lose Qualifications for Advocating Independence in Schools." *Hong Kong Free Press*, August 15, 2016.

Cheng, Lilian. "Lunar New Year Market Stalls in Victoria Park Shut Down by Officials over Hong Kong Protest Displays." *South China Morning Post*, January 20, 2020.

Cheung, Elizabeth. "Fight over Lennon Wall Leaves Two Men Injured as Tensions Escalate between Anti-Government Protestors and Opponents." *South China Morning Post*, September 29, 2019.

Cheung, Tony, and Shirley Zhao. "Hong Kong's Artificial Islands Plan 'Not Ignoring Land Task Force and Public Consultation,' Minister Says, Defending HK$500 Billion 'Lantau Tomorrow Vision.'" *South China Morning Post*, October 12, 2018.

Chim Lo, Yui. "The Last Stand of Colonialism? The Unofficial Members of the Executive and Legislative Councils and the Sino-British Negotiations over Hong Kong, 1982–1984." *Journal of Imperial and Commonwealth History* 48, no. 2 (2020): 370–94.

Chung, Joel. "The Art of Treason." CUP Magazine Publishing, Hong Kong, 2007.

Chung, Joel. "Kowloon King." Asia One, Hong Kong, 2010.

Chung, Joel. *Post No Bills*. Hong Kong: CUP Magazine Publishing, 2009.

Chung, Sze-yuen. *Hong Kong's Journey to Reunification: Memoirs of Sze-Yuen Chung*. Hong Kong: Chinese University of Hong Kong Press, 2001.

Clarke, Sarah. "Hong Kong's Carrie Lam: Protesters Now People's Enemy." Al Jazeera, November 11, 2019.

CNN. "Huge Protest Fills HK Streets." July 2, 2003.

Cottrell, Robert. *The End of Hong Kong: The Secret Diplomacy of Imperial Retreat*. London: John Murray, 1993.

Cradock, Percy. *Experiences of China*. New ed. London: John Murray, 1999.

Dapiran, Antony. *City of Protest: A Recent History of Dissent in Hong Kong*. Melbourne: Penguin Random House, 2017.

Dapiran, Antony. *City on Fire: The Fight for Hong Kong*. Melbourne: Scribe, 2020.

De Fonblanque, Edward Barrington. *Niphon and Pe-Che-Li: Or, Two Years in Japan and Northern China*. London: Saunders, Otley, 1862.

Delbanco, Dawn. "Chinese Calligraphy." *Heilbrunn Timeline of Art History*, April 2008.

DeWolf, Christopher. "Hong Kong's Salty History: Rebellion, Smuggling and Shrimp Paste," *Zolima CityMag*, September 7, 2017.

DeWolf, Christopher. "How Did Christianity Become So Influential in Hong Kong?" *Zolima CityMag*, August 21, 2019.

Dimbleby, Jonathan. *The Last Governor: Chris Patten and the Handover of Hong Kong*. London: Little, Brown & Co., 1997.

Dimsum Daily. "Lennon Wall Message Wall in Fanling Set on Fire by Arsonist." July 14, 2019.

Dung, Kai-cheung. *Atlas: The Archaeology of an Imaginary City*. New York: Columbia University Press, 2012.

Eitel, Ernest John. *Europe in China: The History of Hong Kong from the Beginning to the Year 1882*. Hong Kong: Oxford University Press, 1983.

"Emperors in China Have Always Been Calligraphers." *Colors*, October 2005, 10–11.

Empson, Hal. *Mapping Hong Kong: A Historical Atlas [Hsiang-Kang Ti T'u Hui Chih Shih]*. Hong Kong: Government Information Services, 1992.

Encyclopaedia Britannica. "Convention of 1898."

Fan, Shuh-ching. *The Population of Hong Kong*. Committee for International Coordination of National Research in Demography, 1974.

Fong, Brian C. H. "Stateless Nation within a Nationless State: The Political Past, Present, and Future of Hongkongers, 1949–2019." *Nations and Nationalism* 26, no. 4 (2020): 1069.

Forsythe, Michael, and Paul Mozur. "A Video, a Wheelchair, a Suitcase: Mystery of Vanished Tycoon Deepens." *New York Times*, February 10, 2017.

Gewirtz, Julian. "'Imperial Twilight' Review: An Explosive Mix of Trade and Politics." *Wall Street Journal*, May 17, 2018.

Gracie, Carrie. "Hong Kong's Carrie Lam: 'I Am No Puppet of Beijing.'" BBC, June 21, 2017.

Guyot, Eric. "Tung Chee Hwa Admits China Aided His Shipping Firm in '80s." *Wall Street Journal*, October 24, 1996.

Hase, Patrick H., *Forgotten Heroes: San On County and Its Magistrates in the Late Ming and Early Qing*. Hong Kong: City University of Hong Kong Press, 2017.

Hase, Patrick H. *The Six-Day War of 1899: Hong Kong in the Age of Imperialism.* Hong Kong: Hong Kong University Press, 2008.

"The History of Tai Kwun." 2019. https://mediakron.bc.edu/edges/the-yamen-an-inquiry -into-identity-and-place-in-the-kowloon-walled-city/2019-final-projects/tai-kwun /overview. Last accessed September 17, 2021.

"HK Needs Laws to Protect National Security by Secretary for Security, Mrs Regina Ip." News release, January 28, 2003, www.basiclaw23.gov.hk/english/focus/focus5.htm.

Ho Hing-kay, Oscar. "The Betrayal of the King." *Artlink* 34, no. 1 (2014): 53–54.

Hong Kong Government. "Speech by FS at Asian Financial Forum Cocktail Reception." News release, January 20, 2010, www.info.gov.hk/gia/general/201001/20 /P201001200262.htm.

Hou, Hanru. "How to Remember Tsang Tsou-choi?" In *King of Kowloon: The Art of Tsang Tsou-choi*, edited by David Spalding. Bologna, Italy: Damiani, 2013, 115–33.

Hui, Mary. "In Hong Kong, Almost Everyone, Everywhere—Including Pets—Is Getting Tear Gassed." *Quartz*, August 8, 2019.

Human Rights Foundation. "Complaint Concerning Johnson (Ching-Yin) Yeung." New York, 2020.

Human Rights Watch. "China: Release Abducted Swedish Bookseller." News release, October 17, 2016, www.hrw.org/news/2016/10/17/china-release-abducted-swedish -bookseller.

Jarman, R. L. *Hong Kong: Annual Administration Reports 1841–1941.* Cambridge: University of Cambridge, 1996.

Jing, Lin. "Hong Kong Police Clear Last Pro-Democracy Protests as Leaders Vow Movement Will Continue." Radio Free Asia, December 15, 2014.

Keating, Michael. *Nations against the State: The New Politics of Nationalism in Quebec, Catalonia, and Scotland.* 2nd ed. Basingstoke, Hampshire, UK: Palgrave, 2000.

"'Kowloon King' Is an Emperor without Male Offspring. He Constantly Bears in Mind the Prosperity of His Country and the Peace of His People." *Ming Pao Evening News*, July 12, 1970.

Lahiri, Tripti. "The Teen Protester Shot by Hong Kong Police Faces Charges of Assault and Rioting." *Quartz*, October 3, 2019.

Lam, Jeffie, Sum Lok-kei, and Ng Kang-chung. "Hong Kong Elections: Pro-Democracy Camp Wins 17 out of 18 Districts While City Leader Says She Will Reflect on the Result." *South China Morning Post*, January 25, 2019.

Lam, Yik-fei. *Woh Yuhng: Photographs from the 2019 Hong Kong Protests.* Hong Kong: Brownie Publishing, 2020.

Lau, Chris. "Nine Key Occupy Figures—Including Co-Founders Benny Tai, Chan Kin-Man and Chu Yiu-Ming—Chant Slogans with Hundreds of Supporters at Hong Kong

Court Just before Public Nuisance Trial Begins." *South China Morning Post*, November 18, 2018.

Law, Wing-sang. *Collaborative Colonial Power: The Making of the Hong Kong Chinese*. Hong Kong: Hong Kong University Press, 2009.

Lee, Vicky. "The Code of Silence across the Hong Kong Eurasian Community(ies)." In *Meeting Place: Encounters across Cultures in Hong Kong, 1841–1984*, edited by Elizabeth Sinn and Christopher Munn. Hong Kong: Hong Kong University Press, 2018.

Leung, Po-lung. "Hong Kong Political Strikes: A Brief History." *Lausan*, August 3, 2019.

Leys, Simon. "One More Art." *New York Review of Books*, April 18, 1996.

Lim, Louisa. "Deaths Tell the Story of Life in Early Hong Kong." NPR, August 21, 2012.

Lim, Louisa. "For Hong Kong and Mainland, Distrust Only Grows." NPR, March 23, 2012.

Lim, Louisa. *The People's Republic of Amnesia: Tiananmen Revisited*. New York: Oxford University Press, 2014.

Lim, Louisa. "The Thugs of Mainland China." *New Yorker*, October 8, 2014.

Lim, Patricia. *Discovering Hong Kong's Cultural Heritage: Hong Kong and Kowloon: With 19 Guided Walks*. Oxford: Oxford University Press, 2002.

Lim, Patricia. *Discovering Hong Kong's Cultural Heritage: The New Territories*. Hong Kong: Oxford University Press 2002.

Lim, Patricia. *Forgotten Souls: A Social History of the Hong Kong Cemetery*. Hong Kong: Hong Kong University Press, 2011.

Liu, Shuyong. *An Outline History of Hong Kong*. Beijing: Foreign Languages Press, 1997.

Lo, Alex. "Why the 'Yellow Economic Circle' Is Immoral." *South China Morning Post*, December 31, 2019.

Loh, Christine. *Underground Front: The Chinese Communist Party in Hong Kong*. Hong Kong: Hong Kong University Press, 2010.

Lovell, Julia. *The Opium War: Drugs, Dreams, and the Making of China*. Sydney: Picador, 2011.

Lowe, K. J. P. "Hong Kong, 26 January 1841: Hoisting the Flag Revisited." *Journal of the Hong Kong Branch of the Royal Asiatic Society* 29 (1989): 8–17.

Luk, Elisa, and Sharon Pun. "Collect the Past, Inspire the Future." *The Young Reporter*, April 2017.

Lum, Alvin, and Sum Lok-kei. "'Record 3,000' Hong Kong Lawyers in Silent March against Controversial Extradition Bill." *South China Morning Post*, April 6, 2019.

Ng, Joyce, and Shirley Zhao. "Occupy Central Founder Benny Tai Banned from Supervising Researchers for Three Years Following HKU Donation Scandal." *South China Morning Post*, August 26, 2015.

Ma, Ngok. "The Sino-British Dispute over Hong Kong: A Game Theory Interpretation." *Asian Survey* 37, no. 8 (1997): 738–51.

Macaulay, Thomas. "Minute by the Hon'ble T. B. Macaulay, dated the 2nd February 1835."

Mair, Victor. "Cantonese Tones." February 25, 2017.

Major, John. *John Major: The Autobiography.* New York: HarperCollins, 1999.

Mark, Chi-kwan. "Decolonising Britishness? The 1981 British Nationality Act and the Identity Crisis of Hong Kong Elites." *Journal of Imperial and Commonwealth History* 48, no. 3 (2020): 565–90.

Morris, Esther. *Helena May: The Person, the Place and 90 Years of History in Hong Kong.* Hong Kong: Helena May Institute, 2016.

Morris, Jan. *Hong Kong: Epilogue to an Empire.* Final ed. London: Penguin, 1997.

Munn, Christopher. *Anglo-China: Chinese People and British Rule in Hong Kong.* Richmond, Surrey, UK: Curzon, 2000.

Ng, Kang-chung, and Christy Leung. "Eleven Arrests, Double the Tear Gas Fired During Occupy Movement and 81 Injured: Police Chief Paints Disturbing Picture of Hong Kong Extradition Bill Protests." *South China Morning Post,* June 13, 2019.

Nissim, Roger. *Land Administration and Practice in Hong Kong.* 4th ed. Hong Kong: Hong Kong University Press, 2016.

Obrist, Hans Ulrich. "Foreword: A Protest against Forgetting." In *King of Kowloon: The Art of Tsang Tsou-choi,* edited by David Spalding. Bologna, Italy: Damiani, 2013, 1–9.

Pan, Lu. "Writing at the End of History: Reflections on Two Cases of Graffiti in Hong Kong." *Public Art Dialogue* 4, no. 1 (2014): 147–66.

Pang, Allan. "Manipulating the Past: History Education in Late-Colonial Hong Kong." Undergraduate thesis, University of Hong Kong, 2018.

Parry, Simon. "The Truth About Tear Gas: How Hong Kong Police Violated All Guidelines for the 'Non-Lethal Weapon.'" *South China Morning Post,* August 16, 2019.

Patten, Chris. *East and West.* London: Macmillan, 1998.

Perdue, Peter. "The First Opium War: The Anglo-Chinese War of 1839–1842." In *Visualizing Cultures.* Massachusetts Institute of Technology, 2010.

Perper, Rosie. "Behind the Barricades: Hong Kong Protesters Share What Happened During the Violent Clashes with Police on University Campuses." *Insider,* December 24, 2019.

Platt, Stephen R. *Autumn in the Heavenly Kingdom: China, the West, and the Epic Story of the Taiping Civil War.* New York: Vintage Books, 2012.

Pomfret, David M. "Raising Eurasia: Race, Class, and Age in French and British Colonies." *Comparative Studies in Society and History* 51, no. 2 (2009): 314–43.

Pottinger, George. *Sir Henry Pottinger: First Governor of Hong Kong.* New York: St. Martin's Press, 1997.

Qian, Gang. "Keeping to the Script." China Media Project. January 6, 2019.

Regan, Helen, and James Griffiths. "Man Shot with Live Round in Major Escalation of Hong Kong Protests." CNN, October 1, 2019.

Richburg, Keith. "Words of Calligrapher Perplexing Hong Kong." *Washington Post*, May 12, 1997.

Roberti, Mark. *The Fall of Hong Kong: China's Triumph and Britain's Betrayal.* Revised and updated ed. New York: John Wiley & Sons, 1996.

Sataline, Suzanne. "Hong Kong's Worsening Press Climate." October 11, 2019.

Sataline, Suzanne. "The Other China Emergency." *The Atlantic*, March 24, 2020.

SCMP Reporters. "As It Happened: Hong Kong Protester Shot in Chest, Six Live Rounds Fired on National Day." *South China Morning Post*, October 1, 2019.

Siu, Jasmine, Brian Wong, and Chris Lau. "97 Protesters Hauled to Court over Sunday's Clashes on Hong Kong Island, with Prosecutors Accused of Rushing Charges." *South China Morning Post*, October 2, 2019.

Sotheby's. "Sotheby's Evening Auction: Jean-Michel Basquiat, Tuxedo." 2012.

Spalding, David, editor. *King of Kowloon: The Art of Tsang Tsou-choi.* Bologna, Italy: Damiani, 2013.

Statista. "Average Living Space of Public Rental Housing Tenants in Hong Kong from 2007 to 2020." 2020.

Tam, Johnny, and Stuart Lau. "Education Bureau Rapped over Cantonese 'Not an Official Language' Gaffe." *South China Morning Post*, February 2, 2014.

Thatcher, Margaret. *The Downing Street Years.* London: HarperCollins, 1993.

Ting Sun-pao, Joseph. "1860–1898: The Establishment of Entrepot Trade." In *History of the Port of Hong Kong and the Marine Department*, edited by Lau Chi-pang, Hong Kong: Marine Department, 2017.

Ting, Victor. "Three Hong Kongers Stabbed after Revealing Political Views." *Inkstone News*, August 20, 2019.

Tong, Elson. "Reviving Article 23 (Part I): The Rise and Fall of Hong Kong's 2003 National Security Bill." *Hong Kong Free Press*, February 17, 2018.

Tsang, Steve. *A Modern History of Hong Kong: 1841–1997.* London: I. B. Tauris & Company, 2007.

Veg, Sebastian. "Written Evidence from Professor Sebastian Veg (Cir0030)." Edited by Foreign Affairs Committee. British Parliament, 2019.

Vines, Stephen. "In Hong Kong, Public Consultations Are Effective—at Keeping the Public at Bay." *South China Morning Post*, October 24, 2018.

Vogel, Ezra F. *Deng Xiaoping and the Transformation of China.* Cambridge, MA: Belknap Press of Harvard University Press, 2011.

Wasserstrom, Jeff. *Vigil: Hong Kong on the Brink.* Columbia Global Reports, 2020.

Welsh, Frank. *A History of Hong Kong.* New York: HarperCollins, 1993.

Wesley-Smith, Peter. "Anti-Chinese Legislation in Hong Kong." In *Precarious Balance: Hong Kong between China and Britain, 1842–1992*, edited by Ming K. Chan and John D. Young. Armonk, NY: M. E. Sharpe, 1994.

Wesley-Smith, Peter. "Unequal Treaty, 1898–1997: China, Great Britain, and Hong Kong's New Territories." Revision of thesis (PhD), University of Hong Kong, 1976, 1980.

"Who Wrote 'Glory to Hong Kong'?" *South China Morning Post*, September 24, 2019.

Wong, Alan. "Joshua Wong and 2 Others Jailed in Hong Kong over Pro-Democracy Protest." *New York Times*, August 17, 2017.

Wong, George H. C. "The Ch'i-Shan–Elliot Negotiations Concerning an Off-Shore Entrepôt and a Re-Evaluation of the Abortive Chuenpi Convention." *Monumenta Serica* 14, no. 1 (1949): 539–73.

Wong, Joshua, and Jason Y. Ng. *Unfree Speech: The Threat to Global Democracy and Why We Must Act, Now*. New York: Penguin Books, 2020.

Wong, Minnie, Howard Tang, and Vivienne Tsang. "From Local Identity to the Pursuit of Independence: The Changing Face of Hong Kong Localism." *Hong Kong Free Press*, November 11, 2016.

Wong, Sampson. "When Everything Becomes 'Sensitive.'" The Stand News, July 1, 2017.

Woodhouse, Alice. "Two Disqualified Hong Kong Legislators Arrested." *Financial Times*, April 26, 2017.

Yeung, S. C. "Cosco Takeover of Orient Overseas Fits a Pattern." *EJ Insight*, July 11, 2017.

Zhao, Shirley. "Land Supply Consultation 'Rigged,' Ex–Hong Kong Planning Official Says of Public Exercise to Tackle City's Housing Crisis." *South China Morning Post*, September 22, 2018.